HOW TO PROFIT FROM THE COMING REAL ESTATE BUST

John Rubino

RODALE

Printed in the United States of America
Rodale Inc. makes every effort to use acid-free ∞, recycled paper ♻.

Book design by Judith Stagnitto Abbate/Abbate Design

Library of Congress Cataloging-in-Publication Data

Rubino, John A.
    How to profit from the coming real estate bust : money-making strategies for the end of the housing bubble / John Rubino.
        p.   cm.
    Includes bibliographical references and index.
    ISBN 1–57954–870–9 hardcover
    1. Real estate investment—United States.   I. Title.
HD255.R83   2003
332.63'24'0973—dc21   2003013584

Distributed to the book trade by St. Martin's Press

2 4 6 8 10 9 7 5 3 1 hardcover

CONTENTS

Credit Lines		iv
Acknowledgments		v
Introduction		1

Part 1: A Little Housing History **7**

| 1 | From the Cave to the American Castle | 9 |
| 2 | Boom and Bust | 17 |

Part 2: The Housing Bubble and Its Consequences **39**

3	Anatomy of Today's Bubble	41
4	How It Hits Home	55
5	Impact: Global and Local	61
6	Derivatives, Fannies, and Freddies	75
7	When the Bubble Pops	105
8	Tales from the Dark Side	115

Part 3: Investing for the Housing Bust **129**

| 9 | Preserving Your Capital When the Bubble Bursts | 131 |
| 10 | Making Money When the Bubble Bursts | 171 |

Part 4: Now, About Your House **211**

11	Are You Living in a Bubble Market?	213
12	Your Options	219
13	Minimize Your Property Taxes	239

Further Reading		243
Epilogue		251
Index		255

CREDIT LINES

The quote on page 36 from the *Los Angeles Times,* "Money Boom For Japan, Gilded Age of Riches, by Karl Schoenberger, January 30, 1989, is used with permission.

The quotes on pages 18, 24, and 27 are excerpted from the *Boston Globe* articles "The Space Race/Dot-Com and Other Firms Compete for Dwindling Offices," by Richard Kindleberger, April 9, 2000; "House-Poor Children," by Ellen Goodman, March 28, 1989; and "Building in the Aftermath of the Boom Gone Bust," by Robert Campbell, April 29, 1990.

The quotes attributed to Warren Buffett on pages 75 and 76 are used with his permission.

The quotes on page 96 from *U.S. News & World Report,* "Shelter From the Storm," by Noam Neusner and Matthew Benjamin, July 7, 2002, are used with permission.

The table on page 107 is derived from a study by economy.com and is used with permission.

The quotes from Robert Prechter's *Conquer the Crash* on pages 116–120 and page 189 are used with permission.

Doug Noland's quotes on pages 121–127 are used with permission.

The quotes from Moody's Investors Service on page 180 are excerpted from "Commercial Real Estate Assets in Bank Loan Portfolios," by Les Muranyi, May 2002, and are used with permission.

"Overvalued Markets" on page 216 is reprinted with permission from *Building Market Intelligence.*

ACKNOWLEDGMENTS

This book wouldn't have happened—certainly not in its present form—without the help of several people. Faith Hamlin, my agent, shaped a vague notion into a coherent book proposal. Jeremy Katz, my editor, shaped a raw manuscript into a (hopefully) lucid book. James Turk and Claude Cormier clarified the role that gold will play in what's coming. And Doug Noland and Robert Prechter provided insight into the risks presented by the housing bubble. Thanks to the latter two for allowing me to quote extensively from their writings.

INTRODUCTION

Among economists (some of them, anyhow), there's a rule of thumb that the longer-lived an economic expansion, the deeper the resulting recession. This makes intuitive sense, because the last stage of a boom is when people come to believe that the economic cycle has been abolished, and act accordingly. We buy things we don't need with money we don't have. We invest in—and take jobs at—companies that can only succeed in a perfect world. And the longer this goes on, the greater the mass of bad debts and untenable businesses that must be flushed from the system before growth can begin again.

Because the expansion of the 1990s was the longest ever, and its last few years set records for sheer financial zaniness, you'd think the resulting recession would also be one for the record books. But it wasn't. Instead, we got only a mild slow-down, and at this writing in early 2003, most forecasters seem to think a recovery is under way. What happened? In two words, real estate.

As stock prices headed south in 2001 and 2002, Americans discovered that, thanks to falling interest rates, we could turn our rising home equity into cash through refinancing and home equity loans. Like a huge tax cut, this allowed us to keep spending, propping up the economy and causing us to build and buy homes at a record pace— just about the last thing you'd expect at this point in the economic cycle. As a result, home prices have continued to rise, gradually in some places and dramatically in others, but enough overall to maintain the illusion of continued prosperity.

Unfortunately, the trends that produced the housing boom—falling interest rates, soaring mortgage debt, and plunging levels of home equity—have pretty much run their course. This virtually guarantees a real estate slowdown, and makes a crash, complete with plummeting home prices and mass foreclosures, quite possible. And because housing is the only thing other than the federal deficit that's propping up the overall economy, a broader slowdown (perhaps the really nasty one that should have followed the Roaring Nineties) may also be in the cards. So the question today is not just whether home prices in Boston and San Francisco will fall by 30 percent over the next few years (though if you live there, that's enough to worry about) but whether the bursting of the housing bubble will deflate the rest of the economy. If it does, the middle years of this decade will be tricky—but also exciting, if you take the right steps now. So let's start by defining some terms.

What Is the Business Cycle?

The tendency of capitalist economies to grow for long periods of time and then crash has bugged theorists and policy makers for almost two centuries. Recessions seem so unnecessary, so obviously the result of policy mistakes or outside interference. Like doctors on the trail of a chronic disease, some of the best minds of their times have devoted careers to finding a cure. The great early–twentieth-century economist John Maynard Keynes concluded that an alert government could "fine-tune" an economy—pump it up by borrowing and spending when things were slow and restrain it by raising taxes and running surpluses when consumers and businesses got a little too exuberant. Later, Nobel laureate Milton Friedman suggested controlling the creation of money in order to give the system a steady supply of fuel, thus keeping it on a sustainable growth path. Both seemed reasonable, both were tried in Washington and elsewhere—and both failed miserably, leaving us, in 2003, with the job of cleaning up after the Wall Street/Silicon Valley frat party of the 1990s.

What did the great minds miss? Perhaps they were looking for mechanistic solutions to a psychological problem. History (and common sense) teaches that we're not the always-rational actors of economic theory. Instead, we're highly adaptable, extremely social animals, capable of both caution and recklessness, depending on our experience and the economic environment. Put us in a crowded arena like a financial market, and we pass through predictable mood swings, leading us to act in ways that, in the aggregate, produce booms and busts.

Coming out of a recession, for instance, consumers and entrepreneurs are shell-shocked, and understandably reluctant to take on new debt. This is fine with bankers who, haunted by still-fresh memories of their last batch of bad loans, are in no hurry to lend to any but the most rock-solid borrowers. So, for a while, the national balance sheet gets stronger as families and businesses pay down debt and banks cut back on low-quality loans. Gradually, this caution begins to pay off as fewer borrowers default. Lenders notice that their loan portfolios are profitable again, and start trolling for new customers, offering easier terms and better service.

Consumers and businesses, meanwhile, having paid down their debt and/or avoided taking on new obligations, are in pretty good shape. They begin to test the waters, borrowing a little for commendable purposes like job training and new factories. This works out nicely, and companies start hiring in anticipation of even better times. Individuals notice that they're getting raises, as well as offers from other employers, and the memory of the last recession begins to fade. Maybe this year, thinks middle-America en masse, we can buy that new car *and* take a nice vacation, because next year's raise will more than cover the interest.

Then a new generation of players enters the game, made up of those either naturally risk-loving or too young to remember the last downturn. They fit the times perfectly and, by taking chances in a forgiving environment, make fortunes. (Think junk bond raiders in the 1980s and dot-com entrepreneurs and day traders in the late 1990s). The rest of us, seeing these once regular folks getting rich, gradually buy into the zeitgeist and start making career and financial choices that would have seemed crazy just a few years before. We leave safe jobs to join tech start-ups, buy growth stocks on margin, or borrow as much as possible for the biggest house on the block. Speculation displaces investment in the financial markets. "Hot" money begins to chase whatever is going up, and "bubbles" form in the prices of certain appealing assets. Go back through U.S. financial history and you'll see this happening every decade or so, as a booming economy leads to a systemwide debt binge, which culminates in a buying frenzy in some can't-miss asset: railroad stocks, radio stocks, 1960s tech stocks, the Nifty Fifty of the early 1970s, gold in the late 1970s, junk bonds in the late 1980s, and, of course, the tech stocks of recent, painful memory. This final, mad dance lasts until the sheer volume of bad decisions causes things to unravel. Growing numbers of people and businesses fail to pay their bills, banks find that the bad loans on their books are surging, companies stop hiring and start firing, and the economy sinks into a recession. Then, after a suitable period of wound licking, the game begins again.

Think about why this is inevitable: If the government discovered a perfect mix of policies to keep the economy growing steadily, the risk takers would never have to stop. They could rationally borrow as much as possible because never-ending growth would always allow them to pay off their debts. They would become giants, and the rest of us would eventually see their point: that in a recession-free world, using other people's money to buy what's going up is a low-risk game. Borrowing would soar, and eventually something—a war, an oil shortage, or simply the weight of the accumulated debt—would cause the system to crumble. In other words, you'd get the last few years of a typical expansion when, even in sophisticated circles, the notion takes hold that the good times will never end. So it would seem that as long as there are markets, there will be booms, busts, and bubbles.

What's a Bubble?

Because the theme of this book is that real estate—housing, to be specific—is the latest and in some ways the most dangerous in a long line of bubbles, now might be a good time to admit that serious people disagree about what the term really means. In the late 1990s, there was even a debate about whether tech stocks were a bubble (kind of amazing, when you think about it), with Federal Reserve Board chairman Alan Greenspan famously opining that you can tell such things only after the fact. Maybe so, but in retrospect, the bubbles that everyone now accepts as genuine share certain characteristics. Among them:

- The main indicators in the bubble sector—price, sales volume, employment—hit records and just keep on going.

- Newcomers enter the market with "revolutionary" innovations that look suspiciously like con games but, in the heat of the moment, are hailed as brilliant.

- Established players, in pursuit of enough new business to satisfy Wall Street expectations, begin to evade and eventually ignore their industry's time-honored practices.

- Regular folks begin to make apparently easy fortunes by risking borrowed money on the proposition that the bubble will keep inflating.

- Experts reassure the anxious with logical justifications for rising prices, and promise that even if the current torrid growth doesn't continue, the slow-down will be mild.

Keep all of this in mind as we explore today's housing market.

A Few Words about What Follows

The "financial engineering" parts of this book can be a little opaque. But don't let them bog you down. When you come to something that makes you want to toss the book onto that growing pile in the corner, just skip to the last few paragraphs of the section where I promise you'll find more or less plain English. And if along the way you become convinced that housing is indeed a financial bubble and want some ideas for profiting (or at least protecting yourself) from it, feel free to jump straight to chapters 9 and 10. You can always flip back if you need extra ammunition or moral support. But note that while this book mentions a lot of stocks, mutual funds, and other investments by name, these are *not* recommendations. The months that pass between the writing and publishing of this book can be a lifetime in the financial markets. By the time you read this, some of the companies mentioned will be in very different shape, and others may be gone. So use what follows as a framework for your own research, rather than a source of specific things to buy and sell. That said, here's to the next interesting few years.

PART 1

A LITTLE HOUSING HISTORY

CHAPTER 1

FROM THE CAVE TO THE AMERICAN CASTLE

The craving we all have for a place of our own probably dates back to the first hunter/gatherer who chased a bear from a cave and decided to settle in. And the other major theme of our relationship with real estate—the desire of government to control it—probably emerged that very night, when the tribal chief showed up and said, "Nice cave, Urg, but you understand that all the tribe's possessions belong to the forest god, and as his chosen representative, I really own it. So enjoy it for a while, but when my oldest son captures a bride, he'll be moving in." And so the pendulum has swung ever since, back and forth between individual property rights and society's prerogatives.

According to some accounts, the earliest recorded private property dates from circa 2000 B.C. in Mesopotamia, where the ancestral home was cherished to the point that families sometimes sold their children to cover their property taxes. A little later, the Old Testament tells of Abraham's dropping 400 shekels on some Hittite acreage, not far from what was to become Israel. Yet it wasn't really his, or even his people's, land. In Leviticus 25:23, Yahweh cautions, "The land shall not be sold permanently, for the land is Mine; for you are strangers and sojourners with me."

More familiar to the modern eye are the property laws that emerged in Greece and then Rome, where despite some archaic trappings (selling required a formal public ceremony, children and the mentally disabled were barred from land ownership, and slaves were often thrown in as part of the deal), homes were widely owned and passed from one generation to the next without much interference. Whether these relatively liberal property laws were a cause or a result of the success of those societies is a subject for another book—especially because it didn't last. When Rome fell, so did the concept of widespread home ownership; and in the feudal system that followed, land and everything on it was once again the property of the local king, priest, or lord. Things came full circle with the Norman invasion of England in 1066, when William the Conqueror indulged in the ultimate megalomaniacal fantasy by decreeing that all of England was his by right of conquest. He then parceled out huge estates to his officers, creating the landed aristocracy that embarrasses the country to this day. But even those new dukes and earls owned their lands through "tenure" rather than deed. That is, like Urg the first cave dweller, they kept what they had only as long as the king chose not to take it away. In modern terms, the king was landlord, and the nobleman, tenant.

European tenure laws, as they evolved, took on some truly medieval (in the *Pulp Fiction* sense) aspects. If a landowner was convicted of a felony, for instance, not only did his whole family lose their ancestral home, but the bloodline might be legally broken, preventing the felon's kids from inheriting property from grandparents or uncles. And while a person who pled guilty to a felony lost his home to the local lord or church, if he died without a plea, his next of kin simply paid a fine and kept the property. Not surprisingly, this led to a fair number of pretrial suicides and "accidents." At the risk of committing historical analysis, it's safe to say that one reason for 11th-century Europe's cultural and economic inferiority to Rome of 1,000 years earlier was the former's lack of respect for property rights. Relatively few people had a stake in maintaining and improving their homes, farms, or shops. Large-scale enterprises were virtually impossible to organize privately. Innovation was all risk and no reward, so new inventions were scarce, and were greeted with hostility when they occurred.

This eventually changed, of course. The Renaissance witnessed the rebirth of Classic architecture, with homes on a grand scale adorning the landscape. The Reformation followed, spawning the merchant class, a group eager for home ownership. And, finally, the Industrial Revolution created a wider distribution of wealth and an explosion of city development and growth.

Now let's fast forward to early–twentieth-century America, where private property rights were about to reach their zenith. The Federal government had spent the previous century offering free homesteads to anyone willing to work them, and millions of new immigrants were, for the first time, owners of the beds on which they slept. Yet home ownership—or, more accurately, the financing of home ownership—was primitive by today's standards. Mortgage interest was deductible, as was all interest, and interest rates were low. But mortgages ran for only 3 to 5 years, often with a balloon payment at the end. Down payments were as high as 60 percent, which presented would-be home owners with the choice of scrimping for years to accumulate a big pile of cash or taking out second and third mortgages at very high rates. Too many, especially in the Roaring Twenties, chose the latter, and when the Great Depression arrived, it sent nearly half the outstanding mortgages into default. So in the 1930s, Washington made home ownership even more of a priority, and in the decades since, the time and legislative creativity our government has devoted to the project has been breathtaking. The sheer number of real estate acts, regulations, loan guarantees, and tax breaks would make a complete accounting incomprehensible, so, with apologies to the economic historians out there for the many omissions, here are a few of the highlights.

In the depths of the Depression, Congress created the Federal Housing Administration (FHA) to funnel federal dollars to at-risk home owners, with the goal of keeping them in their homes and out of the tent cities then spreading across so many public parks. The FHA offered shell-shocked banks a guarantee that certain mortgages they wrote would be repaid. This eased bankers' anxieties, lessening the market's distress in the late 1930s and helping World War II veterans settle into suburban homes in the 1940s and 1950s. Along the way, the FHA helped mortgages evolve into the 30-year self-amortizing wonders we've come to know and love. (Today the FHA's mortgage insurance has become a fixture at the low end of the housing market, while its use of federal dollars to smooth out regional housing recessions has saved thousands of families from eviction.)

In 1965, Washington kicked it up a notch, folding the FHA into the newly created cabinet-level Department of Housing and Urban Development (HUD), and expanded the effort to put a roof over every citizen's head. And now HUD, with its $31 billion annual budget, has a finger in just about every part of the housing market. It offers discounts to police officers and teachers willing to move into low-income neighborhoods. It subsidizes the construction and renovation of affordable housing. It runs programs for the disabled homeless, homeless AIDS sufferers, homeless veterans, and just about everyone else in demonstrable need. On the structural side of the market, HUD regulates interstate land sales and sets standards for loan documentation and mortgage issuance. It is automating the mortgage underwriting process by developing statistical tools for assessing borrowers' creditworthiness, and making the resulting data available online.

HUD is still administering all those FHA loan guarantees. The list opposite is just a sampling of what's available. Not surprisingly, all these guarantees have helped HUD become one of the country's biggest property owners, because at any given time it has a huge portfolio of homes whose owners have defaulted on their HUD-insured mortgage payments. HUD buys the properties from the repossessing banks and puts them on the open market—hence the "HUD homes" that show up in real estate brochures

While HUD was funneling federal money into its myriad insurance guarantees and grant programs, the government-sponsored enterprises, or GSEs, were working the mortgage market. Federal National Mort-

HUD MORTGAGE INSURANCE PROGRAMS

Mortgage Insurance for One- to Four-Family Homes

Insurance for Adjustable Rate Mortgages

Single-Family Mortgage Insurance for Disaster Victims

Single-Family Mortgage Insurance for Outlying Areas

Mortgage Insurance for Low- and Moderate-Income Buyers

Graduated Payment Mortgage Insurance

Growing Equity Mortgage Insurance

Mortgage Insurance for Members of the Armed Forces

Mortgage Insurance for Older, Declining Areas

Rehabilitation Mortgage Insurance

Energy Efficient Mortgages Program

Single-Family Cooperative Mortgage Insurance

Home Equity Conversion Mortgage Program

Mortgage Insurance for Condominium Units

Mortgage Insurance for the Construction or Rehabilitation of
Condominium Projects

Manufactured Home Loan Insurance

Manufactured Home Lot and Combination Loan Insurance

Property Improvement Loan Insurance

Source: Housing and Urban Development Web site ■

gage Association (known as Fannie Mae, or just Fannie) and the Federal Home Loan Mortgage Corporation (Freddie Mac or just Freddie) were created by Congress—Fannie in 1938 and Freddie in 1970)—to buy mortgages from local banks, giving the banks a source of fast cash with which to make new loans. Both still retain a connection to the federal government (though its nature and extent is a subject of some debate), while operating as private-sector firms with stockholders and actively traded shares. HUD regulates the GSEs through the Office of Federal Housing Enterprise Oversight (OFHEO), monitoring their financial soundness and directing them to use their capital for socially useful goals like increasing minority home ownership and encouraging low-cost housing. To say that Fannie and Freddie have thrived under this arrangement—and that home ownership as a result is up—would be understating both counts. But because they play a central role in the premise of this book (see chapter 6, Derivatives, Fannies, and Freddies), suffice it to say that they've grown beyond anyone's expectations. Just to pique your interest, their combined total debt now exceeds a trillion dollars (that's right, a trillion), and they're the most important players not only in today's housing market but possibly in the entire U.S. economy.

While Washington's agencies were greasing the housing market's wheels, they were pressuring banks to lend money to the less well-off. The Community Reinvestment Act of 1977 required banks to use affirmative action in lending to "help meet the credit needs of their entire community, including low-and moderate-income neighborhoods." Failure to do so incurred the wrath of banking regulators, and banks have generally adapted by shedding their former reluctance to lend to residents of less affluent communities (though there is some controversy about the extent of this change). And a new, aggressive generation of mortgage lenders discovered the "subprime" market and began offering low-down-payment mortgages (much more about this in later chapters), making home ownership available to people who would otherwise be forced to rent.

Then there's the tax code, in which housing has a place of honor. Unlike credit card and car loan interest, which no longer garners year-end tax breaks, mortgage interest is still deductible. And capital gains on the sale of a home are tax-exempt in most cases, turning home ownership into sort of a real estate IRA, with a tax break on ownership costs and tax-free withdrawals. The annual savings to home owners from these breaks exceed $90 billion. And it's not over. In his first budget, President Bush proposed—and in some cases even offered to fund—a long list of new programs designed to make housing more accessible. The American Dream Down Payment Initiative, for instance, provides $200 million each year for down payments on homes for an estimated 40,000 low-income families. Of that, $45 million goes to housing counseling, to teach people how to become home owners, and $65 million supports "sweat equity" programs, where people earn the chance to own homes by renovating them. There's more—a lot more—but the point is clear: As a society, we really want families to own homes, and we're willing to do whatever it takes to make it happen.

Has it worked? Absolutely! When the world's richest country subsidizes a basic human drive, it tends to get results. So, despite welcoming about a million new immigrants a year, we've managed to build more than enough new homes to accommodate everyone with a job and a desire for a place of their own. Drive through the suburbs of Richmond, Virginia; Fort Collins, Colorado; Spokane, Washington, or any other good-size town, and the similarity is apparent: endless subdivisions full of either newly built homes or construction crews working on the next batch. As you'll see in part 2, by just about every measure, housing is enjoying a golden age. The question is where do we go from here.

CHAPTER 2

BOOM AND BUST

Real estate is everywhere. It's your home, your office, the mall where you shop, and the countryside through which you drive while getting from one place to another. And as a whole, it's immensely valuable. The Bureau of Economic Statistics estimates that the private structures in the United States are worth about $18 trillion, a ninefold increase in the past 30 years. In financial terms, that makes real estate a far bigger part of the economy than stocks, bonds, or cash.

VALUE OF ALL U.S. PRIVATE STRUCTURES

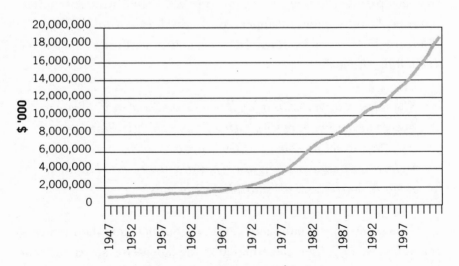

Source: Bureau of Economic Analysis

Because buildings and parcels of land are big and expensive, they must be financed. With the possible exemption of farmland, which marches to a different drummer, this makes real estate one of the most cyclical parts of the economy. That is, its value rises when the economy is strong (and people are willing to borrow to buy big things) and falls when it's weak. With the end of the 1990s boom, you'd expect the price of office buildings, factories, and houses to be way down. And two out of three of them are. The glaring exception is housing. So let's compare the market for office buildings, which is behaving pretty much as it normally does after a long boom, with housing, which isn't.

The Office Market: Weak as It Ought to Be

Because only about 20 percent of office space is occupied by its owner, and glitzy office towers are fun to build, the office market tends to be a highly volatile business. And just as you'd expect, the boom of the 1990s was a wild ride. By late in the decade, there were so many new companies forming in fast-growing cities that available office space had pretty much disappeared. As the *Boston Globe* put it in a 2000 article, "The Space Race: Dot-Com and Other Firms Compete for Dwindling Offices":

> *The Internet land rush is a landlord's dream, even as it threatens to become a nightmare for growing firms with dwindling options on where to set up shop. . . . The emphasis is on choosing the right space and moving in fast. They are in a rush to beat their rivals to market and to establish their brands.*

This is the type of situation that drives builders and their bankers into a frenzy, and office construction in the late 1990s surpassed that of even the frenetic 1980s.

Landlords weren't completely immune from doubt, though, which makes the latter part of the *Globe* article such a perfect example of late-cycle thinking:

> *On the strength of the overall economy, there is not much cause for worry, participants at a seminar held by Spaulding & Slye on the space needs of technology companies were told last week. "We are on the edge of an unprecedented growth period," said an upbeat (name deleted out of sympathy). He went further, saying the strength of knowledge-based economies like Greater Boston's will go a long way toward "ridding us of the business cycle." Even the extreme tightness of the labor market should not derail the expansion, he said in response to a question, predicting the economy would slow in 2001 and 2002 without slipping into recession. As the U.S. economy becomes more capital-intensive, productivity gains are allowing it to stretch its limited labor supply, he argued.*

Thus reassured, developers lined up backing and broke ground on new projects as fast as they could. Then the boom went bust, just as mountains of new office space hit the market in 2001 and 2002. Now most of that space is unoccupied. In a nice piece of media bookending, *Business Week* magazine ran a story in November 2002 titled "The Great Race from Office Space," which noted that tenants were paying penalties to escape from their leases, giving landlords a onetime windfall while saddling them with empty space that the market didn't want.

Equity Office, the nation's biggest owner of office buildings, reported that tenants returned 1.8 million square feet of floor space in the third quarter of 2002. Escaping tenants included Inktomi, a once high-flying Internet firm that paid $50 million to walk away from a never-occupied building in Silicon Valley, and tech icon Sun Microsystems, which forfeited $85 million when it shed some San Francisco office space. The resultant surge in so-called sublease space, combined with all the new space coming on line, has driven down rents while pushing vacancy rates to their highest levels since the 1990–91 recession. After bottoming out at about 9 percent in 1997, office vacancies nationwide hit 18 percent in 2002. But that's just the average. Markets as diverse as San Francisco; Columbus, Ohio; Dallas/Fort Worth; and Atlanta ended 2002 with vacancy rates over 20 percent. Rents were down by 60 percent in San Francisco and 30 percent in Boston, and the rate of return on office space investment was down from the 1996 average of 19 percent to less than 3 percent.

U.S. OFFICE VACANCY RATE

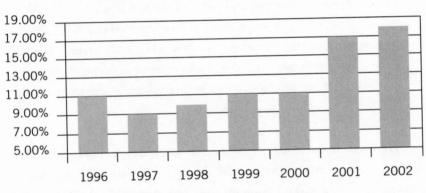

Source: Mortgage Bankers Association

Now "the office markets appear to be in a state of suspended animation," said real estate firm Cushman & Wakefield in a 2002 report. New construction is dwindling as builders and banks lick their financial wounds and as landlords struggle to pay their debts. And a recovery is a long way off. In San Francisco, for instance, 1 million square feet of office space was rented in the boom year of 1999. But in 2001, tenants abandoned more than 5 million square feet, leaving about 9 million available from a total stock of 42 million. Even if demand returns to 1999 levels, it will take 5 years just to nudge the vacancy rate below 10 percent. More likely, that space will be taken up at a rate of 500,000 square feet per year, bringing the vacancy rate down by mid-decade to only the high teens—still very bad for landlords and their bankers.

In most recessions, as you'll see in part 3, housing acts much like office space. In good times we get a little overexcited and build too many homes. And when things turn down, we stop building and buying, prices fall, and we look elsewhere for excitement for a few years. That's what gives the chart below such a nice, wavy pattern—housing rises in good times and plunges in bad. Starts fell by more than 50 percent between 1977 and 1982 and by about a third in the early 1990s.

U.S. HOUSING STARTS

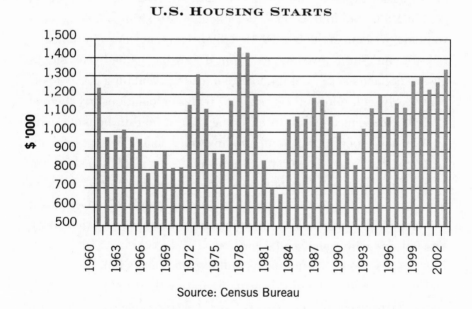

Source: Census Bureau

But looking at this chart, you'd never know the 1990s boom was over. Home building started rising in 1992 and hasn't let up, which implies that something unusual is going on. In the chapters that follow,

I'll argue that housing has become the latest in a long line of financial bubbles, with all that that implies. But first, just in cast you've been swayed by the general sense that this time it's different, let's see how the hottest housing markets behaved in the last recession.

It Was Different Then, Too: Real Estate Bubbles of the Recent Past

One of the characteristics of a bubble is the pervasive sense that it will always be thus. Things have been so good for so long that participants expect the object of their irrational enthusiasm to keep rising forever. That explains how otherwise cautious investors loaded up on gold in 1980, and junk bonds a decade later. And it explains the conventional wisdom of the late 1990s, which said that stocks were nearly risk-free long-term investments. Even if they have a bad year, stocks always bounce back, went the logic, so load up, and plug that 10 percent yearly gain into your retirement savings calculations. By the end of 2002, the same kind of thinking had taken hold in housing, with pundits and reporters repeating the line that housing was a "safe" investment that would eventually rise in value even if it had a slow year or two. They may be right, but even a cursory reading of this market's history reveals that bubbles happen all the time, and when they pop, it can take close to a decade—sometimes quite a bit longer—to recover. The following are some good examples.

New England: The Short-Lived Miracle

In his 1988 presidential bid, Massachusetts Governor Michael Dukakis never missed a chance to take credit for the "Massachusetts Miracle." This is interesting today not because it turned out to be so wrong but because it seemed so plausible at the time. His state was indeed booming, and it did indeed seem like a miracle. Sleepy little mill towns like Lowell and Brockton, which had faded into obscurity when textile and shoe-making jobs moved south, were bustling once more, and buttoned-down Boston had become the East Coast's answer to Silicon Valley. Office buildings were going up everywhere, home prices were surging, and state tax coffers were bulging. And everyone involved, from the governor down to the average home owner, was feeling like a genius.

They were disastrously mistaken, and in retrospect we know what happened. Ronald Reagan, elected in 1980 on the promise of a massive military build-up, kept his word. And New England, home of defense contractors like Raytheon and General Dynamics' Electric Boat division, became the recipient of a torrent of federal dollars. At about the same time, local tech companies such as Wang, Data General, and DEC caught the wave of technology's Next Big Thing, minicomputers. Defense contractors and computer firms started hiring engineers like crazy and drawing venture capital from all over the country. And jobs, really good jobs, were suddenly available for the asking.

In a small region with a stable population and little available land for building, the result was dramatic. In 1983, the median home resale price in Boston was $82,600, just 17 percent above the national median of $70,300, while in Providence, Rhode Island, homes were 26 percent *below* the national median. But when the money started flowing, home prices surged. Boston resale prices rose 21 percent in 1984, 34 percent in 1985, and 19 percent in 1986. By 1987 the city's median home price was $177,200, 115 percent higher than in 1983 and more than twice the national median price (which had increased by only 22 percent during the same four years). Providence went from $59,000 to $137,000 in 5 years, and by 1988 housing in New England was more than twice as expensive as comparable housing in most other parts of the country. And the people who had bought early in the decade found themselves suddenly and mysteriously wealthy.

Newspaper articles of the time illustrate the bemusement—but also the sense of inevitability—that began to take hold. From a 1989 *Boston Globe* piece titled "House-Poor Children," by Ellen Goodman:

> *They were talking about real estate. It is, to be frank, one of their favorite subjects. Each of them had a story to tell. One had bought a house in 1973 for $40,000. It had just been valued at $265,000. Another had a neighbor who sold her house, tripling her money in 10 years—the right 10 years. A third figured carefully the inflated value of his home into his retirement plans. There were no oil wells in their backyards, but the homes had made a more spectacular return than any gusher.*
>
> *But then the subject turned to their children, grown children. Could their children afford to buy the houses they had grown up in? A second set of stories poured out, more troubled than the first. They had working children wholly unable to save a down payment that might equal the parents' entire first mortgage. They had married children who needed two jobs to afford what they had supported with one. Most of their offspring were double-income and house-poor.*

Now, it's the nature of a bubble (indeed, the bubble couldn't have happened otherwise) for the participants to come to see the good times as permanent, and act accordingly. So instead of using the resulting surge in tax receipts to lower the region's traditionally high tax rates, New England state and local governments accepted the double-digit annual revenue increases as their birthright and went on a spending spree, hiring people and putting up spiffy new office buildings. During the 1980s, Massachusetts state spending more than doubled even as its tax rates went up, causing locals to start referring to their state as "Taxachusetts." And instead of selling when their homes tripled in value, residents borrowed against them to buy bigger homes or rental properties, or, like the man in the Goodman article above, began to factor their real estate riches into suddenly much rosier retirement plans. The region's banks, instead of leaning against the wind by tightening loan criteria and diversifying away from hot sectors, did the opposite. Between 1983 and 1989, real estate loans rose from 25 percent of New England bank assets to 51 percent.

And then everything fell apart. As the tide of the Cold War turned in our favor, military spending peaked and then, in 1986, began a steady decline. The computer industry shifted away from minicomputers and toward desktops from Silicon Valley upstarts like Apple and Compaq, forcing Digital Equipment and Wang to lay off workers and shift operations to cheaper locales, such as Texas. And state and local governments' drunken orgy produced massive deficits, which brought the era of ever-higher spending to an end.

Real estate—as it frequently does when a bubble pops—operated in denial mode for a while, with nonresidential building permits rising until 1988. "Confidence had taken the place of fundamentals in driving growth," noted BankBoston economist Richard DeKaser in a 1998 white paper. "Properties were justified on past rates of appreciation," rather than on how they would perform if there was a recession.

But once the growth engine shifted into reverse, no amount of wishful thinking would suffice. New England state governments, now short of funds, began firing the people they had hired during the previous boom. In Massachusetts between 1989 and 1992, the state payroll fell from about 70,000 to 55,000. Overall, the state lost 11 percent of its jobs, compared with less than 2 percent for the country as a whole. The number of construction jobs fell from 150,000 to 65,000.

Because of the long lag between approval and completion for big projects like office buildings, commercial property kept coming on line through the early 1990s, producing a massive oversupply. Vacancy rates soared, rents plummeted, and loan defaults hit records. Northeastern banks, now overexposed to a moribund sector, began to die as well: 16 of them failed in 1990, 52 in 1991, and 43 in 1992. The resulting losses—$1.3 billion in 1990, $5.5 billion in 1991, and $2.8

billion in 1992, accounted for 45 percent, 91 percent, and 77 percent respectively of Federal Deposit Insurance Corporation failure-resolution costs in those years. The survivors pretty much stopped lending for real estate of any kind, making a bad situation disastrous. Permits for new homes fell by two-thirds between 1986 and 1992, while the amount of repossessed property in Massachusetts jumped from $339 million to $1.5 billion. One 1992 study calculated that since 1987, the value of Boston office property had fallen more than 70 percent.

NORTHEAST HOME BUILDING PERMITS

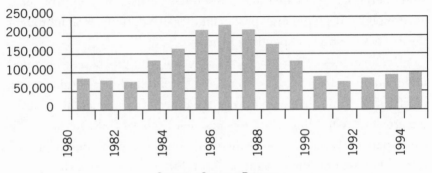

Source: Census Bureau

Things were so bad that one Boston real estate firm simply halved the price of the condominiums in one of its developments. And a banking analyst with a Maine brokerage house organized a 40-mile guided tour of New England real estate lending disasters for potential investors, which included highlights like "a rubble-strewn development site in the Boston suburb of Weymouth, with a ghostly row of unfinished condominium units long abandoned by builders."

"It was the worst regional recession in the United States since the end of the Great Depression," wrote Fred McMahon, senior policy analyst at the Atlantic Institute for Market Studies, in a recent study. As for home prices, they fell an average of 20 percent across the region and took most of the following decade to recover. In Boston, it was 1997 before the average home returned to its 1988 peak.

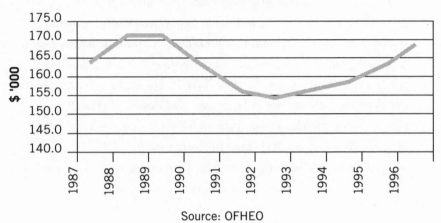

BOSTON HOME PRICES

Nine years to Recover

Source: OFHEO

And so gloom came to replace euphoria. Catching the tenor of the times nicely was a 1990 *Boston Globe* piece titled "Building in the Aftermath of the Boom Gone Bust":

> *What does an architecture critic write about when everyone stops building buildings? Writing about architecture today is like being a movie critic when the screens go suddenly black. Like being a music critic when the horns and violins fade away. Like being a book critic in the world of 1984. . . . I took an anonymous random survey of local architects—anonymous because no firm is willing to talk for the record about the fact that it's hurting for work. The consensus was that 1990 is going to be the worst year for architects since the legendary recession of 1975. Some fear the situation could be even direr than that.*

Big, heavily hyped private developments such as the Campeau and Commonwealth Center projects on Washington Street have—at the most euphemistic assessment—been pushed to the back burner. The state, the cities, and the towns are cutting back radically. Banks have stopped lending. High-tech companies are threatened by Japan. For architects, the pain goes all down the line. "I've had to lay off more than a third of my people," says one prominent architect. "Communities are not approving capital programs," says another. "If the school roof is leaking all over the kids, they'll fix it, but that's all. . . . The development community is basically shut down. Maybe 20 percent of local architects—maybe more, at a guess—have been laid off. As many as 500 came to Boston in the 1980s from depressed parts of the country such as Louisiana, Colorado, and especially Texas. Now many are again moving on."

Southern California: Golden Age of the Golden State

What can you say about California that hasn't already been said? Sixteen thousand miles of sometimes maddening highway, 1,100 miles of often breathtaking coastline, home to Hollywood and Silicon Valley, a multicultural melting pot—pretty much what the rest of the country will look like in 50 years. Toss in really nice weather, and it's no surprise that people have been flocking there for decades and that it now accounts for about 13 percent of U.S. gross domestic product (GDP). Standing alone, it would be the world's seventh-biggest economy, right up there with France.

Because of its size, collective brainpower, and affinity for the new and strange, California tends to blaze trails for the rest of us. And by the late 1980s, the southern half of the state was enjoying an epic real estate boom. Orange County's median home price jumped 32 percent in 1987 to $231,200, the highest for any large market in the country. Los Angeles County prices were up 24 percent to $191,200, and San Diego's 18.6 percent to $157,200, all during a year when the national median home price rose just 3 percent to $88,000. A typical Los Angeles–area house that cost $24,500 at the beginning of the 1970s sold for nearly $200,000 at the end of the 1980s. And the smaller, trendier neighborhoods were out of sight. The average Beverly Hills house was worth $1.5 million, with La Jolla ($686,000) and San Marino ($639,000) moving up as well.

But whereas southern California's many previous booms were due mostly to waves of immigration, this one had more interesting and diverse roots. First, there was the Japan connection. As that country emerged as a global power, its soaring exports of Toyotas and Sonys passed, in large part, through southern California ports. And while Americans were buying Japanese stuff, the Japanese were buying California. When NEC or Hitachi set up regional headquarters in their biggest foreign market, their executives needed classy digs. And because, as you'll read later in this section, Japan's real estate bubble was even bigger than California's, a $700,000 beachfront house in La Jolla seemed like a steal to Tokyo expatriots. So a big part of our suddenly growing trade deficit with Japan was recycled through southern California real estate agents. In 1988, RE/MAX's Rancho Palos Verdes office doubled its sales to Asians to $100 million. And by decade's end, 75 of the 400 full members of the elite Rolling Hills Country Club (dues: $109,000) were Japanese.

An even bigger fire under the housing market was lit by the Reagan-era defense build-up, which funneled billions of dollars into southern California's military bases and defense contractors. Local aerospace firms, now working on massive new contracts, sucked up engineers the way Silicon Valley firms would add programmers a decade later. California's job rolls increased, on average, by more than 400,000 a year in the late 1980s, with the biggest part of that coming in the southern half of the state. Local banks, once again following the money, increased their exposure in commercial and residential real estate to about double the national average.

While all this was going on, a few contrary signs were creeping in, unnoticed in the frenzy. The soaring number of cars on southern California roads had created a blanket of smog, to which Sacramento reacted with some of the world's toughest anti–air-pollution rules. That this dramatically raised the cost of doing business was seen as irrelevant in a place that was attracting people and businesses faster than it could accommodate them. Defense spending, meanwhile, peaked in 1986 and began to drift lower, though this too was lost in the din of the wealth creation party. But when the Pentagon began closing bases in 1989, southern California took some of the biggest hits. The first round of closures alone eliminated two local air force bases and a naval base, and when the dust finally cleared in 1993, California had lost 22 of its 72 military installations, most of which were in the south. And even when bases were spared, key operations were moved, as when the pentagon shifted several hundred employees of the Office of Special Projects, a developer of top top-secret spy satellites, from El Segundo Air Force Base to Washington, D.C. As the *Los Angeles Times* reported, "Just when South Bay civic leaders were hoping they had endured the economy's last punch to the gut, the Air Force landed another one Friday. . . . Stunned and bewildered local officials, reeling from the loss in recent years of at least 20,000 aerospace jobs, say they do not know at this stage how serious an impact the Air Force decision will have on the area's stumbling economy." All told, while the national defense budget fell by just $13 billion—to $277 billion—between 1998 and 1994, California's share fell by 25 percent, from $60 billion to $45 billion.

And finally, in 1990, came the coup de grâce. Saddam Hussein invaded Kuwait, sending consumer spending down and oil prices through the roof, just the wrong combination for a trade dependent, car-centric region. Companies began fleeing the coast for cheaper, less regulated addresses in Arizona and Colorado. And all of a sudden, buying a pricey southern California bungalow seemed kind of silly. Housing starts statewide fell by two-thirds, from 300,000 in 1986 to fewer than 100,000 five years later, and construction workers joined their aerospace counterparts on the unemployment lines.

Angelenos suddenly found themselves in the unfamiliar position of losing money on their homes. And in place of breathless stories of new real estate wealth and shocking price increases, the press began to dwell on how far prices were falling. There was the Orange County geologist who paid $315,000 for a house in a new San Clemente subdivision, only to see the next batch of nearby homes be auctioned off for $70,000 less. And the owner of the 30,000-square-foot mansion who cut his offering price by one-third, to $14.95 million, yet still couldn't attract a buyer. According to one Orange County real estate broker, by the end of 1990, sales of $1 million–plus homes were down by more than half from the pace at the beginning of the year.

LOS ANGELES/LONG BEACH HOME PRICES
Nine years to Recover

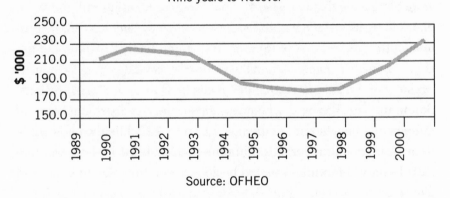

Source: OFHEO

The average southern California home didn't suffer quite so spectacularly, but its value did fall by about 20 percent between 1989 and 1992. For the home owners who held on, it was 9 years before their property values returned to 1989 levels.

Japan: The Mother of All Real Estate Bubbles

Japan's path to modernity could not have been more different from that of the United States. Whereas the U.S. was settled by waves of immigrants, which made it messy but relatively open from day one, Japan in the 1600s was a closed society, needing little from abroad and wanting less. Its feudal structure resembled a cleaner and more orderly version of medieval Europe's, with a semidivine emperor as figurehead, a shogun and his loyal aristocracy (called daimyo) making the real decisions, samurai (think medieval knights sans the armor) acting as enforcers and soldiers, and virtually everyone else consigned to life as a merchant or a peasant. Only a few Dutch traders were allowed to live and work in the port city of Nagasaki, and if a foreign sailor had the misfortune to be shipwrecked on the Japanese coast, as often as not he was summarily executed.

Not surprisingly, this system didn't produce much in the way of technological progress, a fact made painfully clear in 1853 when Commodore Perry's gunboats sailed into Tokyo Bay and informed the Tokugawa Shogunate that henceforth Japan would be trading with the West. Shocked by its sudden weakness, Japan set out to catch up. But instead of adopting the relatively freewheeling capitalism of Britain and the United States, it simply shifted the focus of its feudal system from management of the land to production of goods. During the Meiji Restoration in the late 1860s, the Japanese government redistributed land to farmers and bought out the daimyo, instantly capitalizing a new business class. Samurai became plant foremen and white-collar workers called salarymen, while peasants became factory workers. Mergers and partnerships were encouraged, leading to the formation of large, interlocking banking/industrial entities called *zaibatsu*. In an early hint of what this disciplined culture could accomplish when it set its collective mind to a task, within half a century Japan had become the new bully on the Asian playground, humbling the Chinese army in 1895 and Russian navy in 1905.

Other than a little copper, limestone, and zinc, Japan had few natural resources, so, like its European counterparts, it concluded that the path to greatness was paved with external colonies. Given its location, this meant controlling Korea and at least part of China, so it annexed the former in 1910, took Manchuria in 1931, and invaded China proper in 1937. This brought it into conflict with the Europeans and Americans, who had designs of their own on the region. And in 1941, threatened with the cutoff of oil and steel from its Western suppliers, Japan made perhaps the dumbest move in modern geopolitical history by launching a surprise attack on the U.S. naval base at Pearl Harbor. The result was a crushing defeat, and an occupation and radical reorganization at the hands of victorious General Douglas MacArthur, who set out to eliminate the power of Japan's militaristic elites and build a Western-style democracy.

Postwar occupied Japan looked like anything but a future world power. Its system of government was discredited, big parts of its major cities were wastelands, and its economy was barely functioning. Who knows what it would have become if the occupying authorities had carried out their original plan to break the *zaibatsu* into their constituent parts. But fate intervened.

Distracted by the Korean War and rising tensions with the Soviet Union, MacArthur and his successors allowed many of the connections between banks and industrial companies to endure. So instead of fragmenting, the *zaibatsu* extended their reach, evolving into even bigger industrial alliances now known as *keiretsu*. The result was a perfect fit for the postwar world. Whereas in the United States, banks, insurers, and manufacturers are simply one another's customers, and the government is a regulator and/or adversary, in Japan the players worked together, with *keiretsu* banks providing patient, long-term capital and manufacturers sharing research and development with suppliers and then offering long-term contracts, which allowed suppliers to build factories with minimal risk. And they all owned one another's stock, lessening outside pressure for quick results.

Meanwhile, government guided the process, directing *keiretsu* efforts toward what the Ministry of International Trade and Industry (MITI) saw as the most vulnerable Western markets. To protect local industries, regulators evolved multitiered approval and licensing processes, enforced by layers of ministries and agencies. Like good feudal lords, the *keiretsu* offered their workers lifetime employment in return for loyal service. And workers, like proper samurai and peasants, sang the company song in the morning, put in long hours for modest pay, and—this point is crucial—saved huge chunks of each paycheck. U.S.-style consumerism was never part of the plan.

Because the products that would drive the global economy—including cars, consumer electronics, and mass-produced steel—had been or soon would be invented by the West, Japan's industrial conglomerates focused on the production process, cutting costs and flooding the world with low-priced copies. This worked brilliantly, and by the early 1970s, Japan had become a lot like today's China, an efficient maker of low-end, ubiquitous stuff. Readers of a certain age will recall that "made in Japan" was for a while synonymous with cheap and shoddy. But by continuing to refine the manufacturing process, Japanese companies moved steadily upstream, from lawn mower engines (Honda's early forte) to motorcycles to small cars, and from cheap transistor radios (Sony's first big hit) to color TVs. At each stage, the keiretsu dominated by paying better attention to detail than did jaded Western competitors such as Harley-Davidson, Ford, and General Electric. And by the late-1980s, Japan was churning out stereos and cars that were vastly better than anything made in the West. Books like *Japan in the Passing Lane* both terrified and awed us, while business magazines predicted that with computers and TVs merging, Sony and Hitachi would one day subsume IBM and Intel, shifting the center of twenty-first–century economic gravity to Asia.

By the late-1980s, Japan had become a kind of high-tech version of Texas; everything about it was huge. Its banks dwarfed Chase and Citibank. Several of its brokerage houses could have swallowed Merrill Lynch whole. Its computer chip makers dominated the world; its carmakers were pushing the U.S. Big Three out of trendsetting California. It was the biggest creditor nation, its people had the longest life expectancy and the highest per capita GDP, and its manufacturers were pioneering the use of industrial robots, holding out the promise of pristine factories run by one salaryman in a control room, making obsolete not just American products but the whole U.S. workforce.

By consuming little and exporting a lot, Japan was racking up billions in trade surpluses, with which its people did three things: They bought Japanese stocks, sending the Nikkei Index on a tear similar in scope and duration to the U.S. tech stock bubble of the 1990s. They squeezed ever more impressive office towers into the manmade anthills of downtown Tokyo and Osaka. And they gave themselves, at long last, a little privacy, by buying tiny homes or apartments. In part because of the tsunami of cash washing over the island, in part because of the limited amount of land available, and in part because of antiquated laws that kept what land there was locked into unproductive uses, the value of the real estate that made it to market soared beyond anything the human race had ever seen. Between 1986 and 1988, the price of commercial land in greater Tokyo doubled. In 1988 alone, it soared by 68 percent, making a choice site in Tokyo's Ginza shopping district worth $269,000 per square meter. At the bubble's peak, the total value of land in Japan (which is about the size of Montana) was four times that of all the land in the United States. Heck, Tokyo alone was worth more than the entire United States.

As goes land, so go home prices, and by the late 1980s, Japanese homes (though cracker boxes to the Western eye) were beyond the dreams of the most optimistic San Franciscan. A modest house within a 45-minute commute of downtown Tokyo was about $500,000 in 1989, with bigger, closer places running into the millions. Because this was a little high even for the newly well-off salaryman, local banks—providing their essential bubble-enabling service—began offering 100-year mortgages. And Japanese—convinced by two decades of success that their incomes would always rise and homes would always appreciate—began snapping them up. That these intergenerational loans would saddle not just their children but their grandchildren with huge debts was brushed aside in the general euphoria.

"Leverage," as it always does, began to move from the high-rises to the suburbs. As the *Los Angeles Times* reported in 1989, "People lucky enough to own land have perfected the art of borrowing against their property to pump money into the stock market for lucrative capital gains." As in New England and California, Japanese society began to stratify according to real estate ownership. From the same *Los Angeles Times* article: "Many ordinary Japanese who did not own property before the spiral began cannot dream of buying any now, when a modest home on the outskirts of Tokyo sells for upwards of $2 million. The have-nots must resign themselves to a lifetime of renting." And see if this sounds familiar: "A boom in the sale of luxury items, meanwhile, is being driven by the young offspring of people who own land and can easily borrow against it for a windfall in riches."

But then, against all odds, U.S. companies began to stage a comeback. Instead of going head-to-head with Japan's masters of efficient manufacturing techniques, innovative upstarts like Microsoft and Cisco simply bypassed them, creating whole new industries around PCs and the Internet. The Japanese suddenly found themselves in the slow lane, making commodity products like memory chips, which kept getting cheaper, while each new version of Windows cost the same $89.

At this point the script once again departs from the American experience. Whereas New England and California banks were simply allowed to fail and home owners to default, Japan chose not to let the bubble burst so violently. In part this was due to the previously mentioned structural differences between the two economies. Japanese banks owned vast amounts of stock in the companies to which they lent money, and used the stock as capital against which to make more loans. As the Japanese market soared, the banking sector's capital base exploded, giving it ever more money to lend out. Because capital, as economists like to say, chases inflation, the banks, of course, chose to lend to their booming real estate developer clients. In 1989, they boosted their loans to such businesses by 26 percent, with the underlying real estate serving as collateral for many of the loans.

When things began to sour, the banks found that their virtuous cycle had turned vicious. As stock prices fell, the banks' capital shriveled, and whereas an American bank might have pulled the plug on a failing construction company and written off the loan, the Japanese banks felt compelled to lend more to prevent the company's stock from collapsing and taking the bank's capital base down with it. Thus was created a whole generation of "zombies," real estate companies—and their codependent banks and insurance firms—that would die within a month were it not for continuous infusions of outside capital. With far too much national wealth tied up in vastly overvalued real estate and with no way to get out of it, Japan sank into a kind of torpor, with consumer spending flat, and stock and real estate prices falling a little

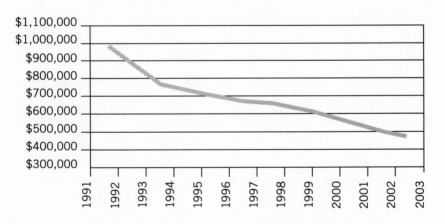

JAPANESE HOME PRICES

Down for Twelve Straight Years*

*Price of a Tokyo-area home with a 1990 market value of $1,000,000.

Source: Japan Ministry of Public Management

each year. The Nikkei stock index fell from its 1989 peak of 38,900 to 8,000 by early 2003. And real estate prices began a decline that, as this is written, is in its twelfth year, with no letup in sight.

But wait; it gets worse. The Japanese government had cut interest rates to zero and borrowed vast sums for "public works," mostly big construction projects, to keep the economy from sinking from recession to depression. The result was a migration of millions of workers away from shrinking industries, such as retailing and electronics, and toward, of all places, construction. By the end of 2002, 10 percent of the Japanese worked in fields that one way or another relate to building things. The government's debt, as a result of its largely ineffective stimulus spending, is now at 120 percent of GDP, about twice the U.S. level. And the banking/construction/insurance nexus is weaker than ever. No one really knows how much bad debt is festering in banks' balance sheets because much of it won't come to light until the banks turn off the loan spigots. But brokerage house HSBC Securities (Japan) estimates that the total is around 15 percent of Japan's gross domestic product, which explains the country's paralysis. There's no way for Japan's economy to recover without liquidating this mountain of misallocated capital, but there's no way to liquidate it without causing something akin to a depression.

PART 2

THE HOUSING BUBBLE

AND ITS CONSEQUENCES

"If one person calls you a horse's ass, be curious. If three people . . . be reflective. After five people . . . buy a saddle."

—DOROTHY PARKER

CHAPTER 3

ANATOMY OF TODAY'S BUBBLE

The aftermath of every bubble leaves its participants shaking their heads and wondering why they didn't see the bust coming. Well, why didn't they? Perhaps because the human mind doesn't shift gears that quickly. Once we form an opinion—that tech stocks will always go up, for instance—we're resistant to anything that conflicts with our comfortable mindset. We ignore the first wave of contradictory news that comes along and begin to question our beliefs only when the weight of evidence becomes overwhelming. And only then, when it's too late, do we, as Dorothy Parker advises, start shopping for saddles. So let's round up some evidence that the housing bubble is about to pop, and see if it qualifies as overwhelming.

Home Sales Are Higher than Ever

Normally, housing is one of the more cyclical parts of the economy, which makes intuitive sense, right? In good times, you're feeling flush and it's both easy to envision yourself in that 3,000-square-foot transitional at the end of the classy cul-de-sac, and easy to make it happen. In bad times, on the other hand, when your stocks are down and your neighbor just got laid off and your boss is huddling with her boss behind closed doors, the last thing you want to do is buy a big new house.

So it was predictable that home sales would surge throughout the fever dream of the late 1990s, setting records in 1998, 1999, and 2000. But after the tech stock crash, the World Trade Center attacks, and the implosions of Enron and WorldCom, when the rest of the economy took a nerve-racking but completely predictable rest, homes kept selling. In 2002, when the NASDAQ fell by 30 percent, a record 976,000 new homes were bought, up 8 percent from the previous year. Meanwhile, building permits set a record in December 2002, indicating that the first part of 2003 would be just as hot.

NEW HOME SALES

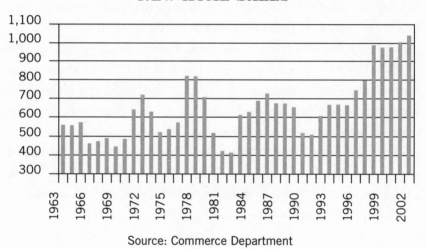

Source: Commerce Department

Mortgage Rates Are at a 37-Year Low

Consider a $250,000 house, bought with a 20 percent down payment on a 30-year mortgage. Using the mortgage cost calculator that's available at financial institutions and on most personal finance Web sites, we see the difference that a few percentage points can make. If mortgages are at 12 percent, as they were back in 1986, the house will cost $2,057.23 a month. Drop the rate to 8 percent, as happened in the early 1990s, and the cost falls to $1,467.53. Step down to 6 percent, the rate that prevailed at the end of 2002, and the cost falls to $1,199.10. With each drop, tens of millions of families become able to refinance their existing loans at lower rates, while millions of renters suddenly qualify for home loans.

In March 2003, the average 30-year fixed-rate mortgage fell to 5.6 percent, the lowest level since 1965. The 15-year fixed rate touched 5.0 percent, and 1-year adjustable-rate loans were going for 4 percent.

MORTGAGE RATES

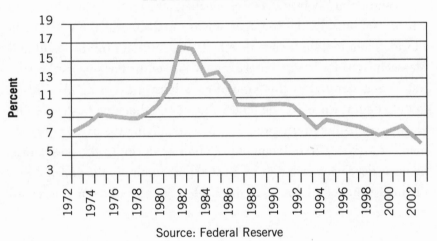

Source: Federal Reserve

Home Prices Are Soaring

For the first time since the 1930s, economists are starting to toss around the D word. Not depression; the other one, deflation. Prices of many things are actually falling, and companies in virtually every field are finding that they have no choice but to go along. DVD players debuted in 1997 at about $500 and now sell for less than $100. General Motors' 2002 cars sold for about 2 percent less than comparable models a year earlier, and used car prices are falling at double-digit rates. Duracell cut its 2003 battery prices by about 13 percent. Air fares are down on many routes. Stock prices have fallen for three straight years. One recent study calculates that even in a broad category like "general merchandise and apparel," prices were falling at a 2.5 percent annual rate in early 2003.

Yet through it all, home prices keep rising, steadily in many places and dramatically in some. According to the Office of Federal Housing Enterprise Oversight, which tracks price changes in repeat sales or refinancings on the same houses, the average U.S. home is up by 181 percent since 1980. In the past 5 years, it's up by 38 percent. And since the start of the post-1990s slowdown, while Whoppers and Accords and Palm Pilots are getting cheaper, home prices haven't missed a beat. Nationwide, the average increase in 2002 was 6.6 percent. In Florida, comparable homes rose by 9 percent, and in Maryland and Massachusetts by 10 percent. Given the size of the housing market, the numbers generated by this kind of growth are staggering. According to the Federal Reserve, the total value of U.S. housing has soared by close to $5 trillion during the past 5 years, giving the average household net worth a $70,000 bump. In California during 2002, the average home owner's net worth rose by $3,000 per month. By the end of 2002, the total value of all homes in the United States had risen to a record $13 trillion.

HOT HOUSING MARKETS

CITY	PERCENT CHANGE IN LAST 5 YEARS	PERCENT CHANGE 2002
Boston	73.24	9.16
Ft. Lauderdale	53.50	13.00
Miami	49.24	13.42
Providence, Rhode Island	55.45	13.48
San Diego	79.12	13.20
National average	*38.50*	*6.60*

Source: Office of Federal Housing Enterprise Oversight

Fewer People Can Afford Homes

Rising home prices aren't necessarily a problem if home buyers' incomes are rising along with them. Historically this has been the case, which is why a house that cost $20,000 in 1950 can go for $200,000 today. So the real key to the future of the housing market is the concept of affordability. That is, can the average family buy the average house, given what they earn and what the house costs? When the answer is yes, then the housing market has room to grow. When it's no, then before growth can continue, either incomes have to rise or home ownership costs have to fall.

There are at least two ways to calculate affordability. The first is to compare the monthly cost of home ownership with the paycheck of a would-be home owner, with the recommended upper limit being around one-third. The second is to compare home prices with average annual incomes in a given area and compare the resulting number with the past two decades' national average of around three (that is, home prices are about three times incomes). But however you approach affordability, in a bubble you'd expect:

1. prices to be rising much faster than incomes, and

2. a large and growing number of people to be unable to afford the average home in their town.

That's clearly the case in the hottest markets. In Boston, as recently as 1995, the local median income was almost enough to buy a median-priced house. But home prices there have doubled in the past seven years, while incomes have barely budged. Today a family making the local median of $61,000 can afford the monthly payments on a house worth only a little more than half the median price of $395,000. In Tucson, the *Daily Star* newspaper crunched the local numbers in late 2002 and found that only 12 of the area's 27 zip codes fell within the affordability zone. The story is more or less the same in Miami, Denver, and much of California; home values are rising faster than mortgage rates are falling, thus pricing a growing number of residents out of what they would consider adequate homes. Unlucky locals who haven't already jumped on the housing gravy train find themselves making more money than their parents, yet unable to afford the kind of house they grew up in, "an odd inversion of the American Dream," as the *New York Times* put it in November 2002. And dramatic divisions of wealth are developing, with families who bought homes in the early 1990s getting richer, while those who rented find home ownership, not to mention financial independence, slipping from their grasp. (Note the similarities here to the New England, California, and Japan bubbles recounted in chapter 2.)

The hottest markets, of course, aren't the whole story. In places such as Columbus, Ohio; Syracuse, New York; and Tallahassee, Florida, prices are up only modestly, and home ownership is still within most families' reach. So what about the nation as a whole? Ian Morris, an HSBC Securities USA economist, attempted to answer that question in January 2002 by comparing home prices with household incomes to create a kind of price-to-earnings ratio for the housing market. Here's a chart based on his methodology, using Federal Reserve data on home

REAL ESTATE WEALTH VERSUS DISPOSABLE INCOME

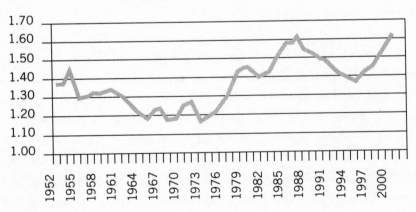

Source: Federal Reserve

values and disposable income. If the numbers are accurate, then overall affordability (or lack thereof) hit a record in 2002.

Home Equity Is at a Record Low

Among World War II–generation Americans, there was once a quaint tradition called the "mortgage burning party." This was a celebration of perseverance in that, after 30 years of scrimping to make those regular monthly payments, a family had at long last whittled their mortgage down to zero. On or around the day of the very last payment, they would invite their friends over to drink beer, eat burgers, and cheer enviously as they tossed the mortgage contract into the fireplace of their 100-percent-owned-free-and-clear home. Do a Google search today under "mortgage burning party" and you'll still find a few, some with uploaded snapshots of good people justifiably proud of their little piece of the American dream.

But they—that is, people who own their own homes free and clear—are a small, shrinking minority these days. As a society, we've spent the past decade going in reverse, consuming our home equity rather than growing it. As you can see from the chart below, in 1945

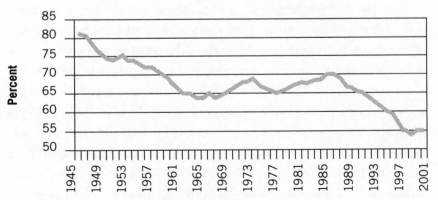

AMERICA'S SHRINKING HOME EQUITY

Source: Federal Reserve

Americans owed the bank an average of about 20 percent of their homes' value. Today that number has grown to 45 percent, which is another way of saying that our equity in our homes, the biggest investment most of us will ever make and our main shelter from life's financial storms, has shrunk to a record low. Why are we doing this? Because we can, thanks to three recent innovations.

Home equity credit lines. Say your house has appreciated in recent years while you've been dutifully making those mortgage payments. As any modern banker will tell you, you've got idle capital, in the form of home equity, just sitting there waiting to be unlocked. Simply sign on the dotted line, and the bank will lend you money against this buried treasure. The interest rate may be lower than that of your existing mortgage, and the interest is often tax deductible.

Cash-out refinancings. When interest rates drop, savvy home owners refinance their mortgages by taking out new, lower-rate mortgages and using the funds to pay off the old ones. Going from a rate of 8 percent to 6 percent, as millions of mortgages have done in the past few years, can cut hundreds of dollars from each month's payment and/or allow the loan to be paid off years earlier. As rates plunged between 2000 and 2002, close to $2.5 trillion in mortgage debt was refinanced, an amount equal to about 40 percent of all mortgage debt outstanding.

This would be a very good thing, if a refinance (refi) simply lowered a home owner's monthly mortgage bill. But in the 1990s a new twist on the theme emerged; instead of refinancing the same-size mortgage, home owners borrowed the maximum against the new, appreciated value of their homes, paid off the old mortgage, and pocketed the difference. The Federal Reserve Board calculates that in 2002 Americans pulled about $170 billion out of their home equity via cash-out refis and home equity loans, versus only $35 billion in 1999. Fully 45 percent of refis in 2002 were cash-outs, compared with about 35 percent in 1999. From 1999 to 2002, the average extraction jumped from $18,240 to $26,723. Meanwhile, only about 10 percent of mortgages refinanced in the second quarter of 2002 had lower new loan amounts.

By January 2003, refis were still going strong. According to the Mortgage Bankers Association of America (MBA), applications for new loans jumped 29.1 percent, versus a year earlier to the highest level in 7 weeks, bringing the current refi boom into its 29th week, versus only about 3 months each for the two previous spikes, in 1998 and 1999.

And even this might be a good thing, if cash-out proceeds were going to pay off other debt. But in 2002, only 26 percent of extracted equity was used this way. Instead, 35 percent went for home improvements, 16 percent for consumer expenditures, 11 percent for stock market or other financial investment, 10 percent for real estate or business investment, and 2 percent to pay taxes. The National Association of Realtors estimates that about 47,000 second-home purchases per year now involve equity drawn from a first home, up more than 60 percent from the pre-2000 average. First-home equity plays a bigger role in the acquisition of a vacation or rental house than do stock sales, inheritances, gifts, or proceeds from the sale of other assets.

HOW WE'RE SPENDING OUR REFI MONEY

Home improvements	35 percent
Repayment of other debts	26 percent
Consumer expenditures	16 percent
Financial investments	11 percent
Real estate or business investments	10 percent
Taxes	2 percent

Source: Federal Reserve

Low or nonexistent down payments. Once upon a time, it was generally accepted that to buy a house, you had to put down 20 percent of the purchase price. That way the banks would have a little cushion against your defaulting or the market's turning sour or whatever, and your payments were held to a manageable level. Most people probably still think this is the norm, but of course they're wrong. A down payment is exactly the kind of anachronism that, because it slows down the deal flow, tends to get tossed overboard in a bubble. And sure enough, in the past few years so many ways have emerged to get around the 20 percent rule—and in fact to bypass the concept of a down payment altogether—that millions of people who in less financially creative times would be expected to rent for a few years and save up a few thousand dollars or buy considerably less house are now signing on the dotted line and moving right in.

Mortgage giant Fannie Mae sponsors a series of low-down-payment mortgages such as MyCommunityMortgage 97, which, according to Fannie's Web site, "includes a minimum contribution of 1 percent or $500, whichever is less (from the borrower's own funds)." And that's the stringent one in the series, which includes the Community 100 Plus, "a more aggressive zero percent down payment mortgage with flexible credit guidelines for borrowers with limited cash resources."

If zero isn't low enough for you, Ditech.com offers the Freedom Loan, a second-mortgage program that "puts you in the driver's seat of your finances by letting you borrow up to 125 percent of your home's value." Call the 800 number and a polite staffer will explain that the rate on this loan can run up to 12.5 percent, depending on your means. But hey, if you're paying 18 percent on a bunch of credit cards, it may not be such a bad move. As Ditech's Web site says, "Many use the Freedom Loan to eliminate high-interest-rate credit card balances, pay for home improvements, or buy a new car—there aren't any restrictions on how you use your money."

But wait; it gets even better. It seems that a while back the Federal Housing Administration (FHA), which guarantees mortgage loans to low-income Americans, decided to allow gifts from charitable organizations to be used as down payments on FHA mortgages. Nothing much came of the idea until 1994 when Don Harris, founder of a tiny Sacramento-based, church-sponsored charity called Nehemiah, met a frustrated real estate developer with an inventory of hard-to-sell foreclosed townhouses. According to an *American Banker* magazine profile, "The conversation got Mr. Harris, who is also a real estate lawyer, wondering: What if he could help get people into homes through down payment donations, or gifts, from private industry? After researching federal law, he found a mechanism that lets charitable organizations make such gifts."

Now, by any standard this was a truly unassailable idea, to help those in need enter the economic mainstream through home ownership. And for a while the volume of help that Nehemiah offered was too small to have any real impact beyond a handful of happy first-time home buyers. But then the home-building companies figured out that they could donate money to charitable organizations—or even create such groups from scratch—and direct them to fund down payments on the builders' homes. Down payment assistance (know as DPA) gift volumes began to surge, attracting the attention of the Department of Housing and Urban Development (HUD), which proposed a rule to prohibit borrowers under the FHA program from using down payment gifts provided "directly or indirectly" by builders and sellers. But pressure from the players—now quite numerous and powerful—in the DPA game forced HUD to back off. And with the regulators on the sidelines, DPA has exploded. By the end of 2002, Nehemiah had gifted down payments for 130,000 mortgages valued, by one estimate, in excess of $13 billion. Around 20 percent of new FHA loans now use various DPA programs, for a total of $42 billion of new DPA mortgages each year.

And, hewing perfectly to the bubble script, just about everyone in the business is now grabbing a piece of the DPA action. Wells Fargo, the number-three U.S. mortgage lender, says it uses about 600 different down payment help programs. "It's an extremely important avenue for us to get mortgage volume and also to reach consumers who wouldn't have been able to afford a home," said a Wells Fargo vice president in a recent interview. The Web site of Neighborhood Gold, another DPA "nonprofit," crows, "From Bank of America to Wells Fargo, we work with some of the largest lenders in the nation. . . . You just fill out the one-page application online or fax it in and Neighborhood Gold takes care of the rest." The organization's Web site allows visitors to type in an area code and access a list of local homes participating in Neighborhood Gold DPA programs. In January 2003, 168 homes were listed as available in Denver's 303 area code.

Yet another purveyor of DPA, Genesis Program, bills itself as "a National Down Payment Assistance Program that provides home buyers with FREE GIFT MONEY to use toward the down payment, closing costs, and other funds needed to purchase a home. Genesis will gift up to $22,500."

Meanwhile, with those pesky conflict-of-interest considerations out of the way, in January 2002 Nehemiah formed a "strategic alliance" with Homebuilders Financial Network (HFN), which creates and manages in-house builder mortgage operations. Then, in May 2002, Fidelity National Financial, the nation's largest provider of title insurance and real estate–related products and services, bought a 75 percent interest in HFN.

So the circle is complete, and down payments are, for a growing segment of the population, a thing of the past. Put another way, mortgage lenders and home owners are now acting exactly the way you'd expect in the late stages of a bubble. They're ignoring the tried-and-true in favor of whatever works to get the deal done, and they're taking on risks that would have seemed insane a decade ago.

Home Ownership Is at an All-Time High

Now that it's possible to become a home owner with no down payment and a mortgage rate of 6 percent, you'd expect the percentage of the population that owns a home to be rising, and it is. After treading water in the mid–60 percent range for decades, the rate of home ownership began to rise in the early 1990s and, by the end of 2002, was at 68 percent, the highest level ever recorded in the U.S. And the mortgage and home-building industries are determined to push it higher, with at least one major player publicly aiming for 70 percent by 2010.

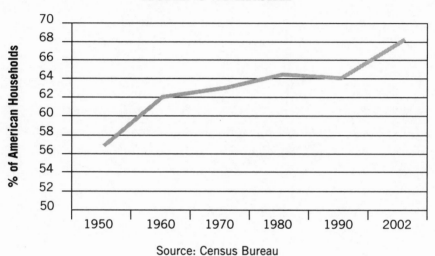

HOME OWNERSHIP

Source: Census Bureau

CHAPTER 4

HOW IT HITS HOME

Job Creation Has Stalled

One of the reasons the late 1990s were so much fun is that new jobs were everywhere. From Main Street (where Help Wanted signs became a permanent part of most stores' window displays) to Silicon Valley (which imported tens of thousands of engineers from India and Russia because we weren't producing enough domestically), everyone needed help and had no choice but to pay up. The fact that nearly a million manufacturing jobs disappeared between 1989 and 1999 seemed insignificant next to the 20 million new service jobs that were created. Retailing, air transportation, and communications each added 3 million new people during the decade, while state and local governments added about 2.5 million. And "business services"—a broad category that includes everything from supply-chain management software to accountants—added a whopping 9 million jobs.

But each of these sectors hit a wall in 2001. Communications employment has imploded as the glut of fiber-optic cable that was laid during the boom keeps pushing prices for long-distance service closer and closer to zero. Retailers, under assault from relentless cost cutters like Wal-Mart, are learning to do get by with fewer people, as illustrated by Kmart's January 2003 plan to close 300 stores and lay off 37,000 workers. State and local governments, as we'll see a few pages hence, are in the process of firing most of the people that they hired in the late 1990s. And "business services" is seeing "the greatest decline in employment in the last 43 years," according to the Bureau of Labor Statistics.

Manufacturing, of course, continues to shrink as we move more and more productive capacity to places like China, where people who can do algebra will work for $2 an hour. And now the globalization process is going upstream. With broadband connections getting cheaper all the time, it has become possible for, say, Microsoft to set up in India a customer service desk staffed by well-trained techies who speak perfect English—and are happy to make $10 an hour. In cities like Bangalore, U.S. banks now process credit card claims and mortgage applications, U.S. hospitals analyze CT scans, and U.S. chip companies design next-generation cell phone components—all work that until recently was done in the United States. And Wall Street has discovered that Indians and Russians can crunch merger and acquisition numbers just as efficiently as can Harvard MBAs—for literally one-tenth the starting pay. As a result, one study estimates that 500,000 financial jobs will move overseas in the coming five years. Another study puts the total at 1.5 million by 2015. Whatever the final

U.S. EMPLOYMENT

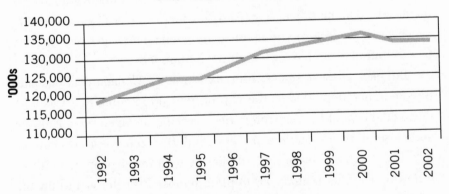

Source: Bureau of Labor Statistics

number, it seems that white-collar workers are about to share some of the pain of their blue-collar neighbors.

On the positive side, there's . . . well, there's baggage inspection, though that cohort of 250,000 has pretty much already been hired. And the military build-up should produce some aerospace work, but beyond that there really isn't a growth industry in the wings waiting to take up the slack.

Consumers Are Maxed Out

With both home sales and cash-out refis booming, it should come as no surprise that Americans are carrying a lot of mortgage debt. But just how much we're carrying—and how fast it's been growing—is still a little shocking. From 1988 to 1997, mortgage borrowing averaged about $220 billion annually, but in 2002 alone we added $820 billion. Since 1995, the amount of mortgage debt outstanding has risen by around $3 trillion, to nearly $7 trillion. As a result, despite

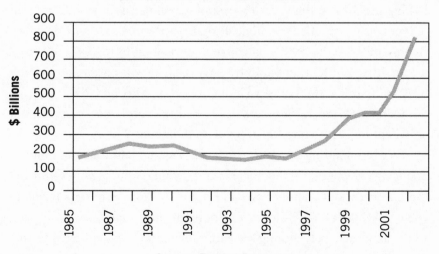

MORTGAGE BORROWING

Source: Federal Reserve

the plunge in mortgage interest rates, more than 6 percent of Americans' disposable income now goes to mortgage payments—close to the record set just before the 1991 recession, when mortgage rates were 10 percent.

Once again, this isn't automatically a bad thing. For years, financial planners and media talking heads have been telling people to dump their high-rate credit cards in favor of cheaper, tax-deductible home equity credit lines and refinanced mortgages. After all, if you can borrow at 7 percent against your house and pay off a 14 percent credit card balance, you're cutting your interest bill in half. Very smart—*unless you turn around and max out the cards you've just paid off.* And unfortunately, that seems to be what we as a nation are doing. According to the Federal Reserve Board, consumer credit (plastic and auto loans, mostly), after contracting slightly in the early 1990s, has surged recently and now accounts for nearly 8 percent of disposable income, the highest level since just before the 1987 stock market crash. As a result, the combined cost of mortgage and other consumer debt is 14 percent, close to an all-time high.

That's not the way it's supposed to work. As you can see from the chart below, in good times we borrow, and in bad times we cut back. During the 1980s, the carrying cost of consumer debt rose from 12.5 percent to nearly 14.5 percent of disposable income, and then fell steeply in the early 1990s as consumers reacted to the Gulf War and the savings and loan debacle by paying off credit cards and cutting back on luxuries. But notice what happened in 2001 and 2002: Despite the tech stock crash, September 11, and the mini-recession, we not only kept on borrowing; we stepped up the pace.

So who's lending us overleveraged consumers all this new money? Some very desperate finance companies, that's who. Again, following the bubble script, lenders are offering ever more generous terms to good risks (General Motor's zero-percent auto loans, for instance), while simultaneously mining the subprime market by lending to people

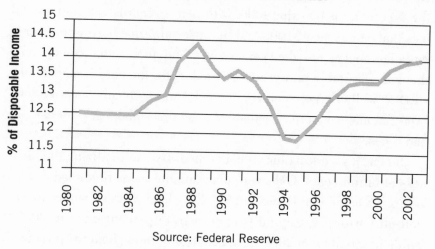

CONSUMER DEBT BURDEN

Source: Federal Reserve

with bad or nonexistent credit records. The low- and no-down-payment mortgages being written these days are subprime by definition, of course, because the borrowers can't scrape up the traditional 20 percent. And the credit card companies, as anyone with a mailbox knows, seem willing to lend money to anyone who will take it. In early 2003, Citibank's AT&T Universal MasterCard was offering zero percent interest for up to 15 months, while the MBNA Elite Rewards Platinum Plus MasterCard was at zero percent for 9 months on both purchases and cash advances. Nearly 40 percent of Capital One's new credit card business is subprime. And Citigroup's CitiFinancial subsidiary made nearly $200 billion of subprime loans in 2002.

Why are the consumer credit companies traveling such a perilous road? Because this late in the day, no other road is open. After years of solid and sometimes spectacular earnings growth, these companies' investors expect superb numbers—and their executives own so many stock options that continued growth is the difference between retiring super-rich and being unceremoniously fired. Besides, subprime credit cards are really profitable, often charging 16 percent rates rather than the 9 percent or less that folks with better records get, and annual fees that can exceed $100. And because subprime borrowers tend to miss more payments, they get socked with late fees that can often be the most profitable part of the whole deal for the card issuer. As the CEO of Wells Fargo recently summed it up, with subprime lending, "you can make a lot more money in good times and lose a lot more in bad times."

So far, it's working for all concerned. By cannibalizing the business of future years, GM's zero percent auto loans produced a sales gain of 36 percent in December 2002. By lending more money to less well-off borrowers, Capital One earned 35 percent more in 2002's fourth quarter than in 2001's. And so it goes, throughout the leveraged finance business, all at a time when history says consumers should be pulling back.

CHAPTER 5

IMPACT: GLOBAL AND LOCAL

Total Debt Is at an All-Time High

After all those years of worrying about "the national debt," we seemed to turn the corner in the late 1990s. A torrent of capital gains and income tax revenues converted federal deficits to surpluses, and for a brief, giddy couple of years, the political debate revolved around whether we should spend our never-ending surplus on the currently needy, use it to eliminate the federal debt in the coming decade, or pay it out in rebates to taxpayers. What fun.

The surplus disappeared along with the tech stock bubble, of course, and Washington is once again running deficits. But look a little deeper, and you'll find a story that's vastly scarier than today's headlines. Federal debt, it turns out, is just one piece of the American debt pie, and neither the biggest nor the fastest growing. And even during the sanguine 1990s, while the Treasury was balancing its books, the rest of us were actually on a borrowing binge. Between 1990 and 2001, U.S. households and businesses borrowed more than $13 trillion (that's trillion with a *t*). And total national debt (the sum debt of government, business, and household borrowing, as well as the obligations of federal trust funds) climbed to $32 trillion. That's eight times the $4 trillion we owed in 1957 (in inflation-adjusted 2001 dollars), and comes to $115,000 per citizen, versus $25,000 in 1957.

And—are you tired of hearing this yet?—the pace is accelerating. More than one-third of our total debt has been added since 1992. That year, private borrowing was $200 billion, and since then it has risen every year; it surpassed $1 trillion in 2002. The government, after retiring a few hundred billion in the late 1990s, is now borrowing more than $300 billion per year, bringing the ongoing annual debt buildup to more than $1 trillion. Early in the current binge, it was telecom companies loading up the wagon. Now, as you know, it is home owners.

But rising debt is manageable if it's put to productive uses that make us richer in the process, right? Sure, if we were generating a positive return on our borrowing—that is, if national wealth as measured by gross domestic product (GDP) was going up as fast as total debt. As you can see from the chart below, that was more or less the case until the late 1970s. Total debt was increasing at close to the growth rate of national income, despite lingering obligations from World War II and the cost of the Korean and Vietnam wars. But in the past 20 years, the

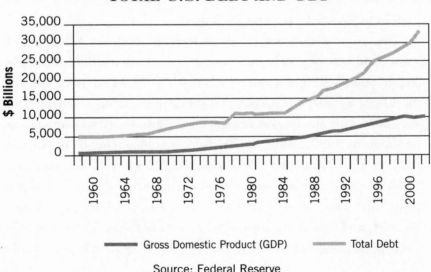

TOTAL U.S. DEBT AND GDP

Gross Domestic Product (GDP) — Total Debt

Source: Federal Reserve

two lines have diverged, with GDP growth slowing a bit and debt accumulation soaring. In the 1980s, real debt increased by $9.5 trillion, while national income grew by $2.4 trillion, meaning that we borrowed more than three dollars for every dollar of new wealth we created. And in the 1990s the gap widened further, with debt increasing by $15 trillion and GDP rising by only $3 trillion, a five-to-one ratio of new debt to new wealth.

What does this mean? Two things. First, it appears that the only way we can keep growing is to borrow ever-increasing amounts of money. Second, the return we can expect on each new dollar of debt is diminishing.

The Dollar Is Suddenly Vulnerable

For most of the 1990s, the whole world seemed to want what the United States was selling: computer chips, software, pharmaceuticals, movies, tech stocks, smart bombs—you name it, America made it. Yet somehow we still managed to buy far more from overseas than we sold, which is another way of saying that our biggest export wasn't a product or service; it was—and is—the dollar. Each year, we make up the difference between our imports and exports by sending roughly $400 billion overseas. A trade deficit this big and persistent should, according to economic theory, throw the supply/demand equation out of balance and make the dollar less valuable. But in the 1990s it was a nonevent; the dollar actually got more valuable, so much so that it became a problem for export-dependent industries. But gravity reasserted itself with a vengeance in 2002, and by year end the dollar was heading south against the yen, the euro, and gold. Let the trend continue—as it probably will—and the dollar might just be the needle that pops the real estate bubble.

To understand how this is likely to play out, let's start with why the value of the dollar matters in the first place. The short answer is that to buy something from abroad, we first have to convert our dollars to our trading partner's currency. The terms of the conversion, known as the exchange rate, determine how many yen, euros, or pesos each dollar will buy and thus how much that new Camry, bottle of French wine, or bag of Colombian coffee costs. When the dollar is strong—that is, valuable relative to other currencies—goods from abroad are cheap. When the dollar is weak, imports become expensive, sometimes prohibitively so. In terms of the rest of the world, our savings become less valuable and we become less rich.

What determines a currency's value? Besides the trade balance, two things: The first is the profit that foreign investors expect to make when they buy a given country's stocks, bonds, factories, and buildings. Other things being equal, a country with low taxes, cheap, well-trained workers, and clear laws is an easier place to make money and thus more attractive to foreign investors. China, for instance, offers cheap but smart workers and a growing respect for property rights and now attracts billions in foreign investment each year. The second key is relative interest rates. When you buy a bond denominated in yen or euros or dollars, you get the interest rate that prevails in that market. If Japanese rates are relatively high, then yen-denominated bonds are attractive and global capital is more likely to flow in that direction, pushing up the yen's value.

The dollar was able to shrug off the trade deficit for so long because we got the other things right. Our taxes were low, our laws were clear, our economy was growing, and our interest rates were relatively high. As a result, the United States became the destination of choice for global capital and brains, with Europeans and Asians using their dollars to buy our stocks, bonds, and buildings, and Chinese and Indian engineers eagerly filling slots at CalTech and Microsoft.

In the process, the dollar became the de facto world currency, with central banks using it as their main reserve asset, countries like Hong Kong and Chile linking their currencies to it, and the price of commodities like oil being denominated in it. In the international underworld, suitcases of twenties are as common as Uzis and stolen cell phones, and it is said that more $100 bills circulate in Russia than in the United States. As Federal Reserve governor Donald Kohn put it in a November 2002 speech, "Evidently, savers around the world have anticipated greater risk-adjusted returns on their investments in the United States than in surplus countries. . . . The upward trend in the foreign exchange value of the dollar since the mid-1990s as the deficit was climbing indicates that the rising demand for dollars from capital inflows, and not the rising supply of dollars from the trade deficit, was the dominating force in international transactions between the United States and the rest of the world."

Meanwhile, the trade deficit kept getting bigger, hitting a record $435 billion in 2002. Japan and Germany, meanwhile, recorded a cumulative trade surplus with the world of $160 billion—beating the United States by a shocking $595 billion. Foreigners now own about $8 trillion of U.S. financial assets, including 13 percent of all stocks, 24 percent of corporate bonds, 43 percent of Treasury bonds, and 14 percent of U.S. government agency debt (such as Fannie Mae's mortgage-backed bonds). According to a Bloomberg report in September 2002, about a third of Fannie Mae's debt is sold outside the United States.

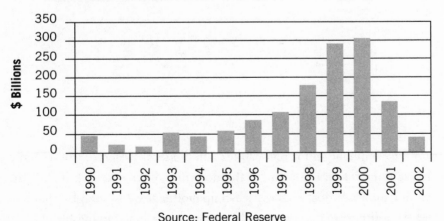

FOREIGN DIRECT INVESTMENT IN THE U.S.

Source: Federal Reserve

Finally, with U.S. stock markets falling and interest rates at record lows, the rest of the world began to look elsewhere for excitement. In 2002 net foreign investment fell by about two-thirds from its 1999 level. Sans the support of foreign investors, the dollar started to drift lower and by year end was down 15 percent to 20 percent against the other major currencies. Now the question is whether 2002 was an aberration or the beginning of a long slide for the dollar. As Hans Guenther Redeker, analyst with major European bank BNP Paribas, put it in a June 2002 report, "So far, the USD decline has been initiated by investors allocating less funds to the U.S. Liquidation of existing positions has not yet taken place, but with the USD dropping fast, the equity and USD decline could become self-feeding."

THE DOLLAR IN 2002

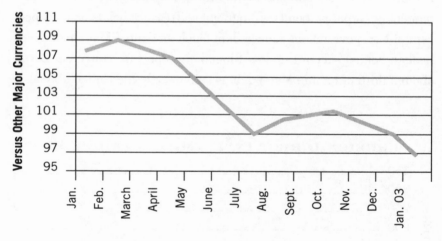

Source: Federal Reserve

The implication for real estate? The Federal Reserve, whose main job is to maintain the value of the dollar, may have to stop its fall by raising interest rates. This will push up mortgage rates, thereby choking off the refi boom and very possibly popping the housing bubble.

State and Local Finances Are a Mess

The last decade of the 20th century was a great time to run a state. Companies were going public and stocks were soaring, producing unprecedented levels of taxable capital gains. Home prices were surging, sending property assessments through the roof, and everyone was working, shopping, playing, and of course paying taxes. The hardest task facing a governor in times like this is deciding how to spend this river of cash. Not whether to spend it, but how. The states, with few exceptions, used their surging revenues to build roads and schools, expand health benefits, and above all hire new workers, who then bought houses and stocks and clothes, paying taxes along the way, and the good times just kept rolling.

Then the music stopped. Plunging stock markets and imploding tech companies caused the tax revenue fountain to dry up, and where growing surpluses once bloomed, deficits now stretch to the horizon. According to the Center on Budget and Policy Priorities, the combined deficits of state governments will reach $60 billion to $85 billion in the fiscal year ending July 31, 2004. And that's on top of the $50 billion hole the states had to plug in 2003. The latest deficit estimates come to about one dollar for every seven in the states' budgets, and for many the gap is even bigger. At the end of 2002, Arkansas' deficit was estimated at 37 percent of its budget, Oregon's at 23 percent, and Missouri's at 20 percent. Add it all up, and states "face the most dire fiscal situation since World War II," said the National Governors Association in November of 2002.

And because most states are required to balance their operating budgets every year, they don't have the luxury of just borrowing, as the federal government is now doing. Instead, they have to choose some combination of spending cuts and tax increases. In Connecticut, Governor John Rowland—who, by the way, was elected on a promise to eliminate the state income tax—proposed a "millionaire's tax," which would take an extra percentage point from the 7,500 highest tax returns. Ohio cut spending by 7.5 percent for most agencies during 2001 and, in December 2002, was considering tax increases on cigarettes and alcohol and another round of spending cuts. Minnesota's governor proposed closing a $2 billion deficit with cuts in nearly every department's budget, and higher taxes on gasoline, tobacco, and some services. And they're all cutting their workforces, through either layoffs or attrition.

Why bring up state finances in a book on real estate? Because we don't buy homes in a vacuum. The decision of whether to extract and spend home equity or to buy a bigger house or a second house—all the things that keep the real estate boom going—depend in large part on homeowner psychology. We do these things when we're confident because jobs are plentiful, raises frequent, and taxes low. In hard times, when taxes rise and layoffs are front-page news, we get cautious. So if state and local governments start raising taxes and laying off workers, they'll offset—maybe more than offset—the stimulative effects of the tax cuts and big deficits now coming from Washington and send a chill down the spine of even the most optimistic borrower.

As usual, California and New York lead the pack both in real estate excess and in fiscal distress, so let's take a closer look at their situations, keeping in mind that on a smaller scale pretty much the same thing is happening in statehouses across the country.

California

By 1998, Californians had put the past decade's defense cutbacks and real estate bust behind them and were back in boom mode. Hollywood had gone global, with the latest Julia Roberts and Bruce Willis films often making more money in foreign markets than domestically. And Silicon Valley had discovered—and been discovered by—this thing called the Internet, and was spawning newborn tech firms on a daily basis. Venture capitalists were pouring in seed money, and investment bankers were vying to take each batch of dot-coms public.

And with every initial public offering, the whole world in effect sent its money to California to buy the shares the company founders were selling. The insiders then paid capital gains taxes on their profits, swelling tax coffers in Sacramento, and used what was left to buy houses, cars, and all manner of grown-up toys.

The state treasury was so flush that, as in Washington, the debate shifted from how to slice a limited pie to how best to spend a never-ending river of excess cash. A quick Internet search under "California budget surplus 1999" turns up all kinds of surreal stuff, like "How Should the Surplus Be Spent? An Investment Budget for California" from a public interest group called the California Budget Project. Being the sort of wish list that surfaces when the public sector loses its inhibitions, the budget sketches out billions in new spending on pretty much everything that a state government can possibly finance, while barely mentioning tax cuts. Governor Gray Davis and his legislature, being both human and politicians, saw the logic of this kind of "investment" and chose to spend most of the tax windfall rather than rebate it to their constituents. They built schools and roads, expanded health care benefits, and of course hired new people to oversee all the new spending. In the last four years of the 1990s, public spending and employment grew by 40 percent and 35 percent respectively, far faster than either inflation or the state's population.

Meanwhile, all the new dot-com millionaires needed appropriate living space, so home prices took off. By 1999, they had fully recovered from the past decade's fall. By 2002, the price of the average California house had soared past $330,000, a 21 percent increase in that year alone. And the media once again were full of tales of instant real estate wealth alongside the trauma of the have-nots who might never be able to afford a home. Yet by the end of 2002 it was as if the housing boom were taking place in a vacuum, because in just about every other way, the state was a total mess.

What happened? The bottom fell out of tech stocks, and market-related tax revenue (mostly capital gains) dipped from $17 billion in

2000 to less than $5 billion in 2002. The $10 billion budget surplus melted away and then some. Because 2002 was an election year, the budget enacted in September "was 'balanced' largely with borrowed money, inflated revenue estimates, and bookkeeping tricks," reported the Cato Institute, a libertarian think tank. Or, as the *Sacramento Bee* put it in January 2003, "Everyone in the Capitol knew that when Davis signed the budget, it was purely political and many billions of dollars out of balance, so no one took it seriously. The only question, really, was how large the hidden 2002–03 deficit and the 2003–04 shortfall would be—what came to be known to insiders as 'the number.'" But even those expecting the worst were shocked when Governor Davis finally announced that the state was $35 billion in the hole. That's roughly $1,000 for each resident, "a hole so deep and so vast that even if we fired every single person on the state payroll—every park ranger, every college professor, and every Highway Patrol officer—we would still be more than $6 billion short," said Assembly speaker Herb Wesson Jr.

As for what Governor Davis and the California legislature will do about it, count on a little of everything. Among the ideas being floated at the end of 2002 were selling $8 billion of "revenue anticipation notes" tied to the state's share of the national tobacco settlement, cutting $10 billion in spending, reinstating stricter eligibility rules for state-sponsored health care, cutting billions from education, raising sales taxes, suspending pay increases for state employees, and increasing various taxes on businesses. The only reason real estate taxes aren't on the list is that they were capped by 1978's Proposition 13 voter initiative.

New York

Get a bunch of Manhattanites together, and sooner or later the talk will turn to real estate. Everyone—and I mean everyone—has a story to tell about the rent they're paying and what it would have bought back in Kentucky, or about the size of their mortgage payments or, more frequently these days, about how much more their co-op is worth than they paid for it.

Putting a roof over your head has never been cheap in New York City, but by the end of 2002 the numbers were beyond most nonresidents' comprehension. According to the Corcoran Group, a Manhattan real estate agency, in November 2002 the average sale price for all categories of Manhattan residential properties was $900,000, compared with $792,000 a year earlier. The average price per square foot was $692, and the average price per room was $209,000. Studio apartments went for $250,000, one-bedrooms for $460,000, two-bedrooms for about $1 million, and three or more bedrooms for $2.5 million. Meanwhile, the "negotiability factor," a measure of the difference between asking and selling price, was -0.3 percent, meaning that the average selling price was actually slightly higher than what the seller was asking.

And this wasn't just a Manhattan thing. In the first half of 2002, Long Island led the nation in price gains of existing homes, with an annual appreciation rate of more than 26 percent. In Queens, home values rose by about 26 percent in 2002. The story was the same upstate, where city folks were buying second homes and pushing the price of everything from raw land to three-bedroom condos up at double-digit annual rates.

That a whole region can live with such housing costs attests to the kind of wealth that Wall Street and Madison Avenue generate in good times. And to call the 1990s "good" is, to steal a line from Dave Barry, like calling the sun "warm." Wall Street supplied the fuel that sent Silicon Valley to the moon, and took a hefty cut of every deal. Whenever a concept—be it networking equipment or business-to-business software or optical lasers—seemed to be working, Manhattan's investment bankers would scour the country for start-ups in the same business and take them public. Who cared if the fields were crowded or the companies not ready for prime time? The market was insatiable, and the fees, well, the fees were too good to pass up. To take just a couple of examples, Salomon Smith Barney analyst Jack Grubman reportedly got a $20 million bonus for a single year during the tech boom, and the team of CS First Boston's star investment banker, Frank Quattrone, reportedly earned 50 percent of the fees they generated from the deals they put together, of which Quattrone's annual cut exceeded $50 million.

Investment banking is a people-intensive business, and as the deals multiplied, so did the number of new hires at Merrill Lynch and Salomon Smith Barney. From 1996 through the middle of 2001, New York State gained 700,000 jobs, which represents a growth rate of 9 percent per year; 425,000 of those jobs were in New York City. And these were, by and large, really good jobs: investment bankers making six and seven figures, analysts making nearly as much, and lots of well-paid support staff. Many came from out of state, drawn by the thrill of huge deals and easy money. And once hired, these new masters of the universe had to live somewhere.

It's not surprising, then, that New York's real estate market looks the way it does. Except for one thing: The boom is over and has been for a couple of years now. Wall Street stopped hiring in 2001 and has been shedding high-priced talent ever since. Merrill Lynch alone cut 18,600 jobs, or 25 percent of its peak workforce between 2001 and 2003. Trading volumes are down on the major stock exchanges, investment banking deal flow is a fraction of what it was in 1999, and class action lawsuits involving thousands of angry investors and billions of dollars have been filed against the brokerage houses responsible for the dot-bomb implosion. And then there are the lingering effects of the World Trade Center attacks, which attracted billions in emergency federal aid and tourist interest in the short run, but called into question the wisdom of a high-profile Manhattan address.

Layoffs and plunging year-end bonuses on Wall Street have led to massively lower tax revenues for both city and state. Whereas in 1999 New York City ran a $1 billion surplus, new mayor Michael Bloomberg took office in 2002 with a deficit in the $4 billion range. Bloomberg's response (rather surprising for a successful entrepreneur) has been to seek new revenues, including an 18.5 percent increase in property taxes and a tax on commuters who travel to the city to work. If these fail to bring in the predicted amount of cash, as big tax increases tend to do, next on the agenda will be cuts in city services, including education and police.

At the state level, New York faced a gap of around $10 billion for fiscal year 2003, out of an overall budget of around $90 billion. Governor George Pataki's initial solution was to cut spending in an attempt to balance the budget without raising corporate or income taxes. Instead, he encouraged state workers to retire early and, like California's Governor Davis, tried to sell bonds backed by money from a court settlement with tobacco companies. The hope was to lessen the impact of the belt tightening by spreading it over several years instead of imposing it all at once.

CHAPTER 6

DERIVATIVES, FANNIES, AND FREDDIES

Derivatives Exposure Is Exploding

Depending on which expert is talking, derivatives are either exhibit number one in the case for financial engineering run amok, or great tools for limiting risk and stabilizing the global financial system. Either way, they deserve some space in a book like this one. Yet, to be honest, I just don't understand them. As the saying goes, it's better to stay silent and appear stupid than to open your mouth and remove all doubt, so I originally decided to bypass the derivatives controversy and hope that the omission wouldn't taint the whole argument.

Then Warren Buffett intervened. The billionaire with a well-deserved rep for common sense had recently used his investment vehicle, Berkshire Hathaway, to buy General Re, an insurance company with some derivative exposure. As he recounted the tale in his 2003 letter to shareholders, what he found left him both confused and worried. His attempts at understanding what he owned were only partially successful, and his efforts to wind down his derivatives exposure would take a "great many years." Like Hell, he told his investors, the derivatives business is "easy to enter and almost impossible to exit." Surveying a global financial landscape that's now enmeshed in such things, Buffett used some uncharacteristically strong language, calling derivatives "weapons of financial mass destruction" that pose the threat of "a mega-catastrophic event."

So much for my plan to avoid the issue. But on the bright side, if Warren Buffett himself doesn't "get" derivatives, then I have some leeway in which to wax ignorant. What follows is a little complicated (if it weren't, there would be no controversy), so please don't leave in disgust. If you get bogged down, just skip to the last few paragraphs of this section.

A derivative is a contract that derives (hence the name) its value from something else. Its function is to divide the risk associated with the underlying asset into pieces, allowing them to be sold to different people, each of whom is theoretically best able to handle it. The concept goes all the way back to ancient Greece. As recounted by Aristotle: A philosopher named Thales, expecting a good olive harvest, bought the rights to some local olive presses. The harvest was a good one, and the value of the presses soared, making Thales a nice profit. Notice how this contract divided up the risks: The owners of the presses got money up front, thus minimizing the risk that a bad harvest would make their equipment temporarily worthless. Thales paid to assume that risk in return for the chance to profit if the harvest was indeed a good one. Both got what they wanted, and presumably each ended up better off.

Today the most familiar variation on this theme is the stock option, which is a contract to buy or sell a given stock at a given price during a given period of time. Another is the futures contract, which works pretty much the same way for commodities like wheat or silver.

To illustrate, assume that a farmer is planting her wheat crop in March and, because she knows her costs, calculates that to turn a profit, she'll need a price of at least $4 a bushel at harvest. She can just grow the wheat and hope for the best— which, the weather being what it is, is financial Russian roulette. Or she can sell her crop ahead of time, using futures contracts and locking the price in at say $4.25 a bushel. The farmer now knows exactly what she'll get, thus eliminating her risk of being ruined by low prices. In return, she's given up the chance for a windfall if the price soars to $6. The speculator (or food processor) who bought the contract has given up the chance to buy cheap wheat if prices fall, in return for a guaranteed supply of grain at a reasonable price (eliminating the risk of a price spike at harvest time). The result: Both parties make an acceptable profit while limiting the threats to their survival.

Or picture a company that sells microchips on the international market. Because it gets paid in yen and euros, its bottom line is at the mercy of currency values. The company can fix this by using futures contracts to lock in its year-ahead exchange rates, in return for giving up the profit it would have made had exchange rates moved in a favorable direction. The people on the other end of the contracts (the counterparties) assume the risk of unfavorable currency fluctuations in return for the chance to profit from favorable ones. Meanwhile, stock options (as you'll see in chapter 10), allow investors to protect themselves against losses, and speculators to place leveraged bets on what they expect to happen.

So far, so good. These examples are fairly easy to understand and, as part of a sound business strategy, useful risk-management tools. If this were the whole of the derivatives business, neither Warren Buffett nor anyone else would be too exercised. But it's not. In fact, stock options and commodity futures are now just a sideshow, and the newest derivatives—again, keeping with the bubble script— are hard for nonmathematicians to grasp, are growing exponentially, and tend to involve financial instruments rather than commodities. And while options and futures are traded on regulated exchanges (like the Chicago Board of Trade), the new derivatives are private contracts between the players and are largely exempt from scrutiny. Some examples:

- **Interest rate swaps** involve exchanging (swapping) interest payments on floating-rate debt for interest payments on fixed-rate debt. These make sense where one party actually wants fixed-rate debt but can get a better deal on floating rate, and the other party wants floating-rate debt but can get a better deal on fixed rate.

Say, for example, that a small bank has a portfolio of fixed-rate loans that pay it the same amount no matter the general level of interest rates. But because the rate the bank has to pay on deposits varies with the market, the bank would prefer an income from its loan portfolio that fluctuates as well. The small bank can go to a dealer, typically a large bank, to swap the fixed rate on its portfolio for a variable rate. The small bank promises to pay the dealer the fixed rate, while the dealer promises to pay the small bank the variable rate. The result: If rates go down, the swap costs the small bank because it owes the difference between the fixed and variable rates. But that's okay because the rate it pays for deposits has fallen as well. If variable rates rise, the bank makes money from the swap; that offsets the higher rates it must pay for deposits. In financial terms, the bank's margin—the difference between what it pays for deposits and what it earns on loans—has been fixed at an acceptable level.

There are lots of other reasons to do interest rate swaps. A company with a high credit rating, for instance, can make money by swapping its lower fixed-rate interest with companies with lower ratings that pay higher interest, with each earning part of the resulting spread. Or companies can play the yield curve by borrowing at variable short-term rates and swapping for longer-term fixed rates. The point, from a financial engineering perspective, is to help participants find exactly the right combination of yield and risk.

Speaking of risk, what exactly is the downside of swaps? It's the same in as regular banking: The company that is obligated to pay the variable rate is exposed to spikes in the market, or, possibly, discontinuities, a situation where credit becomes scarce at any price.

To go back to the small bank in the earlier example, if deposit rates rise faster than that of variable-rate debt—or if people stop putting their money in banks altogether—then taking the variable-rate side of the swap will turn out to have been a bad deal.

- **Currency swaps** are interest rate swaps involving instruments denominated in different currencies. They allow each side to hedge its currency risk and/or cut interest costs. Or they allow an institution to switch from one currency to another. Say a company needs dollars but is better known in Europe, allowing it to raise money at a low fixed rate in the euro bond market. Via a currency swap, the company can switch to dollars at a rate that's lower than it would have been able to borrow directly here. Economists call this "liquidity arbitrage," and it's growing along with world trade.

- **Total return swaps** involve the exchange of the total return from a loan against a contracted fixed return. The first will vary, while the second won't, thereby giving each side a different risk profile.

- **Credit default swaps** involve a seller's agreeing, for an up-front or continuing fee, to compensate a buyer if a given loan defaults, is downgraded, or otherwise runs into trouble. This peels the default risk off the loan without affecting the other risks, such as changes in interest rates or currency values.

- **Portfolio insurance,** also known as dynamic hedging, is a souped-up version of traditional option hedging, where big insurance companies or other money managers use futures and options to lower the risks of their stock portfolios. This allows normally risk-averse companies to benefit from owning stocks, thus freeing up capital that would otherwise be locked into lower-yield instruments like bonds. And, like swaps, when used wisely, portfolio insurance seems to work. As Berkley professor and derivatives pioneer, Hayne Leland, recently noted in an academic paper, "users are discovering that portfolio insurance can be used aggressively rather than simply to reduce risks. Long-run returns can actually be raised, with downside risks controlled, when insurance programs are applied to more aggressive active assets. Pension, endowment, and educational funds can actually enhance their expected returns by increasing their commitment to equities and other high-return sectors, while fulfilling their fiduciary responsibilities by insuring this more aggressive portfolio."

• **Gearing** is, to put it bluntly, gambling, except with derivatives instead of dice or cards. Say that you expect gold to soar in the coming year. You could buy a bunch of gold coins, put them in a drawer, and wait for nature to take its course. But that would be kind of boring, and in any event if gold doubles, you'll make only 100 percent. But by loading up on futures contracts or options, you can leverage your capital to make five or ten times as much as before.

In a much more sophisticated way, this is how some hedge funds operate. They borrow money and then use derivatives to leverage their borrowed capital. A hedge fund, for instance, might put up $100,000 to borrow $1 million, and then buy derivatives that magnify the volatility of this capital by a ratio of 10 to 1. The result: The fund can control $10 million of gold or bonds or yen or whatever with a $100,000 investment. If the commodity rises by 10 percent, instead of making $10,000 as it would have had it been invested just in its original stake, the fund makes $1 million, or ten times its capital. Of course, if gold falls by 10 percent, the fund is wiped out ten times over—not the kind of odds that would let most of us sleep at night, yet this kind of leverage is reportedly pretty common. Long-Term Capital Management, a hedge fund that in the late 1990s set the standard for derivatives abuse, had, at the peak of its hubris, $3 billion in equity, $140 billion in debt, and $1.25 trillion of derivatives exposure. (More on Long-Term Capital Management later in this chapter.) And apparently this company wasn't the only one playing by these rules.

Now, swaps and dynamic hedging and their cousins seem to serve legitimate (if not always obvious) functions. And even with gearing, the counterparty is usually a real business that wants to shed the risk that the speculators are taking on. So what's the problem? Simply put, it's that, as with credit cards and cash-out refis, the tools are not the issue. It's how they tend to be used at the peak of the cycle, when the players get a little too frisky and start building huge, overly complex, and therefore increasingly fragile structures. The critics who see this happening point to the fact that since 1990, the "notional" value (that is, the total face value) of outstanding U.S. derivatives of all kinds has risen from $9 trillion to $55 trillion. In 2002 alone, the amount rose by over $10 trillion. Worldwide, the total is somewhere above $130 trillion. And whereas early on derivatives were used mainly, as in this chapter's first two examples, for hedging agricultural and currency risk via exchange-traded options and futures, today the U.S. Treasury estimates that 86 percent of the notional amount of derivative positions are

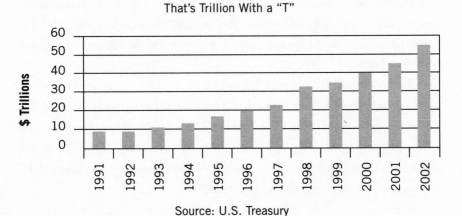

U.S. DERIVATIVES
That's Trillion With a "T"

Source: U.S. Treasury

in the form of largely unregulated interest rate swaps and related contracts. Meanwhile, derivatives exposure is becoming more concentrated, with seven banks accounting for almost 90 percent of the total.

The fact that so many of these contracts involve high-grade debt
means that only a small fraction of the notional $55 trillion is at risk.
This isn't a portfolio of tech stocks, which is why many observers are
unworried. Fed chairman Alan Greenspan remains a fan of derivatives
and in April 2002 noted, "New financial products have enabled risk to
be dispersed more effectively to those willing, and presumably able, to
bear it. Shocks to the overall economic system are accordingly less
likely to create cascading credit failure."

On the other hand, a cynic (at least one who actually understood
how these markets work) might argue that the availability of all this
exotic credit insurance has created a false sense of security, and that
as a result derivatives now wag the dog by driving the creation of liabilities that wouldn't otherwise exist. A cynic might also note that
moving the risk around doesn't eliminate it, and that far from being
unbundled, it looks like these risks are being concentrated in the
biggest U.S. and European banks. Think about it: If Citigroup has $1
trillion in derivative exposure, then the people on the other side of
those deals—the counterparties—are dependent on Citi's ability to
make good on its myriad obligations. The other big banks, meanwhile,
are dependent on the counterparties to make good on their obligations,
and so on, in a system where insurers and insured may be one and the
same and where new exposure is being created at an annual rate equal
to U.S. GDP.

What does all this mean? I don't know, and I have a hard time be-
lieving that anyone does know what currency swaps will do when the
dollar gaps downward or how $100 trillion of interest rate swaps will
behave when bond yields spike. So I'll just leave you with Warren Buffett's take on the subject, which is that derivates carry "dangers that,
while now latent, are potentially lethal."

Fannie Mae and Freddie Mac
Are Inflating the Bubble

As mortgage lending becomes ever more reckless, you might wonder why bankers, smart folks for the most part, are giving so much money to people who are increasingly unlikely to pay them back. The answer is that it's no longer the banks' money. This, more than anything else, is responsible for both today's housing boom and tomorrow's bust.

Back in mortgage lending's dark ages, say, prior to 1980, most banks and savings and loans were community-based businesses that took deposits from local savers and lent the money, often to the same people, as mortgages and business loans. Then the banks held the loans to maturity and earned the spread between what they paid for deposits and what they charged for loans. Because their success—and often their survival—depended on the loans' being paid in full, banks had to be both good at judging creditworthiness and careful about who got their money. Unfortunately, this system had a couple of fatal flaws: By both borrowing and lending close to home, banks were vulnerable to downturns in the local economy. So old-style banking was characterized by rolling regional recessions, in which a rise in loan defaults caused banks to cut back on their lending in order to rebuild their balance sheets. This in turn caused a localized credit shortage, making a bad situation even worse.

Another, more general problem was the structure of bank balance sheets. Banks and savings and loans borrowed their money from depositors via short-term CDs and savings accounts, the rates on which were limited by law, and lent money for longer terms via mortgages and business loans. This made them vulnerable to spikes in short-term interest rates, which usually occurred at the peaks of cycles when the Fed was trying to limit inflation and slow the economy. As rates on nonregulated investments rose, depositors would move money out of their savings accounts and CDs, a process called disintermediation. The banks, starved for funds, would then scale back their lending, often forcing otherwise healthy local businesses into bankruptcy. This came to a head in the early 1990s, when disintermediation—and some startlingly dumb business practices—nearly leveled the whole S&L industry, forcing the federal government to bail depositors out to the tune of several hundred billion dollars.

The solution designed by Wall Street and Washington was to expand the secondary market for mortgages, in which banks, after originating loans, could sell them off to investors. The idea was to attract new cash, which banks could then use to make more loans; this would free banks from dependence on local depositors, smooth out credit cycles, and generally make mortgages more affordable and accessible. So the investment banks teamed with government-sponsored enterprises (GSEs), such as the Federal National Mortgage Association (Fannie Mae) and the Federal Home Mortgage Loan Corporation (Freddie Mac) to buy loans originated by banks, bundle them together into bonds, and sell them off. Known as securitization, this process converts individual, not necessarily comparable, loans into securities that are traded like any other bond. Fannie Mae, for instance, might buy 1,000 30-year fixed-rate mortgages, each worth roughly $100,000, and pool them into one $100 million mortgage-backed security, or MBS issue. Fannie gives the MBS a loan guarantee, in which it promises to pay the interest and principal should the mortgage holders default. A broker like Merrill Lynch or Goldman Sachs then sells the bonds to pension funds and mutual funds in denominations of $1,000 and up.

Now, here's where it gets really interesting. Because the market for this kind of bond is global, and therefore huge, mortgage packagers like Fanny and Freddie, Wall Street's bond traders, and banks and other mortgage originators have discovered that they can write and package pretty much unlimited quantities of mortgages, and sell them off at a nice profit. The result, says Doug Noland, author of the Prudent Bear Web site's Credit Bubble Bulletin and probably the most astute critic of the process, is that securitization as it has evolved in the past decade creates a kind of financial perpetual motion machine.

Old-style banking operated on a fractional reserve system. That is, when the Federal Reserve created new money, the first bank to get it was required to hold part of it (let's say 10 percent for the sake of this example) as reserves, and was allowed to lend out the rest. Hence the term fractional reserve. The recipient of the resulting loan would deposit the proceeds at another bank, which could then lend out 90 percent, and so on, in ever-smaller amounts. This "multiplier effect" permitted a single infusion of cash to generate a much larger volume of loans. But the amount was finite, limited by banks' need to hold reserves against future problems. Fannie and Freddie, however, aren't banks, so they operate free of this kind of restraint, says Noland. "Fannie can give a money market fund an IOU (by issuing commercial paper, a kind of short-term corporate debt), take that money, and use it to buy a mortgage. Whoever sold that mortgage deposits the proceeds into a money market fund, and because there's no reserve requirement, Fannie can go to that fund, give them another IOU, and spend it again. I call this the infinite multiplier effect." In this way, Fannie and Freddie are able to channel effectively unlimited capital from the global bond markets into the U.S. housing market. The only limitation is the ability of banks and other originators to find people willing and able to buy and/or refinance a home. And as we saw in chapter 3, that's no longer a problem.

Between 1995 and 2001, the volume of mortgage loans in the United States increased by a little over $5 trillion. But only a fourth of this ended up on the balance sheets of banks and S&Ls. The rest was packaged into bonds and sold off by the GSE/Wall Street securitization machine. Fannie Mae alone accounted for 35 percent of all the money that flowed into home mortgages during that time. As a result, the amount of GSE-guaranteed debt in circulation now exceeds U.S. Treasury debt.

What does this mean? To put it bluntly, says Noland, the monetary . system has been hijacked by Fannie and Freddie, and mortgage lending has become our main mechanism for financing growth. "We now have a real estate economy. Not a manufacturing economy. Not an information economy. We just trade property deeds at ever-higher prices." The most graphic way to illustrate securitization's dominant role in the monetary system—and how big a risk this presents—is to dig into the GSEs' balance sheets. Fannie, for example (though Freddie would work just as well), holds three categories of liabilities:

Mortgage-backed bond guarantees. Fannie's original role was to help with securitization by guaranteeing that the promised payments would be made. Since 1995, the amount of debt in circulation with Fannie's guarantee has just about doubled, to more than $1 trillion.

Bonds and other debt. When a bank offers to sell a mortgage loan it has originated, either Fannie can work with Wall Street to bundle that mortgage into a bond and sell it off or Fannie can buy the mortgage, keep it, and collect the interest. Fannie used to dabble in the latter strategy, holding a relatively small number of mortgages and earning the spread between what they paid and the cost of the debt it issued to buy the mortgages. But in the past few years, this side of Fannie's balance sheet has exploded. At the end of 2002, Fannie owned mortgages worth $790 billion, up from just $189 billion in 1993. It raised money for this by borrowing in the corporate bond and commercial paper markets, using its government-sponsored status— which seems to imply that Washington will make good on GSE obligations—to get the lowest possible rates. Because Fannie can borrow for a lot less than the average home owner, it makes a nice spread on the deal.

At the end of 2002, Fannie had $764 billion of debt outstanding, most of which it had used to purchase mortgages. To put this in perspective, IBM owes $26 billion, American Express $38 billion, and Exxon $11 billion. No other U.S. company besides Freddie Mac comes close to having this much debt outstanding. At year end 2002, Fannie's debt-to-equity ratio—the portion of its capital structure that it has borrowed versus the part that it has raised by selling equity and retaining profits—was in the neighborhood of 30 to 1. The average commercial bank's is around 11 to 1, yet Fannie is able to borrow at rock-bottom rates because it's a GSE.

Derivatives. Finally, Fannie has derivatives obligations totaling $533 billion. These are primarily interest rate swaps, arcane deals that in theory are designed to protect against swings in interest rates but that in practice might become very unpredictable when their underlying markets start acting up.

Add it up, and Fannie has liabilities in excess of $2 trillion. And the expansion is accelerating rather than slowing down. In 2002, Fannie's book of business—that is, its purchased mortgages plus outstanding MBS it has guaranteed—grew to $1.8 trillion from $1.5 trillion a year earlier, an increase of 20 percent. Its mortgage portfolio grew by 12 percent to $790 billion. By just about every measure, it set records.

A good source of insight into the risks facing Fannie and Freddie, and by extension the economy as a whole, is Roger Lowenstein's book *When Genius Failed: The Rise and Fall of Long-Term Capital Management*. Long-Term Capital Management (LTCM) was a hedge fund

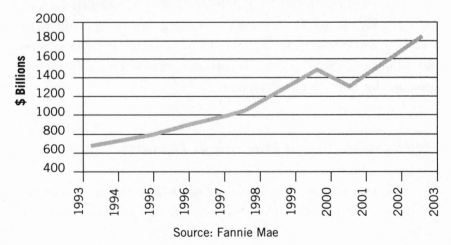

FANNIE MAE'S BOOK OF BUSINESS

Source: Fannie Mae

(i.e., a private, largely unregulated investment company able to dabble in pretty much any market) that was to interest rate derivatives in the late 1990s what the GSEs are to mortgage debt today. The geniuses (literally—they had Nobel prize winners on board) running LTCM thought they had spread their risks around by owning derivatives on bonds from many different countries, *but in reality they were making the same bet in every market*: that spreads between the yields of high and low-quality bonds would narrow as the world's economies became more integrated. When the reverse happened (i.e., when spreads widened), it happened everywhere at once, and LTCM nearly pulled the whole global financial structure down in one spasm.

Today Fannie and Freddie own a wide variety of mortgages and/or have guaranteed mortgages in every part of the United States, so in theory they're diversified against the risk of a regional housing downturn. Yet as mortgage originators lend ever larger amounts to ever more indebted home owners, the risk of rising defaults is growing in every market. And as Fannie and Freddie add to their book of business, they're making essentially one bet: that home owners will continue to make their mortgage payments. And about that federal guarantee: It's an illusion. GSE bonds state explicitly that they are not backed by Washington.

What does this mean? Well, if the economy is running on mortgage debt and Fannie and Freddie *are* the mortgage market, then the whole economy depends on two companies whose combined liabilities exceed $3 trillion and whose growth is accelerating even as the quality of their product declines. You be the judge.

The Securitization Machine Is Hungry

Now we understand why banks are still writing mortgages. But with mortgage debt soaring, why exactly are credit card issuers and carmakers so eager to lend us even more money? Even given the pressure to meet Wall Street's earnings expectations, aren't they worried that our mortgage debt will keep us from paying back our other loans?

Nope, for the same reason that mortgage lenders aren't worried: It's not their money either. To understand why, let's go back to the financial world of, say, 1980. Viewed from a certain angle, it looked like a series of islands. Credit card loans were over there, sequestered on the card issuers' balance sheets. Auto loans were on the car companies' balance sheets, and home mortgages, as you already know, were with the banks and S&Ls that wrote them. These loans were relatively small and dissimilar, with some likely to be paid off in the coming year, others in five years, still others never. Because analyzing and valuing this kind of credit grab bag was so complicated, outside investors were unwilling to buy such debt at anything other than fire sale prices, so the originators of the loans were frequently stuck with them. This tied up their capital, lowering their financial turnover ratios and making them look and feel like Old Economy companies, which they were for the most part. But it also gave them an incentive to lend wisely because they had to live with the results.

Then, in the mid-1980s, the financial engineers had a seminal insight: A bunch of small, dissimilar loans could be bundled together and, with a little finagling, be turned into high-grade bonds that investors the world over would covet. They began with mortgages and credit card debt, but once the machine was up and running, it became obvious that the system could process pretty much anything with an income stream. And now, in the same way that Kellogg's factories turn corn, wheat, or rice into cereal, the U.S. securitization machine stands ready to take nonstandard loans of all kinds and package them into investment-grade, highly liquid paper. (The next few paragraphs get a little technical, so as with derivatives, if you feel yourself bogging down, skip to the last couple of paragraphs. You can always come back later for the details.)

Say that Ford Motor Credit made $100 million of car loans this month but would prefer not to have them cluttering up its balance sheet. Today it can sell the loans to Credit Suisse First Boston, which creates a special-purpose vehicle (SPV) to buy the loans in order to securitize them. The SPV then sells the loans to a trust, another specialized legal entity, for packaging into interest-bearing securities. (The point of sticking the SPV into the middle of the process is to legally insulate the trust from the sponsor, in this case Ford. This "bankruptcy remoteness" keeps future trouble at Ford from affecting the bonds, very important because the bonds will probably carry a higher rating than does Ford itself.)

Because some of the loans are sure to be paid back and some not (though in advance it's not clear which are which), even in the aggregate this batch doesn't qualify as high-grade debt. So the trust engages in a little "credit enhancement," either by fiddling with the structure of the bond offering or by buying it from an outside source. The first strategy might involve "overcollateralization," where the loans are divided into "tranches," generally denoted with letters like A, B, and C. Tranche A is designated as "senior" and gets first dibs on the whole package's cash flow, with the "subordinated" B and C tranches getting whatever's left. Put another way, if a loan in the pool defaults, any loss thus incurred is absorbed by the subordinated securities, which serve as protective layers for the senior tranche, making it highly likely that its interest will be paid. The senior securities are the portion of the asset-backed security (ABS) issue that is typically rated triple-A, while the lower-quality (but higher-yielding), subordinated classes receive a lower rating or are unrated. The term overcollateralization refers to the fact that the face amount of the loan portfolio is larger than the security (tranche A) it backs. There are other strategies in this same vein, with names like yield spread, turboing, and excess spread, all of which involve the structure of the bond issue itself.

The other way to get an investment-grade rating is through "external credit enhancement." The packagers might, for instance, buy credit insurance, paying a credit insurer like Ambac to guarantee that the interest due on the bonds will be paid. Usually this requires some initial internal credit enhancement to cover losses before the insurance coverage kicks in. Here again, there are lots of variations on the insurance theme, including guarantees from noninsurer third parties, letters of credit from banks, and deposits of cash to offset the risk of default. But all serve to improve the bond's credit rating with help from an external source. Once the bonds are packaged, the trust calls a rating agency like Standard & Poor's, Moody's, Fitch, or Duff & Phelps and shows them the credit enhancement insurance and derivative protection. The agency's analysts run the numbers, examine the guarantees, and, duly impressed, endow tranche A with an investment-grade rating. And voilà, the motley collection of car loans has been transformed into good-as-gold, AAA-rated asset-backed securities.

Now Credit Suisse's trading desk hits the phones, calling their global institutional clients to alert them that some literally guaranteed high-grade bonds are available. The institutions happily submit their bids and the bonds are sold. Because the gap between the yields of low- and high-grade debt is so wide most of the time, the price Credit Suisse is able to charge for the bonds is high enough to more than cover the price paid to Ford and the cost of all the processing. The result is a win for all involved. Ford turns its boring car loans into cash, which it can use to make more zero-down SUV loans. Credit Suisse's bankers and traders make nice, fat fees, which translate into those massive year-end bonuses you read about in the paper. The insurers make fees of their own, which translate into big stock option grants for their executives. And—so far, at least—the buyers of these bonds get solid yields with little worry.

The first ABS was issued in 1985, and a total of $1.2 billion of them were sold that year. As you can see from the chart below, we're now producing $400 billion each year, twice the level of 1996, and with no letup in sight. There are about $7 trillion of ABSs outstanding,

ISSUANCE OF NONMORTGAGE
ASSET BACKED SECURITIES

Source: BondMarkets.com

$5 trillion of which are mortgage-based. Of the rest, the biggest pieces are home equity credit lines (more housing debt) and auto loans. Next come credit cards and CDOs (or collateralized debt obligations, which are packages of corporate loans), and student loans. The "other" category includes more specialized loans like equipment leases and mobile home mortgages.

These are all well-understood categories and obvious targets for securitization. But they're not the end of the story because the world contains lots of other loans, and the securitization machine is hungry. Here are some representative next-generation deals.

Asset-Backed Security (ABS) Type Issued in 2002 ($ billions)

Auto	96
Collateralized debt obligations	63
Credit card	69
Home equity	133
Student loan	25
Other	35
Total	420

Source: BondMarkets.com

- The California Statewide Financing Authority recently pooled the expected revenues from litigation against th tobacco companies into a $196 million bond issue. Rated A1 (though subsequently lowered to A2 when Philip Morris was hit with a huge jury verdict in early 2003), the issue was divided into two equal tranches, one of which is to be used for county capital outlays, the other for "endowment funds." This is just one of dozens of such deals where states are converting their expected tobacco settlement funds into cash.

- Hedge funds, because they're free to go both long and short, are frequently profitable and notoriously volatile. Exactly the wrong place, in other words, for a risk-averse pension fund or insurance company to put its money. Yet in May 2002, Credit Suisse First Boston (CSFB) turned $250 million of loans to hedge funds into the first collateralized fund obligation, or CFO. To make the bonds palatable to conservative buyers, CSFB created four tranches, the senior piece consisting of $125 million, with the other three having higher yields and less favorable prospects. The bonds sold, which clears the way for investment funds of all kinds to securitize their cash flows.

- In April 2003, the Brazilian medical imaging equipment distributor MSF Holding floated an $80 million asset-backed bond issue, using a Cayman Islands special-purpose company. The issue was denominated in dollars, and though it contained Brazilian assets, it was assigned a higher rating than the debt of the Brazilian government, thanks to "a groundbreaking transfer and convertibility risk insurance package." The insurance came from the Multilateral Investment Guarantee Agency (MIGA), an affiliate of the World Bank.

In an interview, the investment banker responsible for the deal predicted that this would open the door to the conversion of many more Latin American loans into hard-currency-denominated, high-grade bonds. The gap between the yields of investment- and non-investment-grade debt in the developing world is so wide, he explained, that the gain from packaging and insuring such bond issues far outweighs the costs. Other supranational agencies or insurance companies can provide similar guarantees, and this deal, said the banker, should encourage the others to bring securitization to a region ripe with packageable assets. Home mortgages are spreading, of course, and several Mexican banks now carry credit card loan portfolios in excess of $1 billion. In other words, the securitization machine is retooling to process loans in the developing world.

About the time this book hits the shelves in October 2003, the Asset Backed Securities World Asia 2003 conference will kick off in Singapore. The confab will introduce the Western securitization machine to Asian companies with debt on their books, and, given the tenor of the times, a lot of deals are likely to be struck. Especially fun to watch will be Japan's attempt to solve its banking crisis by securitizing its trillion or so dollars of questionable debt, which might be one of the big financial engineering stories of the next few years.

Now you could make the case that all of the above is not just benign, but pretty cool. If it's more efficient for Ford or Banco de Mexico to securitize what's coming to it, then three cheers for free markets. So what's the problem?

Again, as with derivatives, credit cards, and mortgages, once financial machines are created, they tend to spin out of control. They begin by picking the low-hanging fruit, in this case relatively high-quality loans that would have been created in any event. and that can be packaged into bonds that will almost certainly be paid off. But when that fruit is picked, the machine, in order to keep its operators living the life to which they've become accustomed, must find new raw material. And that's where the trouble starts. In the junk bond mania of the late 1980s, the early leveraged buyouts (LBOs)—in which an investment bank would put together a syndicate to float a low-grade, high-yield bond issue, and use the proceeds to buy control of a company—involved companies such as cable system operators and hospital chains with relatively stable cash flows (a good thing to have if you're going to leverage yourself to the hilt). And they were structured in what passed for a conservative manner in that market. But the supply of such companies was limited, and once they were gone, the LBO industry didn't disband and move on to other things, it began eating through cyclical companies such as railroads and retailers. The result was a wave of giant bankruptcies like Federated Stores and Drexel Burnham Lambert.

A decade later the same thing happened with tech stock initial public offerings (IPOs). The first batch included Amazon.com, Yahoo, and eBay, and were, by and large, real companies with decent prospects. Many of them are still around and some are thriving. But after all the seasoned, legitimate young tech companies had been taken public, the machine, once again, couldn't stop. Venture capitalists plowed their eBay profits into any start-up with a story, investment bankers took them public (often before they had generated their first dollar of revenue), Wall Street analysts assigned them "buy" ratings, and investors ate them up. The process didn't end until the whole thing collapsed. Is that where we are with structured finance? Who knows? But between hedge fund bonds and Brazilian ABS issues, it's hard to escape the sense of familiarity.

Scenes from the Current Bubble

> "There's no risk of a nationwide decline in home prices, period."
>
> **—LELAND BRENDSEL,**
> *chairman and chief executive officer of Freddie Mac,*
> *October 2002*

Statistics are all well and good, but the best way to tell if you're in a bubble is to simply pay attention. As optimism makes its final leap into delusion, you'll see a familiar, predictable pattern begin to form: assets being sold for prices that would have been inconceivable a few years earlier; experts asserting that for a variety of quite logical reasons, prices will always go up; otherwise normal people making millions with seeming ease; and still others using astounding amounts of leverage to build huge, top-heavy portfolios. The tech stock bubble of the 1990s featured an unprecedented amount of this kind of zaniness, so using it as an example, a detached observer in, say, 1999 might have noted the initial public offerings that regularly quadrupled on their first day of trading, Wall Street analysts earning tens of millions of dollars a year who seemed to spend every waking hour on CNBC, and books like *Dow 36,000* riding the mania to best-seller status.

Here, then, are a few signposts on the real estate market's trip down mania lane. In and of itself, each example is easy to dismiss as an aberration. Together they form a pattern that's both hard to ignore and really fun to watch, from a safe distance.

June 6, 2002. In a speech at an Atlanta church, President Bush opines that "the single greatest barrier to first-time home ownership is a high down payment. And so that's why I propose and urge Congress to fully fund the American Dream Downpayment Fund. This will use money, taxpayers' money, to help a qualified low-income buyer make a down payment."

July 7. A *U.S. News & World Report* article, "Shelter from the Storm," notes the rise in real estate prices and concludes that "the price gains are very likely permanent. A shortage of housing, combined with a demographic surge in potential buyers, means that housing will probably be a safe investment for the next decade."

October 15. Capital One Financial, a major issuer of credit cards, reports record third-quarter earnings of $258.8 million, up 56 percent from the year earlier's $165.3 million.

October 17. Permits for new residential construction in September hits the highest level since the current housing boom began.

October 21. *Business Week* magazine publishes "Prices Just Keep Plunging," which notes that across the economy, from airline fares to new cars to clothes to telephone services, prices are falling.

October 21. Leland Brendsel, chairman and chief executive officer of Freddie Mac, addresses a meeting of the Mortgage Bankers Association of America: "There's no risk of a nationwide decline in home prices, period." At the same meeting, Jamie Gorelick, vice chair of Fannie Mae, predicts that, "We can deliver the best decade for housing we've ever seen. Too many Americans still think it's necessary to put 20 percent down on a house or have perfect credit, and don't realize underwriting innovations have allowed home buyers to put down 1 percent—or even nothing—and still purchase a home."

October 28. *Business Week* reports that home equity withdrawals boosted disposable incomes by more than 2 percentage points in the first half of 2002 and quotes a Goldman Sachs analyst to the effect that "consumers are living on borrowed time."

November 11. *USA Today* reports that the net worth of the average California home owner is rising by $3,000 a month as a result of rising home values.

November 12. In the article "Realtors Pressured to Cut Commissions," the *Wall Street Journal* reports that low-cost competitors are squeezing traditional brokers, forcing them to cut fees in order to stay in the game.

November 20. The Center for Housing Policy announces that between 1997 and 2001, the number of families spending more than half their incomes on shelter rose by 67 percent, to over 4 million.

November 25. *Time* magazine publishes "Cash Out Now," which advises home owners to mortgage their homes to buy stocks.

December 2. Fannie Mae and Freddie Mac raise the amount that qualifies as a conventional mortgage by $22,000, to $322,000.

December 4. *National Mortgage News* magazine reports that a record-breaking $729 billion in home mortgages were funded in the third quarter, and predicts that "at the current run rate, mortgage bankers will wind up funding just shy of $2.5 trillion in home mortgages this year." That's up nearly 10 percent from 2001's record $2.1 trillion.

December 5. *American Banker* magazine reports that Bank One and Fannie Mae have created a $12.5 billion loan program in which borrowers can make little or no down payment, and without the usual requirement for mortgage insurance. The loans will also feature "flexible" credit qualification rules.

December 9. The Bureau of Labor Statistics reports that in November about 406,000 people held the title of mortgage broker or banker, up from 349,000 in November of 2001. "The mortgage industry established itself again last month as a hot place to work," crows the Web site MortgageDaily.com.

December 12. "Real Estate Riches: Why Buildings Are Better Investments than Stocks," hits number 3 on *Business Week*'s paperback best-seller list.

December 16. *USA Today* publishes "Consumers Sell Stock to Put Money in Real Estate," which profiles a couple that in the 1990s had 75 percent of their money in stocks. Now "they no longer save; instead, they pour everything into real estate," including a $512,000 home in the San Francisco Bay area. The article also profiles a Washington, D.C., "single mother of two" who paid $263,000—17 percent over the asking price—for a three-bedroom townhouse. For the $26,000 down payment, she cashed in life insurance policies that she had set aside for retirement, and borrowed from her 401(k) account.

December 20. The California Association of Realtors announces that the median price of an existing home in California was $328,310 in November, up 21.5 percent from a year earlier.

December 23. *USA Today* observes in the article "Property Taxes Squeezing Harder" that rising home prices bring rising property tax bills. One Washington state man paid $770 in property taxes on his 1,100-square-foot home five years ago but now pays $1,227—and will probably owe even more this year as the assessment has since jumped by 30 percent.

December 23. The *Wall Street Journal* publishes "Rising Home Prices Cast Appraisers in a Harsh Light," which notes that appraisers are under pressure to go along with unrealistically high home valuations in order to get referrals from brokers. "The truly sad part about this is they are going to find some [expletive deleted] appraiser to do this when I tell them no," said one appraiser.

December 26. San Diego Association of Realtors® announces that San Diego home sales increased 15.9 percent in November, versus a year ago. The median price was up 26 percent, to $378,000. Meanwhile, the annual median family income of San

Diegans was steady at $53,000, according to the San Diego Regional Planning Agency. "What you have now is a median home price that the median earner cannot afford," said an agency spokesperson.

December 27. Nationwide, new home sales rose 5.7 percent in November, to an annualized rate of 1.07 million. The average forecast of economists surveyed by the CBS MarketWatch Web site predicted sales of only 990,000.

December 18. The *Wall Street Journal*, in "Are 'Gifts' from Builders Inflating a Price Bubble?" details how builders now fund "nonprofit" organizations, which then assist home buyers with down payment money—on homes built by the builders.

December 30. In a *Business Week* poll, 53 percent of respondents say real estate is a better investment than stocks.

January 9, 2003. The *Detroit News* publishes the article "More Buy Multiple Homes for Portfolio," which opens with "House-rich Americans increasingly are using their growing real estate wealth to buy— what else?—more houses."

January 13. San Diego Association of Realtors® reports that the average price of a resold local home was $460,894 in December, up 17.2 percent from the $393,144 average in December 2001. The number of resales rose by 12.7 percent.

January 18. A *USA Today* survey of speakers at the Inman News Service "real estate summit" shows a high degree of unanimity: "The market, while poised to cool a bit, is not at risk of a precipitous decline."

January 16. Harvard University's Joint Center for Housing Studies reports that "even with the recent weakness in job growth and consumer confidence, home owners are still investing in remodeling." The quarterly average of $114 billion spent in 2002 by consumers on remodeling was a record.

January 21. UnionBanCal reported that it has been making fewer loans to companies that are not already customers. According to *American Banker* magazine, "To offset the shrinking of its commercial portfolio and falling loan spreads, (the bank) is actively marketing residential mortgages, taking advantage of the home finance boom."

January 24. Countrywide Financial (a major mortgage bank) announces that it funded mortgages worth a record $35.2 billion in December. Total fundings of $102.1 billion in the fourth quarter produced the first $100 billion quarter in the history of the company, and for the full year fundings were up 101 percent. New mortgage applications were coming in at the rate of $1.8 billion per day.

February 24. The *Wall Street Journal* publishes an editorial, titled "Hurray for the Trade Deficit," in which it asserts that the $400-billion-a-year trade deficit is a sign of U.S. economic health and in any event is the only thing keeping the global economy going.

February 24. The *Wall Street Journal* publishes "The Refinancing Boom Spells Big Money for Mortgage Brokers" about how this formerly obscure business is now a way for former truck drivers and salespeople to earn six-figure salaries.

March 6. The Federal Reserve announces that in the fourth quarter of 2002, household borrowing, which includes mortgage and consumer credit, rose at a 10.7 percent rate, the fastest since 1989.

March 6. The U.S. Department of Housing and Urban Development (HUD) begins offering Federal Housing Administration (FHA) insurance for subprime loans. The program is expected to guarantee 62,000 additional mortgages worth $7.5 billion. HUD also expanded its American Dream Downpayment initiative, which helps low-income home buyers with down payments and closing costs.

March 7. The average rate of a 30-year mortgage falls to 5.67 percent, down from 5.79 percent the previous week and 6.87 percent a year earlier.

April 8. The U.S. office vacancy rate hits 16.6 percent, marking the ninth straight quarter of rising vacancy rates and declining rents.

April 8. Apartment vacancy rates hit the highest level in a decade.

April 8. The *Wall Street Journal*, in the article "Fed Weighs Alternative Stimulus Plans," reports that if short-term rates fall much further, money market funds will close down because their expenses will exceed their yields, and that as a result, the Fed is considering other ideas for stimulating the economy, including targeting long-term interest rates by buying bonds on the open market. Fed officials worry, however, that the "exit strategy" of eventually selling the bonds would destabilize the markets.

April 9. The Mortgage Bankers Association revises its forecast for 2003 mortgage originations to $2.6 trillion, from the previous estimate of $1.8 trillion.

April 11. Financial information provider Bloomberg reports that in the first three months of 2003, $594 billion of new debt has been issued in the United States, a 20 percent increase over the same period in 2002. Year-to-date issuance of asset-backed debt was $125 billion, an increase of 25 percent from last year.

April 14. Fannie Mae's first-quarter earnings surge 60 percent from a year earlier, in part because of brisk mortgage demand and in part because of the rising value of its derivatives portfolio.

WHEN THE BUBBLE POPS

How Real Estate Is Propping Up the Economy

So how big a deal is the housing boom for the economy as a whole? Economists have been pondering this question in recent years and they've come up with several different ways to calculate housing's impact, all of which come to the same conclusion: It's very big indeed.

First, there's the previously mentioned boost from cash-out refinancings (refis) and home equity loans. At maybe $170 billion in 2002, this is far bigger than the single-year effect of the tax cut passed by Congress in early 2003. Then there's the change in consumer spending that's caused by rising home values. This is known as the wealth effect, and it's derived from the idea that if we feel richer because our investments are rising in value, we spend more, even if we don't actually cash out any equity. Think about it: If your home's value goes up by $20,000 this year, spending an extra $5,000 on a big-screen TV still leaves you up $15,000. You're building capital and enjoying the fruits of your prescience, which is exactly the way the good Lord intended it.

A recent study by economists Karl Case, John Quigley, and Robert Shiller found that a 10 percent gain in housing prices produces an average 0.6 percent increase in consumption, which is about twice the bang for the buck provided by rising stock prices. Shiller, a Yale University economist whose book *Irrational Exuberance* predicted the bursting of the tech bubble a year before the fact, suggests that real estate wealth has a bigger effect on spending because more people own houses than own stocks, and these days real estate wealth is easier to get at, through home equity loans and cash-out refis, than is stock wealth, which tends to live in inaccessible retirement accounts. Home price inflation is currently adding about $1 trillion a year to U.S. households' net worth, a sum equal to about 10 percent of GDP. So by Shiller's calculation, annual consumer spending is $60 billion higher than it would have been had home prices just stayed at 2000 levels.

But the wealth effect, powerful as it is, just scratches the surface of what housing does for the economy. The real pop comes from the jobs that are created when housing booms. Besides the 407,000 mortgage brokers/bankers who were busy processing refi applications at the end of 2002, the Bureau of Labor Statistics lists more than 1 million people employed in its "real estate services" category. And employment in the construction industry rose from 4.5 million in 1992 to about 6.5 million in 2002, accounting for fully 10 percent of all new jobs created during that time.

Meanwhile, a house isn't a home until it has a fridge, wall-to-wall carpeting, and nice bathroom fixtures, and the companies that make appliances, furniture, lumber, tools, hardware, paint, concrete, and so on employ millions. Appliance maker Whirlpool, for instance, earned $269 million in the 12 months prior to October 2002 and employs 29,000 people. Furniture maker Ethan Allen earned $43 million during this period and employs 7,000. Employees, meanwhile, spend a big part of their paychecks on mortgages, home maintenance, furniture, and so on. The result is a "multiplier effect" in which each dollar increase in direct housing activity leads, according to the National Association of Realtors to an increase in overall GDP of about $1.50. Look at it yet another way: The National Association of Home Builders calculates that putting up 1,000 single-family homes generates 2,448 full-time jobs in construction and construction-related industries, $79.4 million in wages, and $42.5 million in combined federal, state, and local revenues and fees.

And finally, almost 70 percent of all tax revenues raised by local governments in the United States come from property taxes, of which home owners contribute about 43 percent. Economy.com estimates that 2002's new-home construction expanded the local tax base by nearly $200 billion. Assuming a property tax rate of 1 percent of value, the result is $2 billion in new local tax revenues. Overall, economy.com calculates that housing accounted for about a fifth of GDP growth in 2002, with some markets benefiting far more than this. As you can see from the chart below, in 2002 housing was just about the whole show in hot markets like Boston, Denver, and San Francisco.

CONTRIBUTION OF CASH-OUT REFINANCING TO ECONOMIC GROWTH

	percent of 2001 GDP	percent 2002 E
Boston	34	67
New York	37	47
Miami	7	15
Denver	26	86
San Diego	13	23
San Francisco	25	109
U.S. average	17	20

Source: Economy.com

How You'll Know That the Bubble Is About to Pop

All bubbles eventually deflate, but most take their time about it. Look at the price chart for gold in the 1980s or tech stocks after 2000, and instead of an off-the-edge-of-the-table plunge to a new, much lower price range, you'll see a gradual decline that becomes a rout only when viewed in its entirety. So as the air goes out of the housing bubble, there will be plenty of warning signs. They'll be largely ignored by the people who are focused on the past decade's record of easy money and ever-higher home prices. But they'll be obvious to you, if you're looking for them. For example:

Rising mortgage delinquencies. As more and more money flows to subprime borrowers, a growing number of them will start missing payments and default on their obligations altogether. As you can see from the chart below, fewer than 4 percent of "conventional"—that is, relatively high quality—mortgages were in arrears at the end of 2002. But mortgages made by the Federal Housing Administration, which works primarily with low-income borrowers, were falling behind at a rate three times higher, and rising. A fair number of delinquent accounts eventually become foreclosures, in which case the lender actually takes back the house. And by the end of 2002, the foreclosure rate on FHA loans had nearly tripled from the 1986 level.

Mortgage troubles will show up in regional markets before they hit the national averages, so check in periodically with the Mortgage Bankers Association (see Further Reading for their Web address,

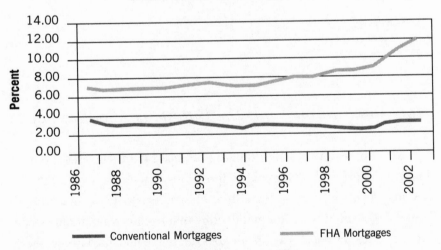

PAST DUE MORTGAGES

Source: Mortgage Bankers Association

along with several other useful ones) for news of which cities are seeing the biggest increases.

Rising credit card defaults. Because of the intimate link between mortgage and credit card debt—and because lenders in both fields have been throwing money at the same group of subprime borrowers—credit card delinquencies and defaults should pretty much echo those of mortgages. So look for rising defaults as a sign that card issuer finances are about to take a turn for the worse and credit availability about to dry up.

The thing to understand about loan problems is that they don't become serious until a bubble begins to pop; before that, so much credit is available that it's relatively easy to borrow against new low-rate credit cards to pay the mortgage and refinance the mortgage to pay the car loan. All but the very weakest borrowers can find a way to keep making those monthly payments. And when they can't, lenders are frequently willing to cut them some initial slack. The Department of Housing and Urban Development (HUD), for instance, offers a series of programs that result, one way or another, in easier terms for hard-pressed home owners. Without these programs, the number of mortgages in default would be far higher than it is today.

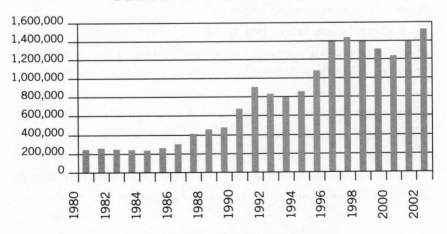

PERSONAL BANKRUPTCIES

Source: American Bankruptcy Institute

Rising personal bankruptcies. As with defaults, bankruptcies tend to rise only modestly while a bubble is expanding because there's always another source of money. So while the 1.5 million personal bankruptcies of 2002 were a record, they were only 8 percent above the 1998 level and nowhere near what they'll be once the credit stops flowing. In the meantime, the slope of the trend line is the key. When it begins to steepen, a tightening of credit standards—and an end to the national debt party—won't be far behind.

A slow-down at the high end of the housing market. Financial analysts joke that you can tell how overvalued a company's stock is by counting the number of Lexus and BMW sedans in its parking lot. The same thing holds for the housing market. When a bubble is inflating, the number of trophy homes of the type you see listed in the *Wall Street Journal*'s real estate section soars. When these castles in the sky stop selling, it's a sign that the more-dollars-than-sense crowd (a trendsetter in both good times and bad) is becoming anxious. Anecdotally, this is already the case in many places. According to a survey *Kiplinger's Personal Finance* magazine published in October 2002, there was a three-to five-year supply of luxury homes on the market in Las Vegas. A different study found a 20-month supply of Atlanta homes on the market for $750,000 and above. And the *Wall Street Journal* noted in August 2002 that "slower growth and instances of price cuts are now becoming more widespread."

Falling home sales, but stable prices. One reason that most real estate experts don't expect home prices to fall is that even in hard times the downside is "sticky." If sellers can't get the price they want, they have the option of just taking the house off the market, and in the initial stages of a downturn, many of them do just that. The result: falling sales but stable prices, which means that home sales are a better indicator of a turn in the market than is average selling price. But sticky doesn't mean stuck. Though perceptions change slowly, they do change, and once those insultingly low offering prices become the norm and sellers accept the new reality, their attitude will become "Let's just get whatever we can for the place." And prices will begin to follow sales downward.

New regulations aimed at curbing abuses. On Wall Street, regulators have spent the past year hammering out deals to clean up corporate governance and remove some of the more glaring conflicts of interest. Brokerage house analysts can no longer be paid for investment banking work, for instance, and company CEOs have to sign off on the accuracy of their companies' financial statements. The result will be less envelope pushing on the part of "financial engineers," which in turn will mean lower revenues and slower growth for Wall Street and for many public companies.

Now it's consumer finance's turn. In September 2002 Citigroup was fined $240 million for predatory lending practices, through which it allegedly piled too much debt onto ill-informed low-income borrowers. In early 2003, Congress, responding to the perception that this kind of thing is widespread, was debating several bills that would set national standards for subprime lending, including one that would cap the allowable interest rate. Also in early 2003, the Federal Financial Institutions Examination Council (FFIEC), a coalition of banking regulators, was cracking down on credit card issuers' abuse of late fees and over-the-limit charges. On some subprime accounts, to take just one egregious example, balances rise even when customers make the minimum payment. Because credit card issuers reportedly make a big part of their profits from their subprime customers, the result of tighter rules will be less credit extended to the low end of the market, and lower card-issuer earnings.

Trouble in the mortgage-backed security market. If the loans that make up mortgage bonds begin to default at a higher-than-expected rate, the markets will begin to sour on this kind of bond. The spreads between their yields and those of risk-free alternatives like Treasury bonds will widen, making it harder for Wall Street to sell new asset-backed bonds. This in turn will dry up the funds available for Fannie and Freddie to buy new mortgages from banks. As St. Louis Federal Reserve Bank president William Poole warned on March 10, 2003, a problem involving Fannie or Freddie "could become acute in a matter of days, or even hours." The possible result: "A crisis in U.S. financial markets that would inflict considerable damage on the housing industry and the U.S. economy."

The Recession of 2004

So here we are. Job growth has stalled. Consumers have burned through a quarter trillion dollars of home equity and now carry more debt than ever before. Interest rates have fallen about as far as they're likely to fall. State governments are running massive deficits. Mortgage lenders and credit card issuers are scraping the bottom of the subprime barrel. And the dollar is weak and getting weaker. What does all this mean for real estate and, by extension, the economy as a whole? Lots of things, none of them good.

- Because states are required to balance their budgets, and have already used up most of the best accounting tricks, the next few years will see big cuts in spending and/or tax increases at state and local levels, perhaps big enough to offset the stimulus coming from Washington's deficit spending and tax cuts. And because state and local governments were, along with housing, a big source of job growth in the past few years, their switch from hiring to firing will mean that in years to come, far fewer potential home owners will have the necessary paychecks to buy houses.

- Consumers normally react to debt burdens of today's magnitude by tightening their belts and/or defaulting. When this happens, the result will be a steep drop in spending on high-end toys like SUVs, big-screen TVs and techie toys, which will result in a wave of layoffs in the industries that make such things.

• The Federal Reserve normally responds to a slow-down in consumer spending by lowering interest rates, to ease the burden of the heavily indebted and to induce the rest of us to borrow more. But by the end of 2002, the Fed had already lowered short-term rates to within 1.5 points of zero, so its quiver is noticeably lacking in arrows. And with the dollar in decline, the Fed may soon face its nightmare dilemma: lower rates to help a faltering economy and risk a collapsing dollar, or raise rates to protect the dollar and risk tipping the economy back into recession.

For the housing boom to continue, pretty much all of the above would have to be wrong. That is, home owners will have to borrow more, as a percentage of their incomes, than ever before. Interest rates will have to fall further into record low territory. Foreign investors will have to keep financing our trade deficit by buying more Treasury and mortgage-backed bonds at historically low interest rates. And who knows—maybe they will. If things have come this far, there's no reason that they can't continue for a while longer. But it's getting harder to come up with a plausible and painless route from here to a new stage of healthy growth. Vastly more likely is something like the following:

Mortgage rates stabilize at the 5.5 percent that prevailed in early 2003. Refinancing activity gradually dries up as everyone who can take advantage of that rate does so. Cash-outs become less attractive because borrowers, by taking out bigger loans at the same rate, will be saddling themselves with higher payments. Without the ability to borrow against one property to buy another, home owners buy fewer second homes and rental properties, and the home-building market contracts.

Home prices, after some initial stickiness, begin to fall, slowly in stable markets, and precipitously in overheated ones like Boston and Miami. (Recall chapter 2 and what happened in New England and Los

Angeles in the early 1990s.) And so the virtuous cycle of rising home prices producing higher incomes producing rising home prices begins to work in reverse. Fewer jobs mean fewer home buyers, falling home prices, and thus fewer jobs in housing-related industries. Meanwhile, a goodly number of laid-off workers will be the same folks who consumed their home equity through cash-out refis or who bought houses with zero down payments. They'll default on their mortgages and credit cards in droves, saddling banks and owners of asset-backed securities with big losses, forcing lenders to scale back their lending. This self-reinforcing cycle ends only when the people who didn't leverage themselves to the hilt start buying up foreclosed homes and busted home builder stocks for pennies on the 2002 dollar. In short, we'll get the recession we should have had in 2001, but three years later, in 2004.

And this is the optimistic scenario. Read on for some other, much scarier possible results of the bursting of the real estate bubble.

CHAPTER 8

TALES FROM
THE DARK SIDE

Recessions, as most people over the age of 35 will more or less recall, are scary but survivable things. So if what's coming is like 1991—or even like 1982 or 1974—it will be painful for most, catastrophic for some, and full of opportunities for the well-prepared few. And it will be over in a year, after which, to steal an image from Adam Smith's classic book *Money Game*, new flowers will push up through the parched earth, and the cycle will begin again.

But what if this time a very different kind of history repeats? What if junk bonds and the tech bubble and the real estate bubble are merely parts of a bigger story, the last chapter of which is much nastier than a garden-variety slow-down? How much nastier? Try a deflationary depression, or an inflationary boom followed by a deflationary depression, complete with 1930s-style unemployment and mass bankruptcies, the kind of decade that scars a whole generation and redirects the flow of human history. I'm not necessarily predicting this, but some other very smart people are, and their scenarios fit the data terrifyingly well. Here are two of them.

Bob Prechter Waves Goodbye

Let's begin with the long-wave theorists, who see economics, politics, and even culture as ebbing and flowing according to regular, repeating patterns. Their story dates from the 1920s, when a Russian economist named Nikolai Kondratieff noticed regular fluctuations in commodity prices going back two centuries, and postulated a 50-year cycle that came to be known as the Kondratieff Wave. Put very simply: Such a wave begins with a slow economic expansion that strengthens over several decades until it begins to generate debt and inflation and finally collapses under the weight of its excesses. The resulting contraction lasts a decade or more, during which bad loans are liquidated (a sterile euphemism for mass bankruptcy and ruined lives), balance sheets are rebuilt, and inflation is wrung out of the system. Then the dance begins again.

Where are we in the Kondratieff cycle? A very bad place. The last wave began in the late 1930s and crested at century's end, which means that we're now a year or two into a downturn that will get far worse before it's through, somewhere around 2010.

But a more interesting and, if that's possible, even more disturbing branch of this family tree is based on the work of Ralph Nelson Elliott, a retired businessman who in the 1930s discovered a different sort of repeating pattern in various, seemingly unrelated economic indicators. Elliott's intellectual successor, a Yale University psychology graduate and former Merrill Lynch technical analyst named Robert Prechter, has built a publishing empire around his *Elliott Wave Theorist* newsletter and best-selling books *At the Crest of the Tidal Wave* and *Conquer the Crash*. As the titles imply, he's convinced that the end is near.

Economics, says Prechter, is more about psychology than finance. And psychology—as expressed through popular culture and international relations as well as stock and real estate prices—goes through long, predictable cycles of pessimism/conservatism, followed by growing success and a steady lightening of mood, and finally wild-eyed optimism. This last stage leads to excesses that produce a devastating crash, and, fast as you can say Herbert Hoover, we're back to pessimism again.

If this sounds familiar, that's because it echoes the description of the business cycle that opened this book. But here's where Prechter takes an interesting turn. These repeating cultural/economic waves, he says, are fractals. That is, they trace out the same pattern when viewed from many different perspectives. Prechter uses the analogy of a coastline: Viewed from a 200-mile-high satellite, it traces a certain irregular-looking pattern. But one can discern the same pattern from a jet eight miles up. Ditto for the view from a mile-high balloon. Likewise, cultural psychology—and its impact on financial markets—traces out the same wave pattern over periods of years, decades, and centuries. In other words, the recession that punctuates the classic, 10-year business cycle has some bigger, more serious relatives that visit less frequently but leave a lasting impression when they do.

In the Elliott Wave universe, a given cycle is composed of five waves that correspond to the psychology of the time. Wave I is the initial bounce off the bottom of the previous downturn. Using the "super cycle" of the 20th century as our reference, that would be 1932's mini-recovery from the 1929 crash.

Wave II is a correction that takes back most of Wave I's gains as people realize that the world is still a nasty place and maybe always will be (think Hitler).

Wave III is a slow-building recovery from the depths of despair as consumers, government officials, and entrepreneurs, still shell-shocked from the recent horrors, focus on only those things that generate high rates of return. This corresponds to the 1940s and 1950s, when the memory of the Great Depression was still fresh and the United States, as a result, was a culturally conservative, financially disciplined place. Lending standards were strict, and to borrow money—or raise it in the stock market—a business had to demonstrate a very clear, productive purpose. Workers were thankful for steady jobs and behaved accordingly, threats from abroad were taken seriously, and sexuality, that riskiest of human impulses, was strictly circumscribed. As a result of all this, corporate and family balance sheets were clean and solid in the 1950s, and company earnings rose steadily, as, eventually, did stock prices. A lot of good jobs were created, and the middle class began once again to expand. The confidence gained from Wave III's steady progress opens a society once again to idealism and experimentation. That would be the early 1960s, with Vietnam and the Great Society.

Then, as night follows day, comes the payback—Wave IV—which corresponds to the late 1960s and early 70s, when budget deficits, rising taxes, military reversals, and rebellious kids threatened to tear society apart.

And finally, we come to the grand finale of Wave V, when society lets it all hang out. Money gets easy, culture becomes increasingly coarse, and the markets boom. For Prechter, this wave began in 1977 and ran for 22 years, to 1999.

THE 20TH CENTURY
SUPER CYCLE

Dow Jones Industrial Average

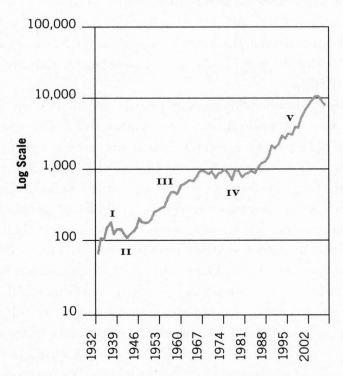

What makes his analysis both disturbing and compelling is the theoretical difference between the expansions of Waves III and V. Whereas both feature fast economic growth and booming stock markets, they're otherwise very different. Wave V seems bigger and better to those who live through it, but in the ways that count, it's actually a pale imitation of Wave III. The table below explains our sense of the greatness of the 1990s: We did it with smoke and mirrors—or, to be more precise, with shocking amounts of debt.

As Prechter puts it, Wave III is built upon muscle and brains, while Wave V is built upon cleverness and dreams. Wave III industri-

THE GOOD OLD DAYS REALLY WERE BETTER

	Wave III (1942–66)	Wave V (1977–99)
Percent average annual real growth of gross domestic product (GDP)	4.5	3.2
Industrial production	5.3	3.4
Peak capacity utilization	95.1	84.4
Average unemployment rate	4.9	6.6
Ending current account trade balance	$1.3 billion	−$96 billion
Ending consumer debt (percent personal income)	65	97
Total debt as a percentage of GDP	150	260

Source: Robert Prechter, Conquer the Crash

alists focus on production to get rich, while Wave V financiers make deals and borrow money to make their fortunes. Seen through the Elliott Wave lens, cash-out refis, the dot-coms, rap music, and *The Osbournes* are all part of the same process of society's slipping the ties that once bound it to a sensible, sustainable path. Because the last wave of a cycle involves massive new debt creation to maintain the illusion of growth, it is inherently unmanageable and produces an inevitable, unavoidable result: a deflationary depression, along the lines of the 1930s, in which a mountain of unproductive debt is written off, huge sections of the economy collapse, and people become as pessimistic as they were optimistic in 1999.

If that's not scary enough for you, recall that this pattern repeats on different time scales, with cycles covering a decade or so, super cycles covering half a century or more, and grand super cycles spanning hundreds of years. And guess what. We just happen to be at the end of a grand super cycle that began in the late 1700s, encompassed numerous smaller cycles, such as the one running from the Depression to the present, and peaked in 1999.

"A bull market that has endured since the time of the Great Depression is definitely ending, and its termination could well mark the end of an uptrend of one degree larger, which has endured since the founding of the Republic," writes Prechter in *Conquer the Crash*. "The deflationary crash that lies ahead will be even bigger than the largest such episodes of the past 200 years."

And real estate? Forget it. Because it's illiquid—that is, it's hard to get out of in a hurry—it's one of the worst possible investments in a deflationary depression.

"At least in the stock market, when your stock is down 60 percent and you realize you've made a horrendous mistake, you can call your broker and get out," writes Prechter. "With real estate you can't pick up the phone and sell. You need to find a buyer for your house in order to sell it. In a depression, buyers just go away. Mom and Pop move with the kids, or the kids move in with Mom and Pop. People start living in their offices or moving the offices to the living quarters. Businesses close down." The result: "a massive glut of real estate."

Now, before you convert your savings into canned food and shotgun shells, be aware that Prechter has been heralding financial Armageddon for a while now. After mistaking the bull market of the 1980s for the whole of Wave V, he turned bearish in the early 1990s and missed the final 8,000 or so points on the stock market's big run. That tarnished his image as a seer and leads him to pepper his analysis with disclaimers about specific timing. But it doesn't invalidate the whole theory, which, like I said, fits the data terrifyingly well.

Doug Noland's Credit Bubble

While Bob Prechter was prematurely forecasting the end of the world as we know it in the late 1980s, a former CPA named Doug Noland was making an early bet of his own by signing on with a bearish San Francisco hedge fund. His new boss "had built an impressive track record shorting the stocks of companies where he could recognize impending problems," recalls Noland. "He was also a brilliant macro thinker, and he was convinced that the U.S. economy and financial system were basket cases after the 1980s excesses." With the Gulf War looming and savings and loans dying like flies, this analysis looked eminently reasonable, and the strategy that flowed from it—betting on a plunge in financial stocks—worked beautifully at first. "Our fund was up better than 60 percent in 1990, and we were considered geniuses. We were turning investors away, and I was daydreaming of what it was going to be like to be wealthy," says Noland.

But instead of collapsing, the economy came roaring back, turning the hedge fund's brilliant short positions into financial black holes. And like a man diagnosed with a disease who researches it until he's knows more than his doctor, Noland began poring over obscure economics texts and Federal Reserve flow-of-funds tables, trying to figure out "how a deeply impaired U.S. system was transformed into the most powerful financial and economic powerhouse the world has ever known." When the hedge fund was finally euthanized in 1996, Noland, older, wiser and still optimistic about a pessimistic future, left the frying pan for the proverbial fire, joining high-profile Texas short seller David W. Tice & Associates—just in time for the tech stock boom to cream that firm's portfolios. "The 1990s were my lost decade," Noland now says.

But the effort was far from wasted. All those long nights of research had given Noland some provocative ideas about where we were headed, and once at Tice, he began posting a weekly Credit Bubble Bulletin on the firm's Prudent Bear Web site. Over the years the column has evolved into probably the single best freely available chronicle of the casino formerly known as the U.S. economy. When a credit card company reports a doubling of its profit, Noland deconstructs its income statement to show that it's all due to subprime loans. When Fannie Mae posts yet another blow-out quarter, Noland compares its burgeoning debts with its minuscule equity and explains the implications. And when he's done with the week's news, he turns to theory, drawing on the ideas of obscure economists who seemed to grasp the dynamics of financial markets more firmly than household names such as Keynes and Milton Friedman.

A case in point is Hyman Minsky, a Berkeley professor who in the 1960s theorized that economies and financial systems change structurally during the course of an expansion, starting out with solid balance sheets and conservative lending institutions and gradually becoming more leveraged—and therefore more fragile—as borrowers and lenders drift from caution to optimism to euphoria. Sort of a long-wave theory of society's balance sheet.

In Noland's take on Minsky, most investments in a newly expanding economy involve "hedge" finance (meaning they're backed by ample and stable cash flows). The resulting system is "robust" and "consistent with stability." A problem with one company or industry doesn't spread because the others are in good enough shape to absorb the shock. Then, as success breeds confidence, the system enters a "speculative" phase, in which ever larger amounts of debt are taken on by ever less credit-worthy borrowers (sound familiar?). And finally, as the various players get cocky and/or desperate, the economy lurches into a "Ponzi" stage, which can be sustained only by continuously adding new liquidity (another word for credit). With everyone leveraged to the hilt, trouble in one place risks a cascade failure of the whole system.

Viewing the 1980s through Minsky's lens, one can easily see how Noland (and Prechter and so many others) mistook the decade for this cycle's Ponzi phase. Junk bond raiders and out-of-control savings and loans executives did seem more at home in a Vegas casino than at a bankers' convention, and after a decade of their shenanigans, the system certainly looked fragile. It easily could have collapsed, in fact, had not the financial engineers discovered securitization, which, you'll recall from chapter 6, is the bundling of risky, dissimilar loans into high-grade bonds. Though it took the first half of the 1990s for the bond packagers to get the concept down, once they did, says Noland, the result was a whole new monetary system independent of government control and ready to turn any spare bit of low-grade liquidity into high-grade paper. And, right on cue, spare liquidity suddenly began flowing like water, thanks to the Federal Reserve.

Beginning in 1997, the global financial system suffered a series of near misses—just as you'd expect during the late stages of a credit bubble. The "Asian Contagion," in which the economies of Thailand, Malaysia, and South Korea imploded, was followed by Russia's default, Long-Term Capital Management's collapse, the Y2K computer bug and the tech stock implosion.

In a more stable global financial structure, each would have been easily contained. But by the late 1990s the global economy was so leveraged—and therefore fragile—that any one crisis could potentially have pulled the whole house of cards. So the Federal Reserve, taking no chances, reacted by flooding the system with liquidity. The government-sponsored enterprises (GSEs) and their structured finance machine turned each new burst of money into mountains of new loans and bonds. Telecom debt soared into the trillions in the late 1990s, and when that industry collapsed, the securitizers turned to mortgages and credit cards.

Now, says Noland, we really are deep in the Ponzi phase of the cycle, where the only way the system can avoid collapse is by creating ever-greater amounts of credit. "The Fed and most analysts continue to believe that the stock market bubble was the problem," he says. But they're wrong. "The equity bubble and now the real estate bubble are just aspects of the ongoing credit bubble." And at this late stage, "the only way to sustain these bubbles is to keep lending to ever-shakier borrowers."

But whereas Prechter sees a deflationary crash looming at this point, Noland wonders if the bubble machine will give up so easily. More likely, he says, "all efforts will be made to sustain this inflationary credit and speculative bubble. The alternative will be deemed unacceptable. . . . Credit bubble dynamics now dictate that enormous and unrelenting credit inflation will be necessary to forestall the undoing of the likes of Fannie, Freddie, JPMorgan, GE, MBIA—the entire Monetary Regime. Inflate or die." In this scenario, the dollar is toast; gold is, well, golden; and real estate, as the center of the last stage of the Ponzi phase, is the source of the biggest "dislocation," another economist euphemism for terrible suffering. "If Minksy were alive," writes Noland, "he would undoubtedly believe that we are today at the precipice."

MORE DOUG NOLAND, IN HIS OWN WORDS

On banking in the age of securitization:

Previously, you had local bankers studying businesses and lending against sound enterprises. We assumed they would hold these loans until maturity. Because they are selling these loans and other trusts to Wall Street, they don't have to live with these loans. They are just trying to originate them and sell them. The whole emphasis on credit analysis with sound lending and sound banking has been turned upside down by structured finance.

We have this very unusual situation where Fannie Mae and Freddie Mac can aggressively go into the marketplace, purchase mortgages and other credit instruments, and reliquefy the system. These institutions are basically quasi-Central Banks, because they have unlimited capacity to issue new debt, to issue IOUs and liabilities, basically to create contemporary money and credit. I look at this as a parallel banking system that has been running without any controls. There are no reserve requirements. There is very little regulation. It has led to lending in enormous excess.

GSE assets began the 1990s at about $450 billion, and have since grown to about $2.55 trillion. Freddie Mac's total assets increased from $35 billion in March 1990 to $722 billion at the end of 2002. This company has another $600 billion of off-balance sheet exposure, all supported by less than $25 billion of shareholder's equity. There are few historical examples of credit excess surpassing what has transpired with the U.S. government-sponsored enterprises over the past decade. Perhaps John Law's Mississippi Bubble scheme is comparable.

Back in 1998, I spoke with many analysts and economists and tried to explain this process and its significance. Almost without exception, I was informed that only banks have the ability to create money and credit. The GSEs and other "non-banks" were simply middlemen taking money from savers and lending it to borrowers. As logical as this conventional doctrine sounds, it is nonetheless incorrect. . . . Money and credit today are little more than journal entries in this enormous elec-

(continued)

MORE DOUG NOLAND, IN HIS OWN WORDS (CONT.)

tronic ledger. There are many players making entries and the Fed does not control the process.

It is this mechanism—with the capability of transforming essentially endless risky loans into perceived safe financial assets—that has so profoundly changed the nature of monetary analysis. And since there is basically insatiable demand for this "money"—the residual of lending—contemporary credit systems enjoy virtually unlimited capacity to create credit. That is, of course, as long as the perception of the soundness of money is maintained.

The Housing Boom

Total Mortgage Credit growth accounted for 88 percent of Total Non-federal Borrowings during (2002's) third quarter (versus 1990's average of 51 percent). . . . Our system has created a Mortgage Finance Monster, with momentous ramifications for the mortgage-back marketplace, the financial system, the U.S. economy and dollar.

This New Age housing cycle is dominated by large national builders with close ties to Wall Street and the mortgage-backed securities marketplace. These builders have unlimited access to cheap finance to pursue their aggressive growth strategies. And not dissimilar to the telecom sector during 1999, the Street, bankers, and Washington are today content to cheer along the construction boom and disregard the consequences. As we have witnessed, the weaker the economy (and more intense the financial stress) the greater the impetus for stoking the Great Mortgage Finance Bubble.

This time around it's mortgage finance that's driving income growth. The problem is that incomes are growing because of mortgage credit growth. . . . We've been inflating (home) prices but making it really easy for home owners to extract equity. If prices go back to where they were even a couple of years ago, they'll be under water. California is especially frightening.

The Credit system was sustained by truly unbelievable (and conspicuous) lending and speculative excess running rampant throughout real estate finance. . . . What's going on in real estate finance is even more egregious than the tech bubble.

Somehow unappreciated, the powerful U.S. mortgage finance superstructure has been a leading provider of "Ponzi" finance, recklessly inflating home prices—assets noteworthy for their lack of underlying cash flow.

Total fourth-quarter 2002 mortgage credit expanded at a record annualized $1.07 trillion, with household mortgage debt surging at an annualized $854.7 billion pace. Household mortgage debt growth is fully 60 percent greater than 2001's record $530.9 billion. To bring additional perspective to the enormity of this credit explosion, recall that pre-bubble 1997 saw total household mortgage growth of $238 billion (nineties average of $250 billion). The fourth quarter saw a lending frenzy at almost four times the pace of only five years ago.

How the Crash Might Come

In the case of the United States, where it appears significant asset price risk has been transferred to a limited number of financial intermediaries and the murky derivatives marketplace, the risk becomes a failure of a key player, consequent market dislocation, collapsing confidence, and a potential breakdown of a monetary system that has come to rely so heavily on structured finance.

At this point the authorities recognize that the only way out is to inflate. Everybody's talking about reflation, and the GSEs are going to be aggressive to try to keep the game going. Does the bond market tolerate this? If not, that's the catalyst.

The day ultra-easy credit availability begins to tighten in mortgage and auto land will prove a major inflection point for the U.S. economy.

The dollar is the greatest wild card for the Wall Street Monetary Regime. If the dollar decline becomes disorderly and currency derivative markets dislocate, all bets are off. ■

PART 3

INVESTING FOR THE
HOUSING BUST

PRESERVING YOUR CAPITAL WHEN THE BUBBLE BURSTS

If you've gotten this far and aren't at least a little worried about your home and other investments, then I don't know what else to say. But if you are worried, take heart because it's possible to protect yourself and/or make a lot of money in the hard times that may be coming. How? By shifting into reverse, financially speaking, and doing the opposite of what worked in the 1990s.

The rest of this book will look at some basic ways to do this. This chapter contains strategies for keeping what you have (which will seem like a miracle when those around you are getting creamed). Chapter 10 outlines some ways to actually make money—maybe a lot of money—by betting against the parts of the economy likely to suffer most when the housing bubble bursts. And chapters 12 and 13 cover what to do with your house. But to repeat the warning that opened this book, the companies and mutual funds mentioned here are examples of whatever strategy is being discussed, not recommendations. Compare them with what you turn up through your own research, but under no circumstances should you buy or sell them simply because they appear in one of the following chapters.

Cash Is King

When things get messy, as they tend to when a bubble is deflating, one of the wisest things you can do is also the simplest: Just pick up your marbles and leave the game, by converting your riskier investments to cash. "Cash" in this case means very short term, highly liquid, and safe investments like money market funds, bank CDs, and Treasury notes. They don't pay much these days because their yields track short-term interest rates, which currently hover around 1 percent. But when real estate and stock prices are falling, a 1 percent gain with zero risk begins to look pretty good. Not all cash is created equal, however. Some kinds are considerably safer than others, so give some thought to the right port in this storm. Among the better choices are:

Treasury-Only Money Market Funds

Chances are, your brokerage account automatically "sweeps" your extra cash into a money market fund. This is a mutual fund that holds the shortest-term, safest commercial paper, such as loans to solid companies that are due to be paid off in a matter of days or weeks. Generally speaking, they're quite safe, though very infrequently one of the issuing companies is unable to pay off even its commercial paper. And

Treasury-Only Money Market Fund	Symbol
American Century Capital Preservation Fund	CPFXX
Dreyfus 100% U.S. Treasury Fund	DUSXX
Fidelity Spartan U.S. Treasury Fund	FDLXX
Schwab U.S. Treasury Money Fund	SWUXX
U.S. Treasury Securities Cash Fund	USTXX
Weiss Treasury Only Money Market Fund	WEOXX

Source: Safe Money Report, Charles Schwab

because a lot of today's supposedly high-grade paper is related t ___ housing boom, standard money market funds may turn out to be unusually bad bets in the years ahead.

Much safer are money market funds that limit themselves to short-term Treasury bills, which are short-term obligations of the federal government that mature in 1 year or less from their issue date. They're issued at a price that's less than their par (face) value, and then rise in value until they mature, with the interest being the difference between the purchase price and maturity price. For example, if you bought a $10,000 26-week Treasury bill for $9,750 and held it until maturity, your interest would be $250. Because the Treasury can just print the money to pay off its debts, the risk of default is as close to zero as is possible in this world.

Most stockbrokers offer clients the option of a money market fund that invests only in government securities, but even here, you've got to be careful. Discount broker Charles Schwab, for instance, has two such funds. The Government Money Fund owns Treasury bills, notes, and bonds along with agency debt, including that of Fannie Mae and Freddie Mac. Schwab's U.S. Treasury Money fund, meanwhile, buys only Treasury paper. In January 2003, each fund yielded around 0.7 percent. But knowing what we now know about Fannie and Freddie, the U.S. Treasury Money fund is clearly the safer choice. If your broker

Web	Telephone
www.americancentury.com	(800) 345-2021
www.dreyfus.com	(800) 645-6561
www.fidelity.com	(800) 544-8888
www.schwab.com	(800) 435-4000
www.usfunds.com	(800) 873-8637
www.tommf.com	(800) 814-3045

offers such a fund, simply inform it that that's where you want your extra money swept, and begin raising cash. Otherwise, refer to the list of Treasury-only funds listed on the previous page.

Treasury Securities, Purchased Directly

The federal government borrows money for different time periods, ranging from a few months to 30 years, by issuing securities in $1,000 pieces. Bills, as you know, mature in less than a year, notes from two to 10 years, and bonds from 10 to 30. For the most part, the Treasury sells its debt to dealers, usually big brokerage houses, which then sell it to mutual funds. But anyone with $1,000 or more can buy Treasuries directly too, commission-free via TreasuryDirect, a government service. It works like this: You set up an online account at the Web site listed at the end of this section and give the Treasury permission to electronically debit your checking account. Then you place orders for the securities you want between 8:00 A.M. and 8:00 P.M. Eastern time, Monday through Friday. TreasuryDirect maintains the account and will reinvest interest and principal according to your instructions, just as a stockbroker would.

Savings Bonds

Remember these? Back before the bull market made them seem antiquated, they were popular savings vehicles because they could be bought with as little as $25 and given as gifts to family members. Now their safety and guaranteed positive yield make them seem like long-lost friends. Savings bonds are bearer bonds, which means they're payable only to the person to whom they are registered. Their principal and interest are guaranteed by the full faith and credit of the federal government; and lost, stolen, or damaged bonds can be replaced. They can be purchased through most financial institutions and through payroll savings plans, as well as directly from the government, all without commissions or other fees. Interest is exempt from state and local income tax, and federal income taxes can be postponed until you cash your bond or until it stops earning interest in 30 years.

Savings bonds come in three flavors. Series E/EE bonds and notes are accrual securities, which means that they don't pay cash interest. Like Treasury bills, they're bought for a price that's lower than their face value, and then "accrue," or rise in value, over time until their maturity, when they're worth the full face amount. The rate for a series E/EE bond is set at 90 percent of the 5-year Treasury rate, which in February 2003 meant they yielded about 2.5 percent. After 6 months, you can cash an E/EE bond at most banks, in increments of up to $1,000 per visit.

Series I bonds earn an interest rate that's linked to inflation, which means they protect you against rising price levels should the economy come roaring back. Like E/EEs, their value accrues, they allow you to defer taxes for up to 30 years, and they are exempt from state and local income taxes.

Series HH bonds are current-income securities that pay cash interest, which is deposited directly into holders' checking or savings accounts. In January 2003, HH bonds were paying interest of 1.5 percent. You can't buy HH bonds for cash; you can get them only in exchange for series EE/E bonds or upon reinvestment of the proceeds of matured series HH bonds.

The savings bond version of TreasuryDirect (on opposite page) is called EasySaver, and works pretty much the same way. Type in your bank account number and specify the savings bonds you want and your account is up and running. It's possible to put the account on autopilot by authorizing regular withdrawals and scheduling bond purchases.

Bank Money Market Deposit Accounts

These are banks' equivalent of money market funds, with a couple of twists. They generally pay a little less than the average money market fund, but in some cases they pay 1 percent or so more because banks are able to increase the interest on these accounts to attract depositors and then lend the proceeds out at higher rates. In early 2003 a handful of such accounts yielded in the 2 percent range. Like other bank accounts, these are insured, up to $100,000 each, by the Federal Deposit Insurance Corporation. To find them, try the search tools of the Web site Bank Rate Monitor.

Treasuries, Savings Bonds, and Bank Money Market Accounts

Bank Rate Monitor	www.bankrate.com
Easy Saver	www.easysaver.gov
Treasury Direct	www.publicdebt.treas.gov/sec/sectrdir.htm
Savings Bonds Direct	www.publicdebt.treas.gov/ols/olshome.htm
Savings Bonds.gov	www.publicdebt.treas.gov/sav/sav.htm

Gold Is Better than Cash

> Paper money always fails. Unfortunately, though, this occurs only after many innocent people have suffered the consequences of the fraud that paper money represents. . . . History and economic law are on the side of gold.
>
> —TEXAS CONGRESSMAN RON PAUL,
> JUNE 14, 2002

The problem with even the most conservative investments, cash included, is that they're denominated in dollars. So their return depends in part on the greenback's maintaining its value. Say, for instance, that Microsoft stock goes up by 10 percent but the dollar falls by 20 percent. As a stockholder, you're down 10 percent in terms of Sony TVs and French wine. If your money market fund is up by 2 percent, then you're really down 18 percent. And because, as we know from chapter 5, the dollar is vulnerable, this is a very real problem.

The solution? Invest in things denominated in more stable currencies like the Swiss franc or possibly the euro (more about these on page 147, "Foreign Currencies—One of Them, Anyway"). Or buy gold, which in its own way is also a separate currency, one that's beyond the control of any government. For most of recorded history, in fact, gold was humanity's money of choice, with good reason. It doesn't tarnish or rust. It exists in limited quantity, making its supply fairly predictable. And it looks and feels comforting, a kind of metallic analogue of ice cream and chocolate. Go to any museum's money section and you'll see worn, dented, but still shiny gold coins dating from civilizations that vanished not long after the dawn of recorded history. And during all of that time, the yellow metal has bedeviled governments. Picture the king, circa 1000 B.C., who wants to build a palace to impress his new young queen or raise an army to invade a weak neighbor. But how, he frets to his ministers, do I pay for it? Because his subjects use gold as their medium of exchange, he can't just decree a bigger money supply, damn it. And poking holes in existing coins and melting the extra pieces to make more is, at best, an imperfect solution because it's visible; everyone in the kingdom would see what was happening. The king, being more or less rational, surveys his options and glumly decides to downsize the palace and put the invasion off for another day (though perhaps he chops off a few advisers' heads in frustration).

This "problem" with gold restrained the growth of government for thousands of years and was only recently "solved" by the introduction of fiat—that is, make-believe—money. Here in the United States the government issued paper dollars and initially promised to redeem them for gold at a fixed price. Because paper is easier to carry around than gold coins, this arrangement made dollars acceptable by guaranteeing their value. But as rising government spending flooded the system with dollars, more and more were converted to gold by rational citizens and trading partners, and in 1973 the Nixon administration severed the link. Henceforth, the dollar was worth whatever the marketplace said it was worth, and in the ensuing three decades it has lost about 70 percent of its value.

Though no longer used as money, gold still functions as a kind of shadow currency, rising when the dollar falls and providing a refuge from government monetary shenanigans for the small but loud "gold bug" community. As you can see from the chart below, in 2002 the dollar/gold inverse relationship was nearly perfect.

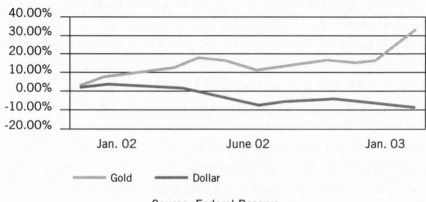

GOLD VERSUS THE DOLLAR

Source: Federal Reserve

How to Own Gold

There are lots of ways to add gold to your portfolio, each with its own pros and cons. The most profitable—when done right—is probably numismatic (collectible) coins, which derive their value from their historical significance and rarity and which therefore usually sell at a high premium over the market value of the gold in the coin. This is a little like buying individual stocks, in that it takes serious study, unbiased information, and luck. Because of this, it's a specialized game that's beyond the scope of this book. If you're interested in gold itself, there are easier ways to get it, including:

Bullion. This is pure gold, which is available in forms ranging from 1/10-ounce coins to 400-ounce bars, and can be ordered over the phone or online. Bullion coins are generally cast by government mints; the most popular are the single-ounce American Eagle, Canadian Maple Leaf, and South African Krugerrand. There are other single-ounce coins out there, including the French Rooster and Chinese Panda, but the less popular (and hence lower volume) coins tend to have higher markups, so if gold is the goal, there's no reason to venture beyond the tried-and-true.

GOLD COINS AND BARS	$ PRICE 3/7/03
Gold Eagle 1 oz	366.60
Canadian Maple Leaf 1 oz	365.60
South African Krugerrand 1 oz	359.25
Gold bar 1 oz	362.10
Gold bar 10 oz	3,600
Gold bar kilo	11,532

Source: Kitco

The same advice holds for choosing a dealer from whom to buy the coins. The precious metals market is shadowy, rife with scam artists and short on competent regulators. So unless your brother-in-law is both a very good guy and a bullion merchant, it's wise to buy from the major dealers who have been around for a while and will likely remain so.

Most will deliver (usually for free) coins and bars to your home. And many offer preselected "portfolios" of various bullion coins and bars for set prices of $10,000 or more. Once your gold arrives, you'll want to resist the urge to keep it in a kitchen drawer and pull it out to impress your friends at dinner parties. Instead, put it in a safe deposit box at a nearby bank and forget about it.

Dealer	Web site	Telephone
American Gold Exchange	www.amergold.com	(800) 613-9323
Blanchard	www.blanchardonline.com	(888) 524-2646
Goldfinger Coin	www.goldfingercoin.com	(805) 482-4425
Kitco	www.kitco.com	(877) 775-4826
Monex	www.monex.com	(800) 489-0839

Mining stocks. If hoarding pieces of metal seems a little, um, pre-technological, you'll be happy to know that an easier, more familiar, and potentially more profitable way to own gold is via the stocks of the companies that mine it. Mining stocks tend to move more dramatically than the price of the underlying metal because for every ounce of gold a mining company produces in a given year, it has tens or hundreds of ounces in the ground. These reserves are revalued by the market when metals prices change, which translates into a volatile stock price. Between 2000 and 2002, for example, gold rose by about 35 percent, while the Amex Gold Index of major gold mining stocks nearly doubled. And many smaller mining companies did even better.

JUNIOR GOLD STOCKS

Company	Ticker	$ price January 1, 2001	$ price February 11, 2003	% Change
Agnico Eagle	AEM	6.07	13.73	126
Glamis Gold	GLG	1.36	11.37	762
Meridian Gold	MDG	6.27	15.60	149
Randgold	GOLD	13.11	30.02	130
Gold		272/oz	370/oz	36
S&P 500		1366	829	−39

To catch the next wave of rising gold stocks, you'll need good sources of information, and luckily there's a thriving gold bug community out there, with Web sites, magazines, and newsletters, some of which are produced by people who have been at this for a long time and have a deep understanding of the field.

Gold-oriented Web site	Web address	Telephone/e-mail
World Gold Council	www.gold.org	(212) 317-3800
Gold Eagle	www.gold-eagle.com	vronsky@gold-eagle.com
Bricks of Gold	www.bricksofgold.com	editor@bricksofgold.com

To choose among the hundred or so gold stocks that are available at any given time, begin by categorizing them according to the following:

Size. The big miners, such as Barrick and Newmont, own many mines with extensive reserves, and produce millions of ounces a year. Mid-tier "juniors" have fewer mines and produce less gold but are less widely followed and frequently have a lot more upside potential. And the emerging miners are generally developing one or two promising mines but not yet producing, which means big risk but huge upside potential.

Hedging policy. Like most other commodity companies, gold miners often sell their production years in advance via the futures market. This guarantees a given price, but it also limits their upside, because no matter how much gold rises, a fully hedged company will get only the contract price. So if your goal is to benefit from a spike in the price of gold, "I would try to avoid the companies that are heavily hedged with a lot of gold sold forward, and stick with companies that are not hedged and would benefit from an immediate price increase," says Claude Cormier, publisher of the newsletter *OrMetal Report.*

Precious metals newsletter	Publisher
Freemarket Gold & Money Report	James Turk
Gold Mining Stock Report	Bob Bishop
Gold Report	Tom O'Brien
Gold Stock Analyst	John Doody
Jay Taylor's Gold, Resource & Environmental Stocks	Jay Taylor
Ormetal Report	Claude Cormier
Resource Opportunities	Lawrence Roulston

Barrick, for instance, tends to be heavily hedged, so while "it's a great stock that will continue to be stable in an environment where gold doesn't move, it will not benefit as much as other companies if gold moves." Newmont is the opposite, with little of its production sold forward and, therefore, more sensitivity to gold's price.

Cost. The cheaper it is to move a given ounce of metal from the ground to the mint, the more profitable the mining operation. Barrick, known for its low-cost mines, has to shell out only $180 to produce an ounce of gold, which means a profit of $170 per ounce at early-2003 prices.

Leverage. The more a miner borrows to build its reserves, the more vulnerable it is to a downturn in price, but the more it makes when metals rise. Add it all up, and the ideal gold mining stock would thus have big reserves; low-cost, unhedged current production; modest leverage; and an obscure, underfollowed stock. Like any other perfect profile, this one is a pretty rare find, of course, so you'll want to pick and choose among the characteristics that suit your temperament.

Gold Mutual Funds. Mining companies can, and frequently do, pour money into unproductive properties, overpay for acquisitions, and sometimes, as with 1997's high-profile disaster Bre-X Minerals—lie

Web address	Telephone	Annual subscription price
www.fgmr.com	(603) 323-8182	$220
www.goldminingstockreport.com	(925) 284-1165	$350
www.tfnn.com/goldreport.htm	(877) 518-9190	$120
www.goldstockanalyst.com	(925) 284-1165	$180
www.miningstocks.com	(718) 457-1426	$123
www.ormetal.com	(450) 653-5527	$130
www.resourceopportunities.com	(604) 697-0026	$225

about what they have in the ground. So it's possible to be right about the price of gold and still lose money in mining shares. The solution, as with any other part of the stock market, is twofold. If you're going to pick your own stocks—which, if done right, is by far the most profitable way to go—you've got to do the work. Find and follow the companies that fit your temperament, subscribe to a good newsletter, pay attention, and be ready to shift gears when things don't go as planned.

If you're unwilling or unable to do this, then let a pro do it for you via one or two good mutual funds, that spread their bets over dozens of stocks. In September 2002, the biggest gold fund, American Century Global Gold, for instance, had in its portfolio 42 stocks, none of which accounted for more than 8 percent of its total. This is about as close as you can get to a pure bet on precious metals mining. The downside of such funds is that with only a few exceptions, they charge excessive management fees, which gobble 2 percent or so of their investors' capital each year. The field is clearly ripe for an index fund that buys just a few dozen established miners and leaves them alone. But until then, the table on the next two pages lists some no-load funds worth considering. To find more, try the "Gold Funds" page at www.gold-eagle.com or the search functions of a good financial site like Morningstar or Charles Schwab.

Gold Fund	Symbol
American Century Global Gold Inv	ACGGX
Evergreen Precious Metals	EKWAX
Gabelli Gold	GOLDX
INVESCO Gold & Precious Metals	FGLDX
Tocqueville Gold	TGLDX
USAA Precious Metals and Minerals	USAGX

Source: Morningstar

Digital Gold. Gold coins and mining stocks are only partial solutions to the dollar dilemma because they don't change the fact that your checking account and other liquid funds are still denominated in a depreciating currency. But a fix is on the horizon, thanks ironically to the Internet. Electronic payment systems have reduced the concept of money to its essence, which is information. Most payments are now simply electronic debits and credits, making it possible do the bulk of your getting and spending via credit cards, online checking accounts, and soon, payment-enabled cell phones. Converted into bits in this way, gold once again becomes a viable—some would say vastly superior—kind of money. Conceptually, it works like this: You transfer some dollars or euros or whatever to a firm that buys gold for you and deposits it in a super-safe vault. You then make payments from this account via credit card or PC, and the gold—without ever leaving the vault—is credited to the recipient's account. If the recipient prefers dollars, the gold is electronically converted by exchanges, just as with the world's other currencies.

The first attempt to turn this theory into reality is called e-gold, the brainchild of Douglas Jackson, a Florida doctor who decided that the cure for monetary instability was a modern (that is, digital) gold currency. His prognosis was correct, and the number of e-gold accounts rose from 3,000 in mid-1999 to 300,000 by the end of 2001. The

3-year average Annual return (%)	Telephone	Web
22.2	(800) 345-3533	www.americancentury.com
25.0	(800) 343-2898	www.evergreeninvestments.com
30.5	(800) 422-3554	www.gabelli.com
17.3	(800) 646-8372	www.invesco.com
27.9	(800) 697-3863	www.tocqueville.com
25.5	(800) 382-8722	www.usaa.com

amount of e-gold in circulation (which by definition is identical to the amount of gold locked away in its vaults) grew from 5,000 ounces in 1999 to 43,000 ounces in 2001, equivalent to the annual output of a medium-size gold mine.

But in 2002—just when e-gold usage would be expected to surge—it began to stagnate. The number of accounts kept growing, but the average account size plunged, causing the amount of gold in the company's vaults to shrink to 37,000 ounces in December.

By early 2003 the momentum had shifted to a new currency called goldgrams, created by James Turk, publisher of the *Free Market Gold & Money Report* newsletter, an all-around big fish in the golden pond. Goldgrams in circulation rose tenfold, to 9,000 ounces in 2002, and in early 2003 rumor had it that by year-end at least one major gold miner would be paying its dividends in goldgrams. All in all, it's a promising beginning.

So should you convert your checking account to digital gold? Not just yet. This concept is still in its infancy, and its growing pains have so far overshadowed its obvious potential. Several e-gold-based payment systems collapsed in scandal in 2002 (hence e-gold's stagnation), and Turk and Jackson are battling over who owns the essential digital gold intellectual property. So digital gold won't become a viable alternative to fiat currencies until two things happen. First, the currencies themselves have to prove that they're as safe and secure as dollars, which means their transaction systems will have to be tested and found acceptable by people capable of assessing those things, like major banks or gold mining firms. And second, a "gold economy" of merchants willing to accept payment in digital gold, banks willing to pay interest on it, and credit cards willing to transact in it has to coalesce around one of the currencies. There's no guarantee that this will happen, but if it does, the impact on the price of gold could be dramatic. Consider: When the supply of dollars increases, it makes each individual dollar a little less valuable, other things being equal. But when someone opens a digital gold account, the operator buys gold on the open market and moves it to a vault. So an increase in the digital gold supply decreases the amount of physical gold in circulation, raising its price. Let a digital gold currency succeed, and the result might be a virtuous cycle in which rising demand for digital gold leads to a higher gold price, which makes existing digital gold accounts more valuable, which leads to higher demand, ad infinitum.

Silver Lining

Virtually everything that can be said of gold applies to its little brother, silver. Silver's price tends to move inversely to the dollar. It can be bought as coins or bars and from the same reputable dealers. Silver mining stocks trade on the major exchanges, and digital silver currencies are being created.

But there are some differences that actually work in silver's favor. Unlike gold, most demand for silver comes from users rather than investors. Silver plays a role in photography, jewelry, medicine, and various industrial products. And lately we've been using more silver than we've been producing. According to the Silver Institute, annual silver demand has grown over the past decade from about 700 million ounces to 900 million ounces, while the annual supply from mines has languished at 600 million ounces. The deficit is being made up through "dishording" as people and governments sell existing ("above-ground" in industry parlance) silver to users. Because few significant mines have opened in the past five years, production isn't likely to expand anytime soon. So the stage is set for a shortage when and if investment demand starts to pick up. As Bill Fleckenstein, a prominent short seller and silver bull, noted in early 2003, "The dollar amount of above-ground stocks in silver is far, far smaller than gold. And central banks don't have silver to sell, as they do with gold. Once silver gets going, it could double more easily than gold could double, simply because the market is smaller."

SILVER AND PLATINUM BARS AND COINS	PRICE 3/7/03
Silver Eagle 1oz	$5.81
Australian Kooka 10 oz	$71.76
Silver bar 100 oz	$546.00
Platinum Eagle 1 oz	$715.15
Platinum bar 1 oz	$713.00

Source: Kitco

Foreign Currencies—One of Them, Anyway

Three decades ago, the world looked a lot like it does today. The Western democracies were emerging from a time of boom and tumult. The United States, though the world's preeminent power, was entangled in foreign adventures that were sapping its strength and causing violent controversy here and abroad. The dollar was the world's preeminent reserve currency and had held its value relatively well in recent years. And despite the many uncertainties, most experts assumed that the future would be more or less like the past: messy but benign.

But a well-traveled college dropout named Harry Browne wasn't fooled, and in 1970 he published what was to become one of the hard-money world's classic texts, *How You Can Profit from the Coming Devaluation*. The dollar is headed for a fall, he wrote, so buy gold and foreign currencies. His timing, as it turned out, was perfect. As the excesses of the 1960s came home to roost, the United States drifted into "stagflation," where prices rose while the economy failed to grow. Gold surged more than twentyfold, and currencies like the Deutschemark, British pound, and Swiss franc trounced the dollar. As you can see from the chart below, the value of a Swiss franc bank account more than doubled in the 1970s.

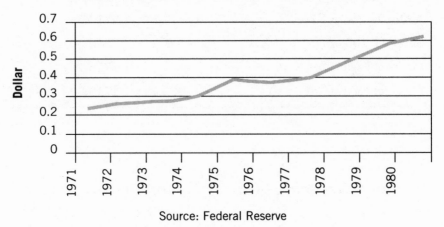

DOLLAR VALUE OF ONE SWISS FRANC

Source: Federal Reserve

This world, like I said, looks a lot like that one, and though history never repeats itself perfectly, the decline of the dollar against the euro and yen in 2002 sure feels like the start of a similar trend. Assuming it is, how exactly do you shift out of dollars and into foreign

currencies, and are the euro and yen, this era's main dollar alternatives, the way to go?

Taking the second question first, with Europe and Japan each running a huge trade surplus, one part of the math seems to be on their
side. But that's where the good news ends. To put it bluntly, both Japan
and the major Eurozone countries are extraordinarily badly run, and
even with their trade surpluses, they seem quite risky.

Japan, as we know from chapter 2, has a banking system that
still must go through the obligatory post-bubble debt liquidation before it can start fueling any kind of growth. Japanese consumers
aren't spending, and its government is borrowing far more, as a percent of GDP, than is Washington. And believe it or not, that's not the
worst of it.

Japan's real problem is demographic. Its population is already
one of the oldest on earth, and its birthrate is so low that the number
of Japanese under 20 years of age fell from 33 million in 1990 to 26
million in 2000 and will, if current trends persist, fall to 24 million
by 2010. By 2025, Japanese over 59 will outnumber those under 25
by two-to-one. The inevitable result, unless Japanese engineers finally get the industrial robot thing working (see chapter 2), is a precipitous rise in government spending to cover the pensions and
health care of these retirees, and a corresponding drop in the ability
of the remaining workers to produce the kind of wealth necessary to
support a world power. So the yen seems at best a trading play in the
hope that the trade surplus gives it a short-run pop before the
banking system collapses and/or the demographic decline turns into
a landslide.

Unlike Japan, Germany and France are a little more open to immigration, which allows them to import (relatively young) workers from
the east and south, thus staving off ossification for a while. But they're
still graying quickly. And their economic systems, in any event, seem
designed to prevent meaningful growth.

To take just a few examples, France in 1997 instituted a mandatory 35-hour workweek, on the economically illiterate assumption that if companies got less work from their existing employees, they would have to hire more, thus boosting employment. This led to the predictable silliness, typified by the (too good to verify) story of French police surrounding an office complex to arrest a group of engineers suspected of putting in overtime to complete a project. The 35-hour workweek was rescinded in early 2003, but the attitude that spawned it in the first place lingers in the form of labor laws that make it virtually impossible to fire someone once they're hired and of subsidies for inefficient farmers—payments that eat up an unsustainable share of the federal budget.

Germany, meanwhile, was seen just a short time ago as the engine that would pull the European economy into the twenty-first century. But overconfidence and a long series of policy mistakes have shattered that dream. Its pension, health care, and unemployment benefits have become ruinously expensive, and its labor laws are something out of the Soviet Union. Speaking of which, when the Iron Curtain fell and West Germany took possession of the eastern half of the country, the East's currency was made convertible one-for-one with the West's, and wages were made comparable, despite the fact that the East's economy couldn't produce anything like that kind of wealth. The result was a massive increase in government spending that has hamstrung German budgets ever since.

Not surprisingly, capital is heading for the exits. Whereas Germany's drug companies once led the world, by 2002 not one was in the global top 10. Its once rock-solid banks are tottering, and its major industrial companies are gradually shifting work to more hospitable climes. Chip giant Infineon Technologies recently made the final break that many others are contemplating, by moving its headquarters to Switzerland. In early 2003, German unemployment was about twice that of the United States, and its budget deficit was bumping up against

the Eurozone limit of 3 percent of GDP. So, yes, the fa[ct that the euro]
zone is running a collective trade surplus might give[it one]
other brief pop, but making a multiyear bet on such a bas[is]
isn't a wise move.

That leaves Switzerland, tiny banking haven in the Alps, not a
member of the Eurozone, famous for staying out of foreign entangle-
ments and therefore not really a terrorist target. Its treasury owns a lot
of gold, and its economy—though in demographic decline as well—
isn't displaying any of the blatant instability of the world's big countries. In any event, mature people make the best bankers, so a graying
population might actually improve the quality of this particular workforce. The downside here is that "it is very difficult for Americans to
purchase Swiss francs (unless you have a few million to throw around,
in which case the big U.S. banks will cater to your requests)," says hard
money guru James Turk. "My recommendation is to open a European
bank account. You don't need to fly there; many banks open accounts
by mail and/or over the Internet." Another possibility, he says, is
EverBank.com, an Internet bank that offers Swiss franc–denominated
accounts.

Cash-Rich Companies

The adage that "cash is king" in a recession applies to companies
as well as to individuals. To understand why, picture two firms that are
equal in every way except that, going into a downturn, one has a lot of
debt and little cash and the other is debt-free, with lots of cash. When
sales start to fall, the leveraged company has no choice but to pull
back, fire the people it spent the past few years training, and put long-
range projects on the back burner. Survival becomes priority one. Its
cash-rich counterpart, on the other hand, isn't bothered by pesky cred-
itors and so can keep on funding research and development, making

acquisitions, and buying back stock, all at a time when the competition is cutting back in all these areas. When the downturn is over, the two companies are no longer equal. The one with the cash is far better able to take advantage of all the opportunities growing markets present. Put another way, while a cash-rich company's operating business might become less valuable in a recession, its balance sheet becomes more valuable. So its stock is less likely to fall as far as its weaker peers and more likely to come roaring back when a recession ends. Here are a few examples from early 2003.

Microsoft's Windows and Office software packages are as close anyone in the tech universe has come to true monopolies. So while the price of every other part of a computer is plunging, each new version of Microsoft's flagship programs carries about the same price tag as its predecessor. Because, once created, software costs next to nothing to reproduce, Microsoft's profit margins are immense, and its annual cash flow exceeds $6 billion. As a result, despite Microsoft's having bought back increasing amounts of stock in recent years, it ended 2002 with a cash balance of $40 billion, without doubt the biggest pile of green ever to grace a single company's balance sheet. So think of Microsoft as two companies. Its Windows and Office franchises are slow-growing but astoundingly profitable, like a New Economy utility, while the other side of the company is the biggest venture capital outfit that's ever been, using virtually unlimited resources for forays into wireless communications, new business software niches, and video games. Whatever the Next Big Thing turns out to be, Microsoft will more than likely own a piece of it.

Cisco is the dominant maker of switches and related gear that manage traffic on the Internet, which was a pretty nice thing to be in the 1990s. Beginning in 1991, Cisco's stock made one of the storied runs in financial history, from a split-adjusted $.30 a share to $77 in 2000. Then it fell back to earth along with the rest of the industry, bottoming in early 2003 at $8 a share. Yet operationally it wasn't really suffering. Sales were flat in 2002, but thanks to stringent cost controls, earnings actually rose to $3 billion. By year end, Cisco was debt-free and had about $22 billion on hand.

Its business isn't a monopoly like Microsoft's, and both computer manufacturer Dell and some Chinese upstarts have designs on some of its highest-margin products. But Cisco is still the big fish in a wireless networking pond that ought to be one of technology's bright spots, even in a recession. The thinking goes like this: Right now there are millions of cell phones, digital cameras, camcorders, and personal digital assistants, all living separate lives. But the next generation of each will be able to tap into wireless data networks, moving information from handset to computer to camera, allowing sounds and images to be shipped around the Internet or saved to a PC hard drive. This transition will involve a lot of gear, much of which will come from Cisco. So weak economy or strong, it will be okay operationally. And because a lot of less well-capitalized tech firms can't say the same thing, Cisco should be able to buy its way into whatever new markets it fancies in the next few years.

Intel, the maker of the brains of most personal computers, had about $13 billion in cash on hand at the end of 2002, but unlike Microsoft and Cisco, it had a fairly clear plan for spending it. While most of the rest of the semiconductor industry is pulling back, Intel is pouring billions into new and upgraded factories, with the goal of dominating the next level of superchips that power cell phones and other wireless devices. In late 2002, Intel's chief financial officer noted that the company's cash gives it the flexibility to increase capacity quickly if spending picks up, and to buy up weaker competitors if it doesn't. Exactly.

Dell isn't just the biggest, most efficient maker of PCs. It's the model that every one else with a supply chain is emulating. By squeezing out inefficiencies at every level of its operation, it has been able to make money in a market where big competitors like Hewlett-Packard and Gateway are struggling. Now it's applying the same principles to other products, like networking gear and computer printers.

And through it all, Dell has been accumulating cash, which totaled about $5 billion in 2002. An example of what this combination of efficiency and financial strength does for a company is Dell's reaction to the post-2000 slump in PC sales. Instead of scaling back as demand dropped, Dell started a price war, figuring that it could handle lower margins better than its competitors. It worked. Dell's sales have barely fallen, while Gateway is hemorrhaging and Compaq and HP were forced to merge.

Nokia, the cell phone giant, has been gaining market share, turning a profit, and building up a $10 billion cash balance while most of the telecommunications industry is in varying states of debt-induced dementia. Now, as the transition from old, voice-only cell phone networks to high-speed voice-and-data systems really gets going, Nokia has the resources to flood the market with camera phones, handheld game consoles, and other toys of the young and cool. One analyst predicts that Nokia's cash pile will rise to $12 billion by the end of 2003.

Cash-rich company	Ticker	price 3/7/03	Market cap $	Net cash $
Cisco Systems	CSCO	13.24	94.2B	22.0B
Dell Computer	DELL	26.73	68.9B	4.7B
Intel	INTC	16.04	106.3B	12.6B
Microsoft	MSFT	23.56	252.1B	40.0B
Nokia	NOK	12.95	61.9B	10.3B

Source: Yahoo Finance, company annual reports

As you may have noticed, all the companies on this list are tech stocks. That wasn't by design; tech is just where the big cash hoards are clustered, perhaps because so much capital flowed into the sector during the 1990s. You may also have noticed that the discussion has been all about cash balances and company prospects, without a mention of valuation or stock price. That's because by the time this book hits the shelves, anything said about early 2003 share prices will be irrelevant. But valuation does matter. Cisco had plenty of cash at $77 a share, but that didn't stop it from falling by nearly 90 percent. So look beyond the balance sheet and make sure a company's price is in line with its prospects. And don't just accept cash as it's given in the balance sheet. The number you want is "net cash," which is cash minus debt, both long- and short-term. A lot of companies that show up on a screen for cash balances will also have as much debt or more, meaning that their net cash balance is zero or negative. Or they'll have items like "investments" and "deferred revenues," which have to be investigated to get at the true level of net cash.

Companies with Pricing Power

Not so long ago, it seemed like the most normal thing in the world for companies to raise their prices a little bit each year. After all, they had to give their people raises, and their other costs were always rising. But in the mid-1990s, this began to change. Whereas computers were once pretty much the only thing that got cheaper every year, and these days companies in virtually every industry report an inability to raise prices, which is another way of saying that their profit margins are being squeezed.

Why is this happening? Two reasons. First, in what is becoming known as the "Wal-Mart effect," a handful of big, hugely efficient operators are squeezing suppliers and forcing price cuts all along their respective supply chains, from raw materials to transportation to finished products. In retailing, of course, Wal-Mart itself is crushing the mom-and-pop retailers and Kmarts of the world with equal relentlessness. In computers, Dell is so much more efficient than Hewlett-

Packard and Gateway that it can undercut their prices and still make money. Competitors have no answer at the moment other than to match Dell's price cuts, accept the resulting losses, and squeeze their own suppliers.

The second factor is massive overcapacity in virtually every major industry. In telecom, a glut of fiber-optic cable is sending the price of long-distance calls and data services into freefall. This is why (one reason, anyhow) America Online, after years of fast growth, actually lost customers in 2002, as competitors undercut its $24-a-month rate by more than 50 percent. And it's why regional phone company Qwest recently began offering unlimited long distance for a flat monthly fee, a development that has to send chills down the spines of managers at AT&T and what's left of WorldCom. And the glut is only going to worsen as China and its billion hardworking citizens enter the global marketplace. Already Chinese factories are undercutting prevailing prices of big-screen TVs and cell phones, with computers and—who knows, maybe cars—on the horizon.

The upshot is that companies in most industries are unable to raise prices, which means they can't generate much of an increase in earnings, which in turn means their stocks are not going to light any fires on Wall Street. But there are a few exceptions, and as pricing gets even more difficult in the coming recession, they'll stand out like stars on a moonless night. Among them:

HMOs. Because health care is one of the last things to be cut in hard times, the companies that run managed-care plans are reasonably well-insulated on the downside. But lately they've been successfully raising prices as well. In 2001 and 2002, the average HMO raised the rate it charges its customers by more than 10 percent annually, and should achieve at least that much in 2003. Why? In part because they have a captive audience. Many markets have only a handful of major health plans, which lowers the incidence of cutthroat competition. And so far no Wal-Mart has emerged in the field to force big changes in pricing. Granted, the HMOs are seeing big cost increases themselves, with a nursing shortage driving up wages and the cost of new drugs rising. But the rate increases they've been able to push through lately have more than covered their higher costs. UnitedHealth Group, for instance, predicted in early 2003 that in the year ahead its costs would rise by 11 percent and its premiums by 13 percent, giving it 20 percent profit growth. And managed care giant Aetna swung from a loss in 2001 to a $.63-a-share profit in 2002 by eliminating unprofitable patients and raising rates on the rest.

There are a couple of obvious risks here. First, costs in this business are always in danger of running wild. New drugs always carry high initial price tags, and quite a few are in the pipeline. New medical devices often work wonders—and therefore can't be denied to patients, but often these devices are far more expensive than those they replace and medical personnel have a tendency to rebel when cost controls weigh too heavily. In Kentucky, for instance, a group of doctors recently won a price-fixing class action case against the area's largest HMOs, including Aetna, Humana, and United Health Care. The likely result: copycat suits in other markets that raise costs for all local HMOs.

Second, you have to wonder how much higher premiums can go before customers revolt. So far they (excuse me, we) have been accepting the increases, but our patience and budgets are not infinite. So pay attention to the trends in both costs and premium increases. As long as the latter is above the former, HMOs will stand out. If the lines cross, then the prognosis will change for the worse. But for the next couple of years, at least, these companies should be among the handful that are able to make double-digit price increases stick.

Medical device makers. The next generation of drugs will be pretty amazing, no doubt. But so will the next generation of medical devices. Imaging devices that create clear, three-dimensional views of our insides, cochlear implants that allow the deaf to hear, noninvasive

Managed care provider	Symbol	Price 3/12/03	% yield	Market cap $
Aetna	AET	45.62	0.09	6.8B
Aflac	AFL	31.25	0.93	16.0B
Anthem	ATH	60.48	N/A	8.3B
Cigna	CI	41.64	3.26	5.8B
Humana	HUM	9.25	N/A	1.5B
Mid Atlantic Medical	MME	37.00	NA	1.8B
Oxford Health	OHP	27.52	N/A	2.3B
Torchmark	TMK	34.70	1.07	4.1B
Transatlantic	TRH	62.70	0.65	3.2B
United Health	UNH	85.71	0.04	26.0B
Wellpoint Health	WLP	68.58	N/A	10.2B

surgery that uses tiny lasers to zap tumors, artificial organs and nerves: The list is endless—and a lot of fun to explore because we'll all need these things at some point. But for our purposes here, the attraction of medical devices is that when they produce a real improvement in the quality of care, health care providers pretty much have to offer them to patients, which means they have to pay what the device makers are asking, within reason. To take just one example, Johnson & Johnson recently introduced a drug-coated stent, a small device that's inserted into a clogged artery to keep it open and clear. J & J's breakthrough is to coat its new stent with a drug that inhibits the formation of junk that clogs arteries; this is expected to keep them clearer longer. The stent works beautifully but costs way more than conventional stents, and both Medicare and the major HMOs have no choice but to pay J & J's price. But note that this field, like the rest of high-tech, is prone to hype. So stick with the leaders, and avoid the small players which depend on only one or two products.

Medical device maker	Symbol	Price 3/12/03	% yield	Market cap $
Biomet	BMET	31.07	0.34	8.0B
Boston Scientific	BSX	44.05	N/A	17.9B
Guidant	GDT	34.21	0.95	10.4B
Johnson & Johnson	JNJ	55.48	1.50	164.8B
Medtronic	MDT	44.07	0.57	53.7B

Recession-Resistant Companies

In the 1990s, many of us felt little need to prioritize because we could have both the SUV and the vacation home and still feed the kids. This may not be the case for much longer, a turn of events that historically has been bad news for the makers of luxury goods, and good news for grocery stores, hospitals, and electric utilities. (The last might even benefit as we spend more evenings at home with our own fridge and a good book.) So relatively speaking, in the next few years the companies that make life's necessities will attract more capital than those selling frivolities. Below is a price chart for Archer Daniels Midland (ADM),

ARCHER DANIELS MIDLAND
What Recession?

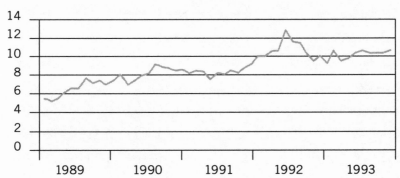

the big food processor and classic recession-proof company. Note that the 1991 downturn was a total nonevent for its stock. Why? Because when we couldn't afford to eat out so often, we bought more breakfast cereal and TV dinners, many of which contain ADM ingredients.

So a portfolio of the best companies in recession-resistant industries might make the next few years more peaceful. If times are hard, you'll conserve your capital and maybe squeeze out a small gain. If you're wrong and the markets set off on another supercycle bull run, you'll underperform the tech indexes but still make money. Here are some likely prospects.

Food processors. These companies buy wheat, corn, soybeans, and other goods from farmers, and turn them into products that we buy in grocery stores and that our kids eat in the school cafeteria. Archer Daniels Midland turns corn and soybeans into the oils and sugars that go into most of what's in your kitchen cabinet. Kraft makes Oreos, Planters nuts, Post cereals, and 58 other brands that most of us recognize and occasionally eat. Sysco sells various prepared and processed foods to restaurants, hospitals, and schools. Those big cans of green

Food processor	Symbol	Price 3/7/03	% yield	Market cap $
Archer Daniels Midland	ADM	10.90	2.22	7.0B
Conagra	CAG	21.74	4.56	11.6B
Groupe Danone	DA	23.67	1.53	15.9B
General Mills	GIS	42.20	2.62	15.5B
H J Heinz	HNZ	29.94	5.43	10.5B
Kellogg	K	28.73	3.55	11.7B
Kraft Foods	KFT	27.30	2.18	47.2B
Sara Lee	SLE	19.01	3.31	14.8B
Sysco	SYY	24.45	1.79	15.9B
Unilever	UL	34.60	4.40	25.1B

beans the lunch lady spoons out? That's where they come from. These and the rest of the big food processors live in a world of intense competition among brands, but pretty stable overall demand. The worst they as a group are likely to see in the coming recession is a shift from brand-name cookies to cheaper store brands—which they make too.

Consumer products companies. Whether we eat in or out tonight, whether we dine on steak or mac and cheese, most of us will still brush our teeth afterward. And if we eat in, we'll wash the dishes. So toothpaste, dish detergent, and other such basic necessities will be among the last things to be cut from household budgets, and the companies making them should get through the next few years without undue stress. These are mostly familiar names: Colgate makes toothpaste and deodorant and soap. Clorox, makes, well, Clorox, and Procter & Gamble makes just about everything that lives under the average sink and in most medicine chests, including Mr. Clean and Crest Whitening Strips. And besides holding up well in recessions, they stand to benefit as the developing world discovers the joys of Right Guard and Pine Sol, giving them a potential growth kicker.

Consumer products company	Symbol	Price 3/7/03	% Yield	Market cap
Avon Products	AVP	51.73	1.64	12.1B
Colgate Palmolive	CL	49.65	1.93	26.7B
Clorox	CLX	42.18	2.09	9.1B
Dial	DL	18.03	0.90	1.7B
Ecolab	ECL	47.93	1.23	6.2B
Estee Lauder	EL	27.95	0.72	6.4B
Gillette	G	31.09	2.12	32.7B
McKesson	MCK	25.70	0.93	7.4B
Newell Rubbermaid	NWL	25.55	3.32	7.0B
Procter & Gamble	PG	80.96	2.05	104.7B

Some of these stocks also have yields that exceed those of money market funds.

Drug companies. For years, the pharmaceutical makers were seen as the perennial all-weather investments, propelled by demographics (an aging populace takes more pills) and science (mood enhancers and cholesterol fighters were pouring out of research labs) that seemed likely to go on forever. But the past few years have forced a revision in this theory as the drug makers' flow of new compounds slowed and some of the old classics, like Prozac, went off patent and attracted generic competition. Even best-of-breed Pfizer lost about a third of its value between 2000 and 2003. But at the new, lower prices, much of the risk has been removed, and because most people are covered by health insurance, drug demand is stable in good times and bad. Plus, many of these companies have a lot of cash, which makes their often-generous dividends fairly safe.

Drug maker	Symbol	Price 3/7/03	% yield	Market cap $
Abbott Labs	ABT	35.45	2.78	55.4B
Astrazeneca	AZN	32.44	3.24	56.6B
Bristol Myers Squibb	BMY	22.80	4.97	44.1B
Johnson & Johnson	JNJ	55.30	1.54	164.3B
Eli Lilly	LLY	56.98	2.39	64.0B
Merck	MRK	52.36	2.77	117.6B
Novartis	NVS	36.25	1.96	89.7B
Pfizer	PFE	29.98	2.04	184.7B
Wyeth	WYE	34.97	2.66	46.3B

Electric utilities. Once we've eaten in and done the dishes, the newly cost-conscious among us will settle in for a little TV or a good book. Both consume electricity. The power companies started out as "public monopolies." In return for the exclusive right to light up the lives in a given area, they were allowed to charge enough to guarantee themselves a reasonable profit. This enabled them to pay big, predictable dividends and made them popular "widow and orphan" stocks. But that changed as deregulation swept the industry, and power generation became, sort of, competitive. This was a success in some places and a total mess in others, like California, and now many states are rethinking their utility rules. As a result, the business is still in flux, but the best-run utilities are once again good defensive stocks, with high, reasonably safe dividend yields.

Electric utility	Symbol	Price 3/14/03	% yield	Market cap $
American Electric Power	AEP	21.77	10.81	7.4B
Dominion Resources	D	54.28	4.68	17.1B
Duke Energy	DUK	13.90	8.47	11.4B
Consolidated Edison	ED	37.89	5.72	8.3B
Entergy	ETR	47.30	3.05	10.2B
Exelon	EXC	48.41	3.72	15.9B
First Energy	FE	29.66	5.00	8.7B
FPL Group	FPL	57.49	4.14	10.5B
National Grid	NGG	30.60	3.75	10.9B
Progress Energy	PGN	38.46	5.63	9.4B

Avoid the grocery chains! Grocery stores might be the most obvious defensive stocks because food is the last thing we cut from the household budget. There's a problem this time around, though, and its name is Wal-Mart. Since it began adding grocery sections to its super-

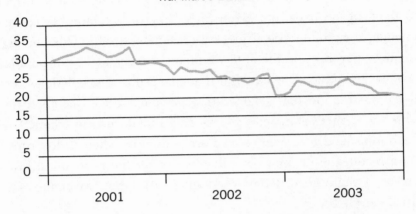

ALBERTSON'S

Wal-Mart's Lunch?

stores a few years back, the retailing giant has taken about 20 percent of the grocery market, and because the business grows only slightly each year, Wal-Mart's gains come at the expense of the existing players, thus messing up the old steady-growth model. As you can see from the chart below, the price of the big grocery chain Albertson's is down by more than a third in the past couple of years, in large part because of Wal-Mart.

Recession-resistant sector fund	Symbol	3-year average annual % return through 2002
Invesco Health Sciences	FHLSX	−15.7
Pimco RCM Global Health Care	DGHCX	12.8
Scudder Health Care	SCHLX	−9.0
Icon Healthcare	ICHCX	1.3
American Century Utilities	BULIX	−19.5
Vanguard Dividend Growth	VDIGX	−3.2
Fidelity Utilities	FIUIX	−26.1

Sector Funds

Sector funds are mutual funds that own stocks in just one industry. This makes them riskier than the average fund because they're not diversified beyond their target industry. But if that's the kind of concentration you're after—and right now it should be—they're a great choice. Below is a list of no-load sector funds in health care and utilities, most of which should hold up better than the overall market in a downturn. But they're not identical, so do some research before buying. Some utility funds, for instance, lump power companies and telecom firms into the same category. So along with Southern Company and Con Edison, you might find AT&T and Sprint in their portfolios. At American Century Utilities, six of the top 10 holdings at the end of 2002 were electric utilities and the other four various kinds of telecom firms, while at Fidelity Utilities the ratio is about 50-50.

This isn't ideal, but because the local phone giants pay good dividends and seem to be winning the latest regulatory wars in Washington, they're reasonable bets in a downturn too.

Web	Telephone
www.invesco.com	(800) 646-8372
www.pimcofunds.com	(800) 726-7240
www.scudder.com	(800) 621-1048
www.iconfunds.com	(800) 764-0442
www.americancentury.com	(800) 345-2021
www.vanguard.com	(800) 662-7447
www.fidelityfunds.com	(800) 544-8888

The other thing you'll notice about the utility funds is that they've been terrible investments of late. That's due to the combination of their telecom holdings (which have tanked along with the rest of the tech sector) and the mess state and local governments have made of power deregulation. Both problems—because they've already happened—should have less of an impact going forward. Further, tighter scrutiny of how these firms do business and their accounting practices should serve to keep them out of the financial quicksand, giving these beaten-down portfolios pretty good prospects.

Some interesting variations on the sector fund theme include:

Exchange-traded funds (ETFs) are pooled investments that look like sector funds but trade like stocks. They come into being when a bank or brokerage house buys shares in a group of companies, wraps them into a trust that can itself be divided into shares and traded like a stock, and turns the fund loose to trade on the major exchanges. Investors can then buy the ETF through their brokers, but instead of getting a single stock, they get small pieces of each stock in the fund. And because they don't employ a lot of high-priced talent to buy, sell, and research their stocks, ETFs have lower operating expenses than most traditional mutual funds.

HOLDRs (pronounced "holders"), or holding company depositary receipts, are ETF variants created by Merrill Lynch. Like ETFs, they trade like stocks. But whereas ETFs can hold varying numbers of companies, each HOLDR is a fixed basket of 20 stocks. Where an ETF might add new stocks when one of its existing positions disappears, HOLDRs do not. Once created, they just trade with whatever companies are left standing. That keeps expenses really low because no one has to maintain them. Besides the brokerage commission, the only other expense associated with HOLDRs is a $0.02-per-share quarterly custody charge paid to Merrill Lynch for holding the shares, and any portion of this not covered by dividends is waived.

ETFs AND HOLDRs	SYMBOL
iShares Dow Jones U.S. Healthcare Sector	IYH
Select Sector SPDR Fund—Health Care	XLV
iShares Dow Jones U.S. Energy Sector	IYE
iShares S&P Global Healthcare Index	IXJ
Select Sector SPDR Fund—Utilities	XLU
Merrill Lynch Utilities HOLDRS	UTH
Select Sector SPDR Fund—Consumer Staples	XLP
iShares Dow Jones U.S. Utilities Sector Index	IDU

Source: NASDAQ

Convertible Bonds

Among the more interesting and least understood ports in a bear market storm are convertible bonds, which—in theory, at least—offer safety, capital gains potential, and income all in one sleek package. "Converts" work like this: A company borrows money by issuing bonds, but to get a lower interest rate, it makes the bonds convertible into common stock. That way, if the market—or the stock in particular—tanks, you still get the interest payments the bond generates. If the stock soars, you get the benefit of the conversion feature. The value of a convert thus comes in two pieces. The bond piece is calculated by dividing the interest rate (or coupon) by the price to find a yield and then factoring in the difference between the price you pay for it and the cash the company has to return to you when the bond matures. The result is called the yield to maturity. If you have a financial calculator, this is easy to derive. Online there are several sites that do this as well (see Further Reading, page 243, for their addresses).

The value of the stock side depends on the proximity of the stock price to the conversion price. If the stock is way below the conver-

Convertible bond fund	Symbol	3-year average annual % return*
Davis Convertible	DCSYX	−4.85
Fidelity Convertible Securities	FCVSX	−7.66
Northern Income Equity	NOIEX	−2.61
Smith Barney Convertible	SCVYX	0.56
Value Line Convertible	VALCX	−11.72
Vanguard Convertible Securities	VCVSX	−7.79

*Through December 31, 2002

sion price—making it unlikely that a bondholder will be able to profitably convert it to stock anytime soon—then the conversion feature doesn't mean much, and the convert trades mostly as a bond. If the stock is near or above the conversion price, the convert will be more sensitive to the stock's movements. This mix of characteristics makes converts more complicated than plain-vanilla stocks and bonds. In some cases they're worth the trouble, though as a group they haven't always lived up to their hype. A lot of high-risk companies issued this kind of debt as the last bull market peaked, and those bonds have done just as badly as the companies' stocks. Telecom is the main offender here, but the whole tech sector contains a lot of land mines. But of course you won't be wandering in that part of town for a few years.

Other points to consider include the fact that converts are usually subordinated debentures (that is, they are not backed by the assets of the company), and other, unsubordinated debts will be paid off ahead of them in case of bankruptcy. Most converts are callable, which means that if the stock price surges, the issuer can take back the bonds for a predetermined price, thereby depriving holders of the chance of the full appreciation. This limits the upside potential compared with that of the company's stock. The yield on a convert is generally less than that of a company's nonconvertible debt. And last but

Web	Telephone
www.davisfunds.com	(800) 279-0279
www.fidelityfunds.com	(800) 544-8888
www.northernfunds.com	(800) 595-9111
www.smithbarney.com	(800) 347-1123
www.valueline.com	(800) 223-0818
www.vanguard.com	(800) 662-7447

not least, at the moment building a portfolio of individual converts is hard because relatively few recession-resistant companies issue them. So the best way to go is probably a mutual fund that holds convertible bonds and preferred stock. Some of the better ones are listed above.

CHAPTER 10

MAKING MONEY WHEN THE BUBBLE BURSTS

Sell High, Buy Low: The Art of Short Selling

In theory, you can make just as much money in bad times as good by seeking out the overvalued parts of the economy and betting against them. But in practice most people find it easy to buy, hard to sell, and *really* hard to actually risk money on the hope that something will go down. That reflects both our nature—it's a lot more comfortable to be on the same side as the smart guys running public companies than it is to oppose them—and our experience, in light of the fact that the overwhelming bias of the stock and real estate markets has historically been up. Beginning in the mid-1930s and running through the late 1990s, buy and hold was a brilliant strategy, better than any in-and-out trading system ever devised.

But there are times—2000 was certainly one of them, and 2004 might be another—when pessimistic is realistic. When housing sinks, it will pull lots of other industries down with it, and each individual shipwreck will be an opportunity for those who saw it coming. So let's look at some ways to profit from falling prices.

Short selling. In the real world, it's generally necessary to own something before you can sell it. Not so in the stock market. If you think a given stock is headed for a fall, you can simply enter a sell order with your broker, and the deed is done. Later, when the stock has dropped, you can buy it back and pocket the difference. This is known as short selling (or selling short, or just shorting), and it's the way hedge funds and other sophisticated investors play overvalued markets.

So let's say that you found chapter 6 compelling, and decide to short Fannie Mae. You call your broker or log onto to his firm's Web site and place a sell order for 100 shares. The broker will "borrow" shares from the account of a Fannie Mae shareholder, sell them for you, and deposit the proceeds (at the February 14, 2003 price of $63, this would come to $6,300) in your account. Once the share price has fallen to, say, $30, you "cover" your short by buying 100 shares to replace those that your broker borrowed. Your profit will be the difference between where you sold and where you bought, or $3,300, minus commissions and taxes.

Smooth, no? But very dangerous. Whereas a long position can only go down to zero, the risk associated with a short corresponds to the upside of a given stock, which is theoretically unlimited. Shorts are thus vulnerable to a kind of buying panic called a "short squeeze," where a large number of short sellers try to cover at the same time, forcing the price through the roof and costing the laggards a fortune. To take just one example, the many people who shorted Amazon.com at $16 in June 1998 saw their target hit $85 within 18 months. Those who held on ended up losing about four times their initial investment—far more, in other words, than even the most obtuse buy-and-hold strategy lost in the ensuing tech stock crash. So "trade, hold, and forget" is not the mantra of short sellers who wish to survive. Instead, it's "sell, and watch compulsively."

And if the stock you short pays dividends, you'll be required to pay this amount to the shareholder whose shares you borrowed. In the Fannie Mae example, if you hold the position for two years, you'll be on the hook for about $3 per share, or $300 for a 100-share short position.

Then there are the various regulatory hoops that a short seller must jump through. You can't short stocks in IRAs, for instance. Instead, short sales must be made in a margin account, in which the broker has agreed to lend a customer money for strategies like shorting and buying on margin. Short sales of most stocks must be made at a higher price than the previous sale (a "plus tick"), to prevent short sellers from driving a stock down to zero. And before allowing you to sell short, your broker will require extra collateral in the account to cover the possibility that the stock will soar. Should your shorts subsequently eat through that cushion, you may be asked for more money.

Yet despite the risk and complexity, shorting is the purest, most popular way to profit from a given stock's overvaluation. So if you're game, let's identify some short candidates by reversing the thought process of the previous chapter. Instead of considering what you'll keep doing and buying in hard times, consider what you'll stop paying for. Bear in mind that as with all the specific companies mentioned in this book, the following are examples only; by the time you read this, their situations may be very different. And the analysis of both companies and industries here is cursory (otherwise, you wouldn't wade through it), which means it misses some of the nuance and variety of the industries mentioned. So before shorting any particular stock, dig much deeper. That said, here are some likely prospects.

Mortgage packagers/credit insurers. This one is a no-brainer. If the housing bubble bursts, it will throw into reverse all the forces that made Fannie and Freddie and their peers such titans. Fannie, as we know from chapter 6, is an inverted pyramid of $2 trillion in liabilities atop less than $1 trillion in mortgages. Let loan defaults exceed what today's rose-colored models indicate is likely, and the talk will quickly turn from Fannie and Freddie's spectacular growth to their desperate need for a government bailout. Their stocks will plunge, and their short sellers will make a quick 50 to 75 percent. The same general outlook holds for mortgage insurers like MBIA, Ambac, and MGIC. Like Fannie and Freddie, they sell their guarantees to the packagers of mortgage-backed securities, and lately this has been a very good business indeed. MBIA earned a cumulative $2.4 billion between 1998 and 2002. And Ambac ended 2002 with a flourish that will live on in the annals of bubble markets, with adjusted gross premiums (that is, the amount of money it received for insuring new bond issues) up 54 percent in the fourth quarter, from the previous year's fourth quarter. Ambac's net financial guarantees in force (the value of the outstanding bonds with its guarantee) rose 24 percent to $557 billion, which comes to about 149 times its year-end capital. As the company's CEO noted, "We enter the new year with significant momentum and an apparent abundance of attractive opportunities."

Therein lies the problem. In good times, writing insurance on mortgage bonds is a license to print money. Low default rates are virtually guaranteed by the availability of credit cards and home equity loans. But models that assume it will always be thus tend to break down when the unexpected happens—which, sooner or later, it always does. As Prudent Bear's Doug Noland points out, insuring bonds isn't the same thing as insuring lives or structures. About the same number of deaths and fires occur each year in a given population of people and build-

Credit insurer	Symbol	Price 2/13/03	% yield	Market cap $
Ambac Financial	ABK	48.63	0.81	5.1B
Fannie Mae	FNM	62.15	2.48	61.4B
Freddie Mac	FRE	54.00	1.62	37.1B
MBIA INC	MBI	36.60	1.85	5.3B
MGIC Investment	MTG	41.15	0.24	4.1B

ings, allowing actuaries to create tables that are accurate over long periods of time. But the credit markets are cyclical. Pricing insurance based on the loss experience of the 1990s leaves these insurers unprepared for the inevitable spike in defaults.

Investment companies. The most obvious winner in a bull market is the investment industry itself. In good times we pour money into brokerage and retirement accounts, which is why, here at the end of a very long boom, there are now more mutual funds than there are stocks on the New York Stock Exchange. Fidelity and Vanguard, the two biggest fund families, control a cumulative $1 trillion. Merrill Lynch, the biggest brokerage house, has 50,000 employees, revenues of $27 billion, and profits of $2.6 billion. Yahoo Finance lists in its "investment company" category more than 70 firms, which together had a market value of $270 billion in early 2003. This is, in short, a vast, sprawling, hugely profitable business, all based on the premise that Americans will pour ever-larger amounts of money into savings, the markets will on balance go up, and companies will keep buying one another out and financing themselves by issuing stocks and bonds. So it has been, with just a few minor hiccups, since World War II, making the investment industry—and its investors—fat and happy. Check out the chart below, and you'll see that owning Merrill Lynch was a brilliant move from the early 1980s through 2000.

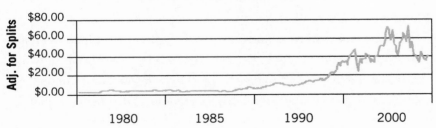

MERRILL LYNCH
The Biggest Investment Company
During the Longest Bull Market

But in recessions, individuals skip their IRA contributions, laid-off workers by definition don't contribute to their 401(k)s and on balance individuals sell more stock than they buy. Companies, as a result, find it a lot harder to sell their stock (and often bonds), and therefore don't go around buying one another out with such abandon. For investment companies, a paucity of fees translates into lower earnings and plunging stock prices, making them great short candidates.

Deciding which investment company's stock to short is a bit of a challenge, though. For one thing, the balance sheets of these companies are tough to analyze. Goldman Sachs has cash that nearly equals its stock price, but debt that's four times its equity. Morgan Stanley has $70 billion in cash, but debt that's five times its equity. And their strategies vary widely. Bear Stearns has traditionally run a very lean operation, which held it back during the boom and makes it one of the most profitable firms on Wall Street now that things are a little slower; Merrill has shed tens of thousands of people in the past few years, which lowers—though by no means eliminates—its exposure to a serious downturn. While the big investment banks like Goldman Sachs make money from trading and doing deals, the Chicago Mercantile Exchange, a futures exchange, depends on trading volumes in listed derivatives; Charles Schwab makes most of its money from individual stock trades; and Franklin Resources manages mutual funds. Winnowing this list down to just a few prime short candidates, in other words, is a big piece of research. On the other hand, since they're all dependent on pretty much the same general trend—our putting money into the game rather than taking it out—all of them will suffer when the spigot is turned off.

Consumer finance companies. Credit card companies' marketing alone makes them logical short candidates. After all, anyone this desperate to give you free money has to be headed for trouble. And thanks to securitization, the mortgage lenders have become just as

Investment company	Symbol	Price 4/21/03	% yield	Market cap $
Alliance Capital	AC	32.51	6.67	2.4B
A G Edwards	AGE	29.98	2.23	2.3B
Ameritrade	AMTD	5.19	N/A	2.2B
Franklin Resources	BEN	36.04	0.85	9.2B
Blackrock	BLK	44.94	N/A	2.9B
Bear Stearns	BSC	69.48	1.00	6.8B
Chicago Mercantile	CME	50.13	1.15	1.6B
E*TRADE	ET	4.78	N/A	1.7B
Eaton Vance	EV	29.44	1.11	2.0B
Friedman Billings Ramsey	FBR	10.75	13.03	1.5B
Goldman Sachs	GS	78.02	0.63	36.6B
Lehman Brothers	LEH	65.61	0.76	15.9B
Legg Mason	LM	55.15	0.82	3.5B
Merrill Lynch	MER	41.15	1.60	38.0B
Morgan Stanley	MWD	46.31	2.05	50.3B
Neuberger Berman	NEU	31.61	0.98	2.2B
Charles Schwab	SCH	9.04	0.51	12.2B
T. Rowe Price	TROW	30.31	2.37	3.7B
Waddell & Reed	WDR	20.26	2.75	1.6B

reckless. As a result, the consumer finance companies teeter. There's the threat of rising defaults from their newest customers, which are only prevented from becoming a tidal wave by the availability of home equity loans and new credit cards. More stringent government regulations are limiting the use of late fees, high rates and other tricks for milking low-income customers. And looming over the industry like a mushroom cloud is the current level of consumer debt. Americans have never increased their borrowing beyond the level achieved in late 2002, so for these companies to maintain their growth, a very unlikely—and ultimately very bad—set of circumstances would have to prevail by mid-decade. Much more likely is a dramatic slow-down in credit demand, followed by a collapse in the credit companies' market value.

Consumer finance company	Symbol	Price 2/13/03	% yield	Market cap $
Americredit	ACF	2.74	N/A	418.9M
American Express	AXP	32.55	0.98	42.4B
Compucredit	CCRT	6.22	N/A	284.4M
Countrywide Financial	CFC	53.46	0.90	6.7B
CIT Group	CIT	17.40	2.71	3.6B
Capital One Financial	COF	29.11	0.36	6.4B
Household International	HI	27.03	3.73	12.2B
Leucadia National	LUK	33.28	0.76	1.8B
Providian	PVN	6.10	N/A	1.7B

Money center banks. In general, banks don't do well in the early stages of a recession, when rising loan defaults outweigh the benefits of falling interest rates. This time, with interest rates already close to zero, JPMorgan Chase's experience in the 1991 recession—shown below—is likely to be repeated across the whole industry.

Or it might be a lot worse. Even though the big banks now hand most of the mortgages they originate off to the packagers, they've kept enough mortgage debt on their books to cause them trouble when defaults begin to rise. And their other lines—auto, business, and personal loans, and investment banking and securities trading—all depend on

J.P. MORGAN CHASE SHARE PRICE

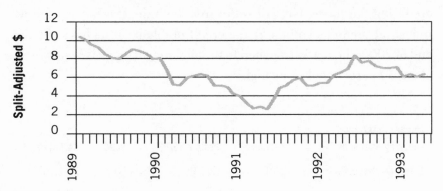

consumers' willingness to borrow and/or the markets' appetite for more structured finance deals. In 2002, JPMorgan Chase, for instance, underwrote 79 asset-backed bond offerings (mostly packaged consumer and home loans) worth $51 billion, with Credit Suisse First Boston and Citigroup not far behind. And, true to form, the big banks are now, at the peak of the cycle, moving aggressively into housing and consumer lending. In 2002's fourth quarter, Bank of America's mortgage banking and credit income rose by 23 percent and 17 percent respectively (versus a year earlier), while the rest of the bank's business lines barely grew at all.

General Electric appears on this list because it has evolved, along with the economy as a whole, from building things to financing them. Originally—and in the minds of most people still—GE was an industrial company that made machines like turbines, engines, and microwaves. And it does indeed still make those things. But over the past decade, its real growth driver, GE Capital, has become one of the world's biggest banks. Like the other big money center banks, GE Capital is made up of numerous divisions—25 in this case—with business lines ranging from commercial real estate to jet plane financing to credit cards and mortgage insurance. In terms of both revenues and earnings, finance is now about 40 percent of the company. So in a credit-led downturn, GE will suffer from both the slowing sales of its industrial products and the rising credit problems at its bank. By the end of 2002, the market seemed to be catching on, and GE's stock was about 50 percent below its high.

Money center and superregional bank	Symbol	Price 2/13/03	% yield	Market cap $
Bank of America	BAC	67.60	3.81	101.2B
Bank of New York	BK	22.54	3.35	17.2B
Citigroup	C	31.84	2.55	161.0B
General Electric	GE	22.80	3.43	219.7B
HSBC Holdings	HBC	53.41	4.31	99.9B
JPMorgan Chase	JPM	21.29	6.32	42.5B
U.S. Bancorp	USB	20.15	3.90	38.5B
Wachovia	WB	34.22	3.05	46.5B
Wells Fargo	WFC	45.60	2.65	76.8B

Regional banks. In May 2002, Moody's Investor Service noted with alarm that "the boom-bust cycle over the late 1980s to early 1990s fundamentally changed the supply of (commercial real estate) financing. Hundreds of thrifts collapsed, and many large domestic and foreign banks withdrew, or substantially reduced their role after suffering spectacular losses." The regional banks, said Moody's, "readily filled the vacuum (in commercial real estate lending) left by the departure of thrifts and big banks. . . . The (credit) ratings of several banks are currently under pressure because of this issue."

Home builders. Next to the mortgage lenders and insurers, the

Regional bank	Symbol	Price 2/13/03	% yield	Market cap $
BB&T	BBT	31.78	3.65	15.2B
FleetBoston Financial	FBF	24.00	5.78	25.1B
Fifth Third Bancorp	FITB	52.58	1.99	30.2B
Keycorp	KEY	23.65	5.21	10.0B
Mellon Financial	MEL	21.22	2.45	9.1B
National City	NCC	27.01	4.56	16.5B
Bank One	ONE	35.00	2.40	40.8B
PNC Financial	PNC	42.20	4.55	11.9B
Suntrust	STI	54.53	3.33	15.4B
State Street	STT	36.33	1.42	11.8B

surest housing shorts are probably the home builders themselves. The most aggressive of them have been setting records the past few years, building more houses, hiring more people, and making more money than ever before. Meanwhile, because the shares of such companies are cheap compared with current earnings, value-oriented investors have been snapping them up. By the third quarter of 2002, home builder Beazer was owned by 121 mutual funds, up from only 21 in 2001. Centex was owned by 280, versus 175 in 2001, and Lennar was owned by 250, versus only 50 in 2000.

The point? True to form, the pros are throwing money at what's hot, regardless of what's coming. As one money manager opined in an October 2002 interview with TheStreet.com, "(housing) stands out to me as the most attractive sector in the market. In a nutshell, you have a major industry in this country that is trading at six-plus times 2003 earnings. And they're growing by more than 20 percent annually, depending on the company." Another analyst, playing his part to the hilt, went on record in the same article with "Investors should ignore the conventional wisdom that home builders are cyclicals that should only be bought early in a recovery, when price/earnings ratios are high, and sold when earnings catch up with stock prices."

What the buyers of cyclical stocks at the peak of their cycles seem to miss every time is that when things turn down, earnings don't just plateau; they evaporate. This time, because housing has been on a historic tear, the comedown should be that much more extreme.

Home builder	Symbol	Price 2/31/03	% yield	Market cap $
Beazer Homes	BZH	56.28	NA	726.1M
Centex	CTX	52.62	0.30	3.2B
D. R. Horton	DHI	18.19	1.51	2.6B
Hovnanian Enterprises	HOV	29.26	N/A	897.3M
KB Home	KBH	44.40	0.66	1.7B
Lennar	LEN	50.94	0.10	3.0B
MDC Holdings	MDC	37.20	0.85	991.3M
Pulte Homes	PHM	48.74	0.32	2.8B
STD Pacific	SPF	25.11	1.26	808.1M
Toll Brothers	TOL	18.82	N/A	1.2B

Title insurers. Title insurance is something that few people think about until they buy a house. And even then, it's just a formality, a few hundred bucks tucked in among all the other nickel-and-dime charges on a loan contract. But billions of dollars of residential and commercial property are sold each year, and the business of ensuring that property titles are free of prior liens is a big, highly profitable one. At least it is until the bubble pops and the number of title searches plunges. The nimbler title insurers will respond as they always do, by shutting down branch offices and laying off employees (who, of course, will drop whatever home-buying plans they themselves might have had). And the companies' stocks will do what they normally do in a recession, which is tank. As you can see from the table below, the big title insurers are hugely profitable, for now.

Title insurer	Symbol	Price 2/13/03	2002 profit $ million	% yield	Market cap $
First American	FAF	22.25	234	1.76	1.6B
Fidelity National	FNF	31.29	532	1.89	2.9B
Landamerica Fin.	LFG	36.50	89	0.76	664.9M
Old Republic	ORI	26.22	392	2.45	3.1B
Stewart Info	STC	21.85	68	N/A	387.3M

U.S. auto makers. GM had a huge 2002, with earnings of $1.7 billion on record revenues of $187 billion. The problem is, it accomplished this with huge rebates and zero-percent-financing deals, turning its financing arm into—you guessed it—a huge, aggressive bank. That GM is keeping its plants running by stealing from future demand is, sort of, accepted by company managers, according to a January 2003 *Business Week* magazine article. It seems that the company's past leaders saddled it with massive pension and retiree health care obligations, leaving it no choice but to go for cash flow in the here-and-now.

Meanwhile, GM—and Ford and the Daimler Chrysler unit formerly known as Chrysler—make virtually all their money from SUVs, pickups, and minivans, which are exactly the markets now being targeted by the still much more efficient Japanese. Toyota already makes a top-rated small pickup, and Honda's minivan is best of breed. So that leaves GM and Ford with losing hands, both financially and operationally. With overindebted U.S. consumers likely to cut back on luxuries—including our penchant for driving 4,000-pound SUVs back and forth to the grocery store—the coming few years look grim for Detroit. And if the Big Three catch cold, their parts suppliers, like Delphi and Johnson Controls, will catch pneumonia.

U.S. auto and auto parts maker	Symbol	Price 2/13/03	% yield	Market cap $
Autoliv	ALV	21.08	2.44	2.0B
Borg Warner	BWA	52.35	1.38	1.4B
Delphi	DPH	8.30	3.41	4.6B
Ford Motor	F	8.69	4.74	15.9B
General Motors	GM	33.04	5.94	18.5B
Gentex	GNTX	27.87	N/A	2.1B
Genuine Parts	GPC	28.74	4.12	5.0B
Johnson Controls	JCI	79.17	1.84	7.0B
Lear	LEA	38.80	N/A	2.5B
Magna International	MGA	54.10	2.54	4.8B

Construction/engineering companies. The big construction firms are an impressive bunch, capable of designing, building, and then sticking around to operate state-of-the-art chip, drug, energy, and defense plants. To take just a few examples, Jacobs Engineering provides "integrated test and evaluation support" at what the Air Force says is the world's largest complex of aerodynamic and aeropropulsion ground test facilities. And Jacobs recently completed construction in Ireland of one of the biggest, most advanced biotech facilities, for Wyeth Medica. Flour, meanwhile, recently built a state-of-the-art cell culture facility for Biogen, and a petroleum-based carbon fiber plant for Conoco.

If you want a good sense of the future of large-scale manufacturing, the Web sites of these companies are great places to start. Meanwhile, for the most part they have solid balance sheets and high margins, which implies management that's prudent as well as creative. Their stocks reflect this: Jacobs, currently an analyst favorite, nearly tripled between 1999 and 2003. Emcor quadrupled, and Chicago Bridge better than quintupled.

Unfortunately, all the brilliant engineers in the world won't keep orders from drying up in a recession, so the next few years won't be anything like the past few, and some of the recent big winners will likely retrace their steps.

Construction/engineering company	Symbol	Price 4/18/03	% yield	Market cap $
Chicago Bridge	CBI	18.44	0.87	821.7M
Emcor	EME	48.43	N/A	722.8M
Flour	FLR	35.60	1.80	2.8B
Granite Construction	GVA	16.57	2.41	683.3M
Jacobs Engineering	JEC	39.70	N/A	2.1B

Property developers. These companies buy land and/or structures, improve them in some way, and then either sell them or operate them for a profit. At any given time they hold big inventories of raw land and half-completed buildings, which they fund with borrowed money. So their success depends on their projects' generating adequate cash income and on rising sale prices after completion. In good times, that's how it normally works. Combine massive leverage with the big markups possible when a wheat field is transformed into a classy subdivision or mall. Toss in a tax break from depreciating all that capital, and you tend to get really attractive levels of cash flow. Check the price charts for the bigger developers, and you'll see that they were great investments in the early years of the decade, doubling or tripling while tech stocks were imploding.

But leverage (as you're no doubt sick of reading) is a two-edged sword that cuts deeply into developers' profits when houses stop selling and office tenants stop renewing their leases.

Take San Francisco–based Catellus Development, which specializes in suburban commercial business parks and subdivisions. Neither seems like a good place to be when our debts force us to stop buying big suburban houses and the services of companies that populate commercial parks. Catellus's debt is 2.75 times its stockholders' equity, it pays no dividend (a big plus for shorting), and its stock more or less doubled between 1999 and 2003.

Cleveland-based Forest City, meanwhile, is all over the place, with regional malls, office buildings, hotels, apartment complexes, raw land, and even a lumber wholesaling arm. Apartments might do relatively well in a housing bust (more about that later in this chapter), but the rest of Forest City's businesses look like sitting ducks. Its debt is 4.9 times its equity, its stock nearly tripled between 1999 and 2003, and its dividend yield is a low 0.7 percent.

Another possibility is New York–based American Real Estate Partners, which is big in gaming, with hotels in Las Vegas and Atlantic City, though it also develops subdivisions and planned communities. It's less heavily leveraged than Catellus and Forest City, but gaming is a highly discretionary specialty (we have to live somewhere, but we don't have to take gambling vacations), it pays no dividend, and its stock is a lot more erratic that those of the other big developers. There are more like this in the table opposite, but the formula is pretty straightforward: Leverage plus depreciating assets equal a falling stock price.

Furniture makers. Recall from chapter 3 that we're spending about a third of the proceeds of our cash-out refinances (refis) on home-related upgrades. A big part of this is furniture, so the story here is

Property developer	Symbol	Price 4/18/03	% yield	Market cap $
American Real Estate	ACP	10.38	N/A	478.5M
Catellus Development	CDX	21.47	N/A	1.8B
Forest City	FCEa	35.08	0.68	1.7B
LNR Property	LNR	35.45	0.14	1.1B
Regency Centers	REG	33.96	6.12	2.0B

fairly simple: Fewer home equity loans and less disposable income equal fewer leather sectionals and Louis XV china cabinets. So Ethan Allen, La-Z-Boy, Bassett, and their competitors, after a decade in which many of them set records, are due for a major breather.

By the end of 2002, some of this was already built into their share prices, which were down an average of about a third from their 12-month highs, and in any event the furniture makers aren't as risky as the financial players mentioned earlier in this chapter. They're solid, well-managed companies that just happen to be in a business that's temporarily heading south. So focus on the balance sheet: Ethan Allen and Hon both have lots of cash and virtually no debt, making them less vulnerable to a sales decline. A better bet, strictly from a balance sheet perspective, might be Herman Miller, with debt that exceeds cash by about $40 million.

Appliance and tool makers. As we've built record numbers of ever-larger homes with ever-slicker kitchens, the companies that make stoves, dishwashers, and refrigerators have enjoyed one of the best stretches in their industry's history. Same thing for the companies that make the tools we use to build, renovate, and maintain all these houses. As a group, these companies have generated growing revenues and mostly solid earnings, and their stocks have held up reasonably well in the tricky markets of the early 2000s. But soon the demand won't be there as American society decides en masse to make due with the old

Furniture maker	Symbol	Price 2/13/03	% yield	Debt/equity	Market cap $
Bassett Furniture	BSET	12.58	6.61	0.01	147.5M
Dorel Industries	DIIBF	24.88	N/A	0.34	778.9M
Ethan Allen	ETH	29.64	0.81	0.02	1.1B
Furniture Brands	FBN	19.80	N/A	0.43	1.1B
Hon Industries	HNI	25.71	2.03	0.01	1.5B
Kimball International	KBALB	13.61	4.71	0.01	518.0M
Legget & Platt	LEG	19.15	2.72	0.47	3.7B
LA-Z-BOY	LZB	19.20	2.06	0.35	1.0B
Herman Miller	MLHR	15.90	0.89	0.98	1.1B
Natuzzie Spa	NTZ	9.12	2.84	0.01	498.7M

fridge, and borrow tools from the neighbors instead of buying new ones. It's not the fault of these companies; like the furniture makers, they're just in a game that's about to change. So while spectacular flameouts (as we'll likely see in the finance sector) will probably be rare, some steep declines are very possible.

In the 1990 housing market downturn, for instance, Whirlpool fell from 24 to 13, and Maytag from 20 to 7. This time the drop in appliance demand should be considerably steeper. So pay attention to balance sheets and recent results, and focus on weakness. Maytag's sales have risen modestly over the past few years, but its total liabilities have risen by 50 percent, bringing debt to a serious-sounding 26 times equity, according to Yahoo Finance. A deteriorating balance sheet in what should be a good market might be a sign of trouble to come.

Also, watch the pension issue. Some of these companies have long histories, which means a lot of retired workers, and keeping their health care and pension plans funded will become much harder when sales start shrinking. The one downside, from a shorting standpoint, is that some of these companies have painfully high dividend yields.

Appliance/tool maker	Symbol	Price 4/18/03	% yield	Market cap $
Black & Decker	BDK	37.23	1.29	2.9B
AKT Electrolux	ELUX	33.30	4.26	5.6B
Makita	MKTAY	7.25	2.10	1.0B
Maytag	MYG	19.29 .	3.73	1.5B
Snap-on	SNA	28.14	3.55	1.6B
Stanley Works	SWK	23.01	4.43	1.9B
Whirlpool	WHR	53.68	2.53	3.6B

Is It Wrong to Profit from Others' Misfortune?

In Adam Smith's book *The Money Game*, the narrator meets a hot-shot trader named the Great Winfield, who convinces him to buy cocoa futures. A few days later Smith gets a phone call from his elated partner. "Civil war!" he cries happily. "The Hausas are murdering the Ibos. Tragedy! I don't see how they can get the crop in, do you?" Readers, and hopefully Smith himself, see both the humor and the pathos here. People are dying in horrible ways, and that's good because it disrupts the cocoa market, driving up the price and making their futures contracts more valuable. Therein lies the short seller's great dilemma, the sense that you're betting—and therefore hoping—that bad things will happen to good people. Follow the strategies in this chapter, and you stand to benefit when friends and neighbors are thrown out of work and lose their homes and nest eggs. And once you've committed, like Adam Smith to his cocoa futures, it's hard not to take secret pleasure in each new layoff announcement and bankruptcy.

Is it worth the resulting angst? That's a question each would-be short has to answer for himself. But it's helpful to draw a distinction between events that you can affect and those that you can only watch. In the next Super Bowl, one team will very possibly be humiliated because that's the nature of that particular game. Neither your bet in the office pool nor your elation when your team dominates will change the outcome. Likewise, if we as a society are doing dumb things with our money—which we seem to be—the inevitable result isn't something that any one of us can change. So we're left with a choice: Do nothing and suffer along with everyone else, or take steps to protect ourselves and our families. If we're right, and other people suffer while we thrive (or at least survive), we'll face a moral dilemma, no doubt. But considering the alternative, it's a dilemma that most people would willingly choose.

Long/Short REIT Combinations

The list of short candidates in the previous section doesn't include what a casual observer might see as the best of the bunch: the real estate investment trusts, or REITs. Without doubt, they'll suffer greatly when the housing bubble bursts. But because of their high dividends— which, you'll recall, the short seller has to pay—they don't attract much short interest. There are, however, some ways around this, so let's start by defining some terms.

A REIT is a company that owns and, in most cases, operates income-producing real estate such as apartments, shopping centers, offices, hotels, and warehouses. Congress created them in 1960 to give the rest of us a chance to play along with the Donald Trumps of the world, and to sweeten the deal, lawmakers exempted REITs from corporate income taxes as long as they pay 95 percent of their cash flow to stockholders. The result is a group of powerhouse real estate firms with very high dividends and, in recent years, very happy investors. The Wilshire REIT Index gained an average of 15 percent a year from 2000 to 2002, while the S&P 500 lost a cumulative 40 percent.

It's logical that REITs would be a great a great idea in good times.

They let individuals own a diversified real estate portfolio and make a nice current income, and they attract capital to the property field, enabling enough new malls and apartment buildings to go up to meet the rising demand. But of course it's the not-so-good times we're concerned with. As Robert Prechter says in his book *Conquer the Crash*, "Make sure you avoid real estate investment trusts, which are perhaps the worst property-related investments during a bear market. Some REITs valued at $100 a share in the early 1970s fell to 1/4 by late 1974, and most of them never recovered. REITs are sold to the public because the people who do the deals don't want to stick with them. The public falls for REITs cycle after cycle. These 'investments' hold up in the best part of bull markets, but they are disasters in bear markets."

Assuming that past is prologue, how do you profit from falling REITs without having to pay those massive dividends? One way is to short them in combination with long positions in the REITs least likely to take a hit. In this way you benefit twice: once when the shorts fall further than the longs (the difference is your capital gain) and again when the shorts cut their dividends more than the longs (the difference is your current income). So let's divide the REITs into short and long camps.

The Good

Health care. The same factors that make drug companies and HMOs solid bets during a recession work in favor of the REITs which own nursing homes, medical office buildings, and clinics. Most of us have health insurance, which will keep paying for our doctor visits, operations, and prescriptions right through a downturn. And the population is aging, which increases the demand for health care a little each year. Another plus is that the health care REITs have already had their recession. Beginning in the late 1990s, lower Medicare reimbursements, a shortage of skilled nurses, and the failure of too many nursing home residents to pay their bills wreaked havoc with these companies, causing some high-profile bankruptcies and a general investor stampede for the exits. But in 1999, Medicare reimbursements were partially restored. And according to a Moody's report from late 2002, the strongest of the health care REITs have become a lot more selective about the properties they acquire and the creditworthiness of their customers, which is translating into improved cash flow and stronger balance sheets.

Some of their recent numbers bear this out. Biotech lab operator Alexandria Real Estate had an occupancy rate in excess of 95 percent at the end of 2002, and was growing at better than 10 percent a year. In 2002's fourth quarter, Health Care REIT grew its revenue and "funds from operations" (REITs' preferred measure of cash flow) by 18 percent and 35 percent respectively. There are more like this, and by and large they should hold up relatively well in the next downturn.

Health care REIT	Symbol	Price 2/14/03	% yield	Market cap $
Alexandria Real Estate	ARE	40.00	5.00	758.9M
Health Care REIT	HCN	25.11	9.29	980.7M
Health Care Properties	HCP	34.45	9.46	2.3B
Health Care Real Estate	HR	27.40	8.83	1.1B
National Health Investors	NHI	14.07	9.93	374.6M
Nationwide Health	NHP	13.00	13.77	639.1M
Universal Health	UHT	25.51	7.22	298.3M

Apartment REITs. Apartment managers might be the only people in America who find nothing uplifting about the surge in home ownership. That's because low-rate, zero-down-payment mortgages have made home buyers of hundreds of thousands of people who would normally rent. This has sent apartment vacancy rates through the roof and forced apartment operators to cut prices via move-in incentives like rent-free months, reduced or waived security deposits, and extra amenities. According to Dallas-based apartment market research firm M/PF Research, the percentage of upscale landlords offering concessions to new tenants more than doubled in 2002, to 34 percent.

The result: lower cash flow for the apartment REITs, and stocks that, by the end of 2002, were trading close to their 12-month lows. But by mid-decade things should look very different, with former home owners moving back into apartments in droves, and occupancy rates, if not rents, rising. Meanwhile, fewer new apartments are being built, which should ease the supply side of the equation. So for the stronger apartment REITs, a housing downturn won't be a recession at all, but more like a return to business as usual.

Apartment REIT	Symbol	Price 2/14/03	% yield	Market cap $
Apartment Investment Mgmt.	AIV	34.85	9.33	3.2B
Archstone-Smith	ASN	20.95	8.10	3.7B
Avalon Bay	AVB	35.80	7.76	2.4B
BRE Properties	BRE	29.75	6.55	1.3B
Camden Property	CPT	30.70	8.21	1.2B
Equity Residential	EQR	23.52	7.32	6.3B
Essex Property Trust	ESS	50.40	6.16	920.4M
Home Properties of NY	HME	31.19	7.81	835.2M
Post Properties	PPS	22.51	13.78	830.9M
United Dominion Realty	UDR	15.22	7.21	1.6B

The Bad

As for which REITs to short, the easy answer is "all the rest." Just about every other category of property stands to suffer in the coming downturn. But a few, as the saying goes, are more equal than others.

Mortgage REITs. Instead of buying buildings, these REITs leverage themselves to the hilt to buy mortgage-backed securities, earning the difference between their borrowing cost and what the mortgages pay. With short term funds available for 2% or less, and mortgages yielding 6%, the result has been spectacular, with the average stock on this list beating the S&P 500 comfortably over the past few years.

The central fallacy at work here was articulated perfectly in late 2002 by an analyst who should definitely remain nameless: "Since (the mortgage REITs) invest chiefly in Fannie Maes, Freddie Macs, and other GSE debt, all of which are backed by the U.S. government, the firms' investments are virtually risk-free."

Wow, what a great business! You borrow at cheap money market rates, and buy things with a *guaranteed* yield three times as high. There's just one little fly in this ointment: As we know from chapter 6, mortgage-backed securities are not guaranteed by the U.S. government. They're guaranteed by Fannie, Freddie, or one of the other mortgage insurers, which is not at all the same thing. So mortgage REITs face two big risks, neither of which is well-understood by the people gobbling up their stocks. First, if mortgage defaults spike, which they almost certainly will, the insurance safety net is likely to fray, if not shred, causing some poorly constructed bonds to plummet. The value of all mortgage bonds will then fall, and mortgage REITs will find themselves owing more than they own. Second, if short-term interest rates rise (for instance, as the Fed tries to defend a falling dollar), the spread between what these REITs have to pay for their cash and what they earn on their mortgage bonds will shrink, possibly to zero and beyond. This is what happened to the S&Ls in the early 1990s—when

their borrowing costs spiked while their junk bond portfolios were imploding—and it virtually destroyed the industry.

An analyst for investment bank Friedman, Billings, Ramsey got it
unintentionally right in a 2002 interview when he said, "These REITs
are financial companies that have elected a REIT tax status because
formation of a REIT is something that a company can opt to do by
simply filing a different type of tax return." In other words, they're not
like S&Ls; they *are* S&Ls. They borrow short and lend long on housing,
and it's entirely possible that they'll end up the same way.

Mortgage REIT	Symbol	Price 7/1/03	% yield	Market cap $
Anthracite Capital	AHR	12.18	11.61	582.4M
Anworth Mortgage	ANH	15.25	11.67	483.8M
Impac Mortgage	IMH	16.26	12.35	799.9M
Novastar Financial	NFI	59.95	15.06	633.1M
Annaly Mortgage	NLY	19.96	12.05	1.8B
Redwood Trust	RWT	40.85	6.51	721.5M
Thornburg Mortgage	TMA	24.87	9.72	1.4B

Office and commercial REITs. With office vacancy rates already sky-high in many formerly hot markets, you'd think the office
REITs would be played out as short candidates. But remember, the vacancy rate at the end of 2002 happened during a time of positive economic growth. In the next recession, they'll go much, much higher.
When analyzing these companies, focus on three things. First, obviously, is leverage, which makes them a lot of money in good times and
can be devastating in bad. So one simple, and probably effective,
strategy is to target the office REITs with the most debt and least cash.
But you can refine the search by looking at where their office buildings
are located.

A good example is Spieker Properties, which back in the late 1990s was a star because it was the biggest landlord in Silicon Valley. It sold out in 2001 to industry leader Equity Office, and you can bet that Equity Office now wishes it had put its money to work in Kansas or Ohio. The location of a REIT's properties is generally available on its Web site, and the Mortgage Bankers Association Web site is a good source for city-by-city vacancy trends.

The final thing to consider is the number of leases due to come up for renewal in 2004 and 2005, which is also available on the REITs' Web sites or in their 10-K reports. Because new leases will tend to be for lower rents, a large proportion of renewals means falling cash flow.

Office REIT	Symbol	Price 2/14/03	% yield	Market cap $
Arden Realty	ARI	20.82	9.57	1.313B
Boston Property	BXP	35.44	6.88	3.377B
Mack Cali Realty	CLI	27.35	9.08	1.574B
Carramerica Realty	CRE	23.51	8.58	1.249B
Cousins Properties	CUZ	23.83	6.28	1.160B
Equity Office	EOP	23.75	8.39	9.766B
Highwoods Properties	HIW	20.90	11.08	1.116B
HRPT Properties	HRP	8.36	9.57	1.077B
Reckson Associates	RA	19.48	8.60	1.163B
SL Green Realty	SLG	29.46	6.23	896.2M

Retail REITs. Last but not least are the REITs that own malls and other shopping centers. Again, the logic is fairly straightforward. If we're going to buy less in coming years, we'll spend less time (or at least less money) at the local mall. Sales of the high-end retailers that anchor most classy malls will suffer, causing some to pull out and others to demand lower rents, leaving the mall REITs with less cash to pass on to shareholders. In 2002, only the first part of this scenario played out, with retail sales moderating but occupancy rates and rents remaining stable at most malls. And for some reason, more malls were sold for higher prices in 2002 than in previous years. But like the housing bubble, this won't last if the rest of the economy is going the other way.

Retail REIT	Symbol	Price 2/14/03	% yield	Market cap $
Developers Diversified	DDR	22.61	6.76	1.4B
General Growth Properties	GGP	50.00	5.72	3.1B
Kimco Realty	KIM	32.02	6.84	3.3B
Macerich	MAC	30.55	7.49	1.5B
Mills	MLS	28.36	7.76	1.2B
New Plan Excel	NXL	18.54	8.80	1.7B
Pan Pacific	PNP	36.60	5.48	1.4B
Regency Center	REG	31.27	6.70	1.8B
Simon Property	SPG	33.50	7.19	6.2B
Weingarten	WRI	36.55	6.02	1.9B

Shorting Derivatives

Shorting individual stocks is how a lot of professional bears bet against the market, and done right, it's the way to make the most money. But as you know, shorting has some serious drawbacks, the biggest one being that any given stock can fool you. Shorting Cisco back in 1999, when it was trading at 80 times earnings, seemed like a no-brainer, based on both historical precedent and simple common sense. But that didn't stop it from doubling the following year. So shorting stocks—just like buying them—requires that you be able to diversify by holding decent-size positions in eight or more unrelated companies, something that is beyond the means, not to mention the attention span, of most of us. Luckily, options offer some solutions.

I know, chapter 6 said that derivatives are a problem, and in the aggregate they may be. But options are from the old, pre-bubble generation of derivatives, meaning that they are both easily understood and, when used wisely, are amazingly powerful and flexible tools. And they're a lot of fun.

As you'll recall from chapter 6, an option is a contract that gives its owner the right, but not the obligation, to buy or sell a specified number of shares at a predetermined price within a set time period. Call options allow a holder to buy (that is, call away) shares, and "puts" confer the right to sell (or put the shares into someone else's account). They're derivatives, in the sense that their value is derived from that of an underlying security, most frequently the stock of a publicly traded company (though options also exist for lots of other things). Stock option contracts control 100 shares of the underlying stock, so a quoted price (or premium) of, say, $2 implies a cost of $200 for a given contract. Because you're paying only for the right to profit from a change in the stock's price, you pay a lot less than if you bought the entire 100 shares outright. Yet if you're right, you gain almost as much as if you owned the shares.

Because options come with a variety of strike prices (the price the underlying stock has to hit before the option can be exercised) and expiration dates, option strategies can be as complex or as simple as you want to make them. As one options trader told me, it's like a three-tiered chess game, with the only limitation being your imagination. But usually—and almost always for a novice—simpler tends to be better, so here are some basic but effective ways to use options in a down market.

Naked puts. This is the option player's answer to shorting a stock. You buy a put on a stock you currently don't own, wait for the stock to go down (which makes the put more valuable), then sell at a profit. If the stock goes the other way, the put expires worthless; your risk is thus limited to the cost of the option, rather than being infinite, as with the shorting of individual stocks. And because a put ties up a lot less capital than shorting, you can stow your excess cash in a risk-free money fund, protecting most of your capital while profiting almost dollar for dollar from a fall in stock prices. But understand this strategy for what it is: a short-term bet on a big move down. If the move doesn't happen, your puts will expire worthless, and you will have lost your entire bet. So don't give in to the temptation of leverage. No matter how sure you are of a coming move, never risk more than a small fraction of your capital on naked options of any kind.

Covered calls. Now, say you own a stock that's just sitting there. You can turn its lethargy to your advantage by selling calls on it, thus earning the price of the call in return for agreeing to sell the stock should it rise to the option's strike price. If the stock goes up, it's called away and you pocket both the sale price and the proceeds from the call. If the stock doesn't rise, the option expires worthless and you're free to write another one. Lots of people earn an extra 10 percent to 15 percent each year this way on their otherwise staid portfolios. But this isn't hedging. You still own the stock, and lose if it goes down. Just not as much.

Married puts. If you're worried about a stock's heading south in the short run, but don't want to sell, you can "hedge" it (that is, eliminate or minimize the risk of its falling) by buying a put. This, remember, allows you to sell at a given price, a right that becomes more valuable if the stock falls. You're thus protected against a price decline, but since you continue to own the stock, you still profit if it goes up. Think of it as term insurance.

Collars. The downside of hedging with puts, as with any form of insurance, is that you're out the premium if you don't collect. A "collar" solves this problem by combining a covered call with a put. The call generates cash to pay for the put, while the put protects you against a drop in the stock's price. Your out-of-pocket cost is more or less zero, and for the duration of the collar, you've pretty much locked in the current stock price. To actually make money on the downside, you can create a "ratio collar" by buying more than one put. This magnifies your profit if the stock falls and, depending on the price of the call you sell, might still be cost-free to set up.

Volatility spreads. Now, let's say you expect a big move from a favorite stock, but you're not sure whether it will be up or down (a pretty common feeling these days). You could buy both a call and a put, so that a big move in either direction makes money and you lose only if the stock just sits there. With a volatility spread, you have to shift mental gears a bit and think of volatility (or "vol," as traders refer to it), rather than the market, as the thing you're buying and selling. When a stock trades in a range for a while, the premiums for both puts and calls tend to shrink as players begin to expect more range-bound trading. Volatility becomes cheap, in the same way a boring stock's P/E ratio tends to become low. Conversely, after a stock has made a big move, option premiums rise as traders bet on more action. Volatility becomes expensive, making volatility spreads less attractive. The market of early 2003 was a good environment for this kind of strategy because it was trading in a range, with—between the Iraq war and the incipient recovery—the occasional violent mood swing.

LEAPS. Traditional options have one huge drawback: They're short-lived. Most run for 9 months or less, so unless you're right on both direction and timing, that naked put you bought with such high hopes will expire worthless, and you'll lose everything you paid for it. Enter LEAPS, or long-term equity anticipation securities, which solve the lifespan problem the way we'd all like to solve it, by living a lot longer. LEAPS run for up to 2-1/2 years, allowing you to be fuzzy on "when" but still make money from a correction sometime up to, say, 2005. So they're a safer, cheaper alternative to shorting a bunch of overvalued stocks.

But not all LEAPS are created equal. So let's explore a real-world example using—what else—Fannie Mae. The table opposite shows

Fannie Mae Puts, February 4, 2003	Last Sale	Bid	Ask	Open Interest
JAN2005 45 ZFNMI	$4.60	$4	$4.30	3231
JAN 2005 50 ZFNMJ	$5.80	$5.30	$5.60	3888
JAN 2005 55 ZFNMK	$7	$6.70	$7.20	88
JAN 2005 60 ZFNML	$9	$8.40	$8.80	466
JAN 2005 65 ZFNMM	$12.30	$10.40	$10.70	4481
JAN 2005 70 ZFNMN	$14.30	$12.70	$13	786
JAN 2005 75 ZFNMO	$19.10	$15.30	$15.60	6
JAN 2005 80 ZFNMP	$19.20	$18.30	$18.60	114
JAN 2005 85 ZFNMQ	$22.90	$21.50	$21.90	54
JAN 2005 90 ZFNMR	$27.90	$25.20	$25.50	428

Source: NASDAQ

how Fannie's 2005 LEAPS puts appeared on the NASDAQ Web site in early February, 2003, when Fannie's stock price was around $63. The first put listed expires in January of 2005 and gives its owner the right to sell Fannie stock at a strike price of $45 until the third Friday of January, 2005. The "Ask" of $4.30 means that a contract for 100 shares costs $430 plus commissions. This option is "out-of-the-money," because its strike price is below the current share price. For such an option to be profitable, Fannie would have to fall far enough below the strike price to offset the premium and trading commissions. That implies a target price of $40 a share sometime in the next two years, which, while quite possible, is a lot to hope for in a relatively short period of time.

Next, scroll down to the bottom of the chart, and check out the "in-the-money" Jan 2005 90. This put can instantly be exercised for about $27 more than the share price. But because the premium, at $25, is over one third of the share price, this option offers relatively little in the way of leverage and requires its owner to risk a relatively large amount of capital. In other words, you're better off just shorting the stock and making money dollar-for-dollar on the way down, thus avoiding the risk that the option will expire worthless if Fannie doesn't fall.

The best bet is in the middle of the table, where the more-or-less "at-the-money" puts reside. The Jan 2005 60 put, for instance, costs $9, meaning that for the put to be worth enough to offset the premium, Fannie has to fall below $51, a more reasonable objective. If the stock goes up, you lose a maximum of $9 share, but if it falls to $40, you make $11, or a 110% profit. And if it really falls—to, say, $20—you triple your investment, while your maximum loss stays the same, at 100%.

LEAPS exist for most of the big banks and finance companies mentioned in the section "Sell High, Buy Low: The Art of Short Selling," page 171. To find them, go to NASDAQ's Web site, and click on "Investment Products," then on "Options and Indices," and finally on "LEAPS."

Options strategies, as they're described here, sound deceptively simple. They're not, and as with most other things, the difference between doing all right and spectacularly well lies in a grasp of the details. In-the-money options, for instance, because they can be exercised instantly at a profit, tend to move just about dollar for dollar with the underlying stock, while out-of-the-money options—because they can't be exercised immediately for a profit—tend to move less than the underlying stock. And the value of an option has a time component that diminishes as the expiration date approaches. The rate of shrinkage is slow at first and accelerates as time runs out, causing the behavior of the option to change. And for any given strategy, there are numerous possible building blocks. Is it better buy the 32 (strike price) put? The 35? The 40? And should you buy the April with 3 weeks left, or go out to June, which costs more but offers more time? Is it more cost-effective to hedge with short-term options and keep rolling them over as they expire, or use long-term LEAPS and forget about them for a while? The better able you are to answer such questions, the more effective your options strategies will be.

There are two ways to develop this kind of expertise. The first is to take advantage of the good free tutorials that are offered by some of the interested parties. The Options Industry Council, for instance, offers a free tutorial CD, available by calling (888) OPTIONS, that walks viewers through the various strategies, from the simplest to the most complex. And the council's call center, says council president Paul Stevens, is staffed with knowledgeable people "who are available to play 'stump the expert.'" Several other good tutorials are listed in Further Reading on page 243.

Most brokerage houses, meanwhile, offer their clients a range of options help. Discount broker Charles Schwab (with which I'm familiar because I both write for one of its magazines and trade through the company) has an online options trading platform called Option-Street, which features some good background, including archived roundtable discussions with industry heavyweights. Its options trading staff publishes an online newsletter, available at www.schwab.com/optionsnewsletter. Each article includes its author's number, and readers are encouraged to call with questions. And Schwab's options trading engine lets clients input details like the shares owned and trading goals, and automatically structures the appropriate strategy. Users just click on the "trade" button and the strategy is implemented. Merrill Lynch, E*TRADE, and the other major brokers offer much the same information.

One final note about trading options: Buy and hold is absolutely the wrong mindset. Because options lose some of their value as the strike price approaches, their risk/reward calculus changes far more quickly than that of the underlying shares. So the most successful options traders close out their positions when they've served their purpose, to avoid the risk of a violent, unfavorable move just before expiration. And when a strategy doesn't work out, they take the loss and move on. So almost unanimously, they advise clients to clarify their goals before beginning trading. For example, is your primary goal to protect what you have or to make it grow? How much cash do you want to generate, and how much risk are you willing to take on? And when you implement a strategy, think through the possible outcomes. If it goes your way, what will you do? If it doesn't, when will you cut your losses? Have a definite answer for each of these questions before you start, and stick to the plan.

Exchange-traded funds (ETFs). Like traditional mutual funds, ETFs and HOLDRs allow you to diversify on the cheap, in this case for a single brokerage commission. But they can also be shorted just like an individual stock (more easily, in fact, because they're not subject to the uptick rule). So instead of, for example, shorting Citigroup individually and running the risk that it will somehow thrive while the rest

ETF SECTOR FUND	SYMBOL
IShares Dow Jones U.S. Real Estate Index	IYR
StreetTRACKS Wilshire REIT Index	RWR
IShares Cohen & Steers Realty Majors	ICF
Merrill Lynch Regional Bank HOLDR Index	RKH
IShares Dow Jones U.S. Financial Services	IYG
IShares Dow Jones U.S. Financial Sector	IYF
Select Sector SPDR Fund—Financial	XLF

Source: NASDAQ

of the banking system tanks, you can instantly spread your risks over a whole sector with a single trade by shorting the right ETF. The table on the previous page lists some possible short candidate ETFs. And here are the main holdings of two of them.

MERRILL LYNCH REGIONAL BANK HOLDR INDEX (SYMBOL: RKH)

Company	Symbol
Amsouth Bancorp	ASO
BB&T	BBT
Comerica	CMA
FleetBoston Financial	FBF
Fifth Third Bancorp	FITB
Firstar	FSR
First Union	FTU
Key Corp.	KEY
Mellon Financial	MEL
Marshall & Isley	MI
National City	NCC
Northern Trust	NTRS
Bank One	ONE
PNC Financial	PNC
Synovus Financial	SNV
Suntrust Banks	STI
State Street	STT
U.S. Bancorp	USB
Wachovia	WB
Wells Fargo	WFC

ISHARES COHEN & STEERS REALTY MAJORS (SYMBOL: ICF)

Company	Symbol
Equity Office Properties Trust	EOP
Equity Residential Properties Trust	EQR
Simon Property Group	SPG
Prologis Trust	PLD
Archstone-Smith Trust	ASN
Vornado Realty Trust	VNO
Public Storage Inc REIT	PSA
Boston Properties Inc REIT	BXP
Apartment Investment & Management	AIV
Duke Realty Corp REIT	DRE

Bear Market Mutual Funds

Most mutual funds are designed for good times. That is, they buy things that tend to go up along with either the market as a whole or a specific sector, and down during corrections. Vanguard's flagship S&P 500 Index fund, for instance, earned an average of 15 percent a year during the 1990s, which was right in line with the broad market. But because the same link works in reverse, this isn't the place to be as the United States heads into a recession. Instead, you want one of the handful of mutual funds that takes the opposite approach, loading up on things that go up if the market falls. These are called bear funds, and, not surprisingly, they've made their long-suffering investors very happy since the bubble burst in 2000.

Like their bull market cousins, bear funds come in two flavors: actively managed and indexed. The first tries to find overvalued stocks and then sells them short—that is, sells them without owning them, in the hope of buying them back later at a lower price, with the goal of outperforming the market on the downside. The index funds structure options, futures contracts, and short sales to match—inversely—the performance of a given index, such as the S&P 500. As with any other category of funds, bears vary dramatically in performance, expenses, and risk. And most charge an arm and a leg in management fees and other expenses, making them questionable long-term investments. But as a way to hedge against or profit from a bear market, they're a clean, simple choice. Among the families of no-load funds with established records are:

Prudent Bear. Run by David W. Tice, a frenetic trader and out-spoken critic of corporate accounting shenanigans, this small Texas outfit operates just two funds, with assets totaling around $700 million. The Prudent Bear fund blends long positions in precious metals with big short bets on overvalued stocks into a mix that was an abject failure for most of the 1990s but a spectacular success once the bubble popped. While the S&P 500 was losing 33 percent in 2002, Prudent Bear was up 88 percent. The firm's Safe Harbor fund, meanwhile, owns high-quality international bonds and gold, making it likely to benefit from a declining dollar. As a bonus, it generates a little income from the bonds in its portfolio.

Prudent Bear's Tice is an interesting character who drove the corporate criminal to distraction with some early and in retrospect prescient criticism of the accounting scams of the late 1990s. His highest-profile exchange was with Tyco, the fast-growing conglomerate and tech bubble darling. Tice accused it, in effect, of accounting fraud, and the company, along with most of its fans on Wall Street, went ballistic, dismissing Tice as a crank and, worse, a short seller, who profits by stirring up trouble. Now, with Tyco's CEO and his minions headed for the slammer, the world wishes it had listened. The Prudent Bear Web site, meanwhile, is a great clearinghouse for dark-side market analysis. Among much else, it features the weekly Credit

Bear market fund	Symbol	3-year average annual % return
Leuthold Grizzly Short Fund	GRZZX	14.9
ProFunds Bear	BRPIX	15.6
Prudent Bear	BEARX	30.9
Prudent Bear Safe Harbor	PSAFX	8.9
Rydex Ursa	RYURX	17.20

Source: Morningstar.com

Bubble Bulletin, written by Doug Noland, whom you'll remember from chapter 8.

ProFunds. This is billed as the biggest operator of index funds, with a total of six in the bear category. Instead of picking individual stocks, it uses futures and options to target a given beta, or volatility relative to a market index. ProFunds Bear, for instance, is designed to go up exactly as much as the S&P 500 goes down, for a beta of −1. The ProFunds UltraBear has a beta of − 2, meaning that it aims to rise twice as much as the market drops. The family also includes funds linked to the NASDAQ 100 and a European large-cap index. The 2-beta funds give you leverage without the need to borrow money, which made them pretty close to the best place to be between 2000 and 2002 (though, like all leveraged investments, they're risky, so beware).

Rydex. This company has been offering bear funds since the early 1990s and now has a solid lineup, including the Ursa and Arktos Funds, which, like ProFund, use derivatives to "inversely correlate" with the S&P 500 and NASDAQ 100 respectively.

Leuthold. Its Grizzly Short Fund won the prize for best timing (which you love to see in a money manager) by opening for business in June 2000, when just about anything could be shorted for a quick profit. Through the end of 2002, it was up a total of 76 percent, and its

Web	Telephone
www.leutholdfunds.com	(800) 273-6886
www.profunds.com	(800) 776-3637
www.prudentbear.com	(800) 711-1848
www.prudentbear.com	(800) 711-1848
www.rydexfunds.com	(800) 820-0888

strategy of staying 100 percent short U.S. common stocks makes it a pure play on a mid-decade bear market. Its management fees of 2.96 percent make it ridiculously expensive as a long-term holding, but as its recent record indicates, it's a good place to be when the market cracks.

PART 4

NOW, ABOUT YOUR HOUSE

CHAPTER 11

ARE YOU LIVING IN A BUBBLE MARKET?

The most obvious piece of advice that seems to flow from all this talk of a real estate bust is to sell your house. But it's not that simple, of course, because a home is more than just an investment. It's the center of most families' lives. In economist-speak, your home is a good that you consume as well as an investment that you hope to sell for a profit. As with a hot car or season tickets to the opera, it is sometimes worth holding a depreciating asset if it offers benefits that offset its loss of value.

Besides, not all housing markets are equally likely to crash in coming years. Real estate, like politics, is at least partly local, so while national trends like economic growth and interest rates will play their part, the action in your neighborhood really depends on local employment, population growth, and land availability. In Massachusetts, for instance, where land is scarce and job growth strong, home prices are up 490 percent since 1980. In Oklahoma, where land is more plentiful than high-paying jobs, prices are up only 65 percent. Towns like Santa Barbara and Boston have seen average home prices double since the mid-1990s, while others like Springfield, Illinois, and Salt Lake City are up less than 20 percent. So the next recession's impact on home prices will be a lot more noticeable in the first two than the last.

Meanwhile, the engines driving each town's economy are different. When Boeing laid off 15,000 workers in the Seattle area in 2002, it took the wind out of what would otherwise be a booming real estate market. Regions dominated by colleges, on the other hand, have more stable real estate markets because their main employers suffer less— and sometimes actually grow—during recessions.

Is your local housing market overheated?

How do you tell an overheated market from a reasonable one? First, look at how prices have changed over the past few years. A good source for this is the Office of Federal Housing Enterprise Oversight (OFHEO), which crunches numbers provided by Fannie Mae and Freddie Mac to produce various comparative lists and indexes. (OFHEO's Web site, along with the others mentioned here, is listed at the end of this book.) Note that the hottest markets tend to be coastal, while the tamest are mostly in mid-country.

HOTTEST MARKETS (% APPRECIATION)

	1-year (2002)	3Q 2002	Last 5-years
Nassau–Suffolk, New York	14.69	4.08	77.76
Barnstable–Yarmouth, Massachusetts	14.18	2.20	89.79
Yolo, California	14.17	3.80	71.79
Brockton, Massachusetts	13.86	2.91	76.83
Chico–Paradise, California	13.84	3.17	48.41
Redding, California	13.63	3.65	39.85
Providence, Rhode Island	13.48	2.41	55.45
Miami	13.42	2.81	49.24
Fresno, California	13.23	3.61	35.23
San Diego	13.22	3.36	79.12

Source: Office of Federal Housing Enterprise Oversight (OFHEO)

LEAST HOT MARKETS (% APPRECIATION)

Area	1-year (2002)	3Q 2002	5-year
Greensboro–Winston-Salem, North Carolina	2.34	0.14	22.77
Little Rock–North Little Rock, Arkansas	2.28	0.24	20.58
Janesville–Beloit, Wisconsin	2.28	0.62	19.45
Sheboygan, Wisconsin	2.25	−0.73	21.03
Rockford, Illinois	2.24	−0.16	14.83
Springfield, Missouri	2.19	−0.33	14.30
Raleigh-Durham–Chapel Hill, North Carolina	2.18	0.23	22.31
Baton Rouge, Louisiana	2.17	−0.18	22.75
Salt Lake City–Ogden, Utah	2.16	0.92	15.46
Provo–Orem, Utah	2.13	0.26	15.86

Source: Office of Federal Housing Enterprise Oversight (OFHEO)

Next, you'll need some way of equating local home prices with the ability of locals to buy them. Here, the experts are on the case: John Burns, an Irvine, California-based real estate consultant and publisher of the Building Market Intelligence newsletter, combines local home prices and incomes to produce a "barometer" reading, where anything over 5 is a housing bubble. Anything over 7, meanwhile, is "a large housing bubble," where current prices are unsustainable. To take the most extreme example, Burns calculates that the average Boston house costs 7 times the average resident's yearly income, and would require mortgage payments equal to 45 percent of that income. Note the difference between Boston and Indianapolis, where the average house costs only about two years' pay. Other things being equal, a Boston homeowner clearly has more incentive to sell.

OVERVALUED MARKETS

Market	Barometer reading	Price/income ratio	Mortgage payment/income
Boston	9.3	7.0	44.9%
San Diego	7.8	6.7	43.1%
Ft. Lauderdale	7.6	4.5	29.1%
San Francisco	7.3	7.3	46.7%
Miami	7.1	4.7	30.0%

Source: the newsletter *Building Market Intelligence*

Another approach comes from Michael Sklarz, chief valuation officer at Fidelity National Information Solutions, who throws job growth and the pace of home building into the price/income mix. His pick for most overpriced market is Tacoma, Washington, where the median home price of $170,000 was, he estimated, 23 percent too high at the end of 2002.

Economy.com of West Chester, Pennsylvania, cites as the most overvalued market Naples, Florida, where home prices have nearly doubled since 1995, far outpacing incomes.

UNDERVALUED MARKETS

Market	Barometer reading	Price/income ratio	Mortgage payment/income
Philadelphia	0.0	2.5	16.2%
Indianapolis	0.0	2.1	13.4%
St. Louis	0.6	2.1	13.3%
Dallas	0.8	2.4	15.5%
Hartford, Connecticut	1.0	3.3	21.0%

Source: the newsletter *Building Market Intelligence*

As you can see, the experts are finding plenty of overvalued markets, though they tend to disagree on where they are. So you'll want to consult a couple of them and ideally look into price, job, and income trends yourself. Once you have a sense of where your local housing market sits on the bubble continuum, you can make an educated guess as to how far prices will have to fall to move back in line with incomes. In Boston, for example, home prices would have to fall by 50 percent or more to reach Philadelphia's price-to-income ratio.

It's not possible, of course, to make precise predictions about exactly how far home prices will fall in a given market. But it is possible to say that if you're in a market where prices have been rising faster than incomes, you're at considerable financial risk. The question is, what should you do about it?

CHAPTER 12

YOUR OPTIONS

Sell

Trade down. Can you get by with less house? If so, it might make sense to reverse the trend that has dominated most baby boomers' lives, and trade down. Sell the five-bedroom, $500,000 house on the prestigious cul-de-sac, and use your capital gain as a down payment on a smaller place in a more modest neighborhood. The price of your new home will still fall when the bubble pops, but less drastically than that of your current, more expensive one. And because the gain from your

THE BENEFITS OF TRADING DOWN

	$500,000 house	$300,000 house
Mortgage balance	256,000*	$100,000**
Monthly payment at 6%	$1,530	$600
Annual property tax bill	$3,000	$2,000
Equity loss if local prices fall by 20%	$100,000	$60,000
Total cost over 3 years	$164,224	$87,600

*Assumes a $320,000 purchase price 5 years earlier, 20 percent down payment, refinanced in 2002 at 6 percent.

** Assumes you clear $244,000 on the sale of your old house and put $200,000 down on the new one.

current house will make your next mortgage smaller, your monthly payments will be a lot lower. The table on the previous page, though admittedly a very rough calculation, shows how such a move might be worth roughly $25,000 a year.

Sell and rent. I can see you shaking your head and just skipping this part. But let me make two points, or maybe four, depending how you parse what follows. First, there are some very nice apartments and rental houses out here. A quick Google search under "luxury apartments Boston" turns up some spacious two- and three-bedroom rentals in what claim to be prestigious locations for $2,000 to $4,000 a month. Typical of the middle of this range is the following listing, plucked more or less at random from a realtor's Web site.

> *$3,200. The best view in the city can be seen from this stunning Beacon Street two-bedroom unit. The living room windows show off the expansive sailing area of the Charles River. Sip tea and watch your favorite Brokers flip over Cape Cod Mercury sailboats on a brisk fall afternoon. The elevator opens right into the apartment, which has hardwood floors, high ceilings, and a great location. Parking available.*

Now, the most common reaction to rents of this magnitude is "Are you on drugs? Why pay that kind of money and have nothing to show for it at the end of the year?"

That's a valid sentiment when home prices are rising, but when they're falling, "not having anything to show" for home ownership means avoiding a big loss. If you have kids, you may be concerned that they need the stability of a house with a yard and a tree-lined street and all that those things imply. Maybe, but many apartment complexes are full of kids, in very close proximity and with no busy streets to cross. Young families thrive in such surroundings.

And finally, home ownership is such an ingrained part of our concept of the American Dream that we tend to forget just how much work is involved in mowing the lawn, pulling up weeds, fixing the garbage disposal, and all the other things that keep the average suburbanite out of trouble on weekends. Eliminate these chores by moving into an apartment, and you get a massive free-time bonus. Think of three years in an apartment that saves you $100,000 in home depreciation as an extraordinarily well-paid vacation, and all of a sudden it becomes less of a hardship.

Skip town. Throughout the West, there is only one truly despised minority: Californians. For the past decade, they've been cashing out of their ridiculously expensive real estate and buying McMansions in neighboring states, to the bemusement and sometimes resentment of the locals. Because most ex-Californians are wonderful people, their new neighbors eventually forgive them their origins, preventing this from becoming a major civil rights issue. And in any event the Californians are clearly onto something: The world is full of very nice

---

RELOCATION GUIDES

The Great Towns of America by David Vokac (paperback, $17.47)

The 100 Best Small Art Towns in America by John Villani (paperback, $11.97)

Choose a College Town for Retirement: Retirement Discoveries for Every Budget (Choose Retirement Series) by Joseph M. Lubow (paperback, $10.47)

America's 100 Best Places to Retire by Richard L. Fox, editor (paperback, $16.95)

Making Your Move to One of America's Best Small Towns by Norman Crampton (paperback, $13.97)

National Geographic Guide to Small Town Escapes (paperback, $17.50)

Places Rated Almanac (Special Millennium Edition) by David Savageau (paperback, $17.47)

Source: Amazon.com ∎

places, some of which, at any given time, are affordable. And moving from an expensive area to a cheap one offers the choice of more house for the same money or the same house for less money. Either way, you win in both terms of bank account and, frequently, lifestyle. So if you're in a hot market and you occasionally fantasize about greener pastures, you now have the financial wind at your back. Whereas three years ago you would have been crazy to sell and miss out on the raging bull market, now you can safely indulge your wanderlust—and get paid for it. This isn't a travel book, so I won't dwell on the idea of moving, except to say that there are tons of good sources on choosing a new home, a few of which are listed on the previous page.

Hedge

Now, let's say you're twice blessed. You live in San Diego and you own a house that's doubled in value, to $400,000. You've checked with *Building Market Intelligence* and *Economy.com* and discovered that home prices in your area are way above what local incomes can support, and you accept—intellectually, anyway—the possibility that your home's value may fall in coming years.

Yet you love it here. Your kids are happy, the schools are good, and your spouse's head would explode if you insisted on moving to Idaho or, worse yet, an apartment. So you choose lifestyle over net worth and decide to stay. Does that mean you're fated to drop a $100 thousand when the housing bubble pops? Not at all. You just employ some of chapter 10's bear market strategies to "hedge" your real estate. Hedging is simply the act of investing in something that's likely to move in the opposite direction of an existing asset, thereby—if done right—locking in your gain in return for foregoing future gains. Corporations are enthusiastic hedgers of all kinds of things, including currencies, commodities, and even their publicly traded shares, and there's no reason that individuals can't do the same. So consider these two approaches. The first is to assume that as the national housing scene goes, so goes your local market, and construct a general hedge. The second is to zero in on the hedges that relate most closely to your local housing market. Let's take each in turn.

Designing the Right Hedge

General. This is the fast approach because it involves simply betting against the broad housing bubble by shorting the bubble's beneficiaries. Such a hedge might include the following:

GENERAL HEDGE

Short sale candidate	Symbol	Bear market fund
Fannie Mae	FNM	Prudent Bear Fund
Capital One Financial	COF	Rydex Ursa
Citigroup	C	Leuthold Grizzly
Ambac Financial	ABK	
Lennar	LEN	

When San Diego real estate begins to fall, it will more than likely be because of national trends (a slowing economy, rising interest rates, or some combination thereof). So the companies listed here, as the major national brands in mortgages, consumer finance, and home building, will probably fall along with your home's value. Short them, and you'll be reasonably well-hedged. Or buy some bear funds, which will be operating on the same principals, with a little gold and foreign currency exposure tossed in for good measure.

Area specific. It's always possible that local events will affect local real estate in ways that take it out of step with the rest of the country. So the best hedge would focus on the companies that build, finance, or otherwise benefit from the local housing bubble. And the best way to compile such a list is to ask someone who knows. A veteran stockbroker at one of the better regional stockbrokerage houses, for instance, would have the major housing players at his or her fingertips. Another good source is the local business journal, which covers the area's business community and each year compiles a book of lists in which the editors rank the biggest companies in most fields. Here you'll find the mortgage lenders and home builders that are either based in the area or do a lot of business nearby. San Diego has two business journals, the *San Diego Business Journal* and the online San Diego Source (www.sddt.com). Both offer free listings of the biggest companies in various fields, along with general information on how much business they do and how many people they employ locally. Pull the top few names from the relevant categories, and you've got a custom-made short list. Here's what San Diego Source had in February 2002.

San Diego housing stocks	Symbol	Business	Market cap $
D. R. Horton	DHI	Home building	2.7B
Centex	CTX	Home building	3.5B
Hovnanian Enterprises	HOV	Home building	1.0B
Bank of America	BAC	Bank	103.4B
Wells Fargo	WFC	Bank	77.0B
Union Bank of California	UB	Bank	6.2B
Downey Financial	DSL	S & L	1.1B
Washington Mutual	WM	S & L	31.9B

Source: San Diego Source

California superregional banks like Wells Fargo and Union Bank of California are obvious choices because they're headquartered in-state and write tons of mortgages and business loans in San Diego.

Downey Financial and Washington Mutual are big West Coast savings and loans that lend billions to San Diego home owners. And D. R. Horton, Centex, and Hovnanian are home builders that dominate the San Diego market.

The right-size hedge. Exactly how much do you need to commit to a hedge to offset a falling home price? Maybe "exactly" was the wrong choice of word in the previous sentence because there are too many variables here to come up with a precise number. No one can predict how far the value of a given house in a given city will fall in the next real estate downturn. Likewise, while it's easy to be right about the direction of bank and home builder stocks, how far they fall will vary from stock to stock, making the particular fate of Wells Fargo or Centex anybody's guess. So hedging, done this way, is an art rather than a science. But a partial hedge is better than none, so let's say that based on history, a housing market as hot as San Diego's should correct by 20 percent when all is said and done. For your $400,000 house, that means a loss of $80,000 of home equity. And let's say further that in the same tough housing market, the companies on your short list would be expected to fall by 50 percent. To generate an $80,000 gain on your hedge, you'll need to begin with a $160,000 short position. A big number, yes, but thanks to the real estate bubble, big numbers are now your lot in life.

Hedging with LEAPS. Recall from chapter 10 that in early 2003, for about $900 an at-the-money LEAPS contract would have given you temporary control of $6,300 of Fannie Mae stock. Assuming the same ratio holds across the other stocks you might short, a $160,000-equivalent hedge can be created using LEAPS for only $22,000. That's a bargain, but with one very big drawback: If you short actual stocks and the housing market doesn't crash, your short positions might just sit there, costing you only the transaction costs and dividends. But if you hedge with LEAPS, they'll gradually lose value until they expire worthless in three years.

LEAPS Hedge					
LEAPS put	Symbol	Bid	Offer	Open interest	Stock price 2/21/03
Citigroup JAN 2005 30	ZRVMF	$5.10	$5.40	2716	$33
Fannie Mae JAN 2005 60	ZFNML	$8.60	$8.90	568	$64
Freddie Mac JAN 2005 50	ZFMMJ	$7.40	$7.60	838	$54
MBNA JAN 2005 15	ZKMC	$3.60	$3.80	434	$14

Source: NASDAQ

Other hedges. In early 2003, some other interesting experiments in home price hedging were being conducted. They were too new to be recommended here, but by the time this book hits the shelves, that may have changed. For instance, Real Liquidity, based in Washington, D.C., was testing a home price insurance product in Syracuse, New York, that, for a one-time premium of 1.5 percent of a home's value, insures for 30 years against a fall in local home prices. The policy is tied to an index of local home prices rather than the individual home and, after a 3-year grace period, will make up the difference between the price a home owner receives for an insured house and what it would have sold for if the index had not fallen. If the product succeeds in Syracuse, Real Liquidity hopes to roll out the concept to other cities in late 2003. Though it's classified as insurance by state regulators, this is really an at-the-money put option on local home prices. If the premium is 3 percent, as Real Liquidity predicts that it will be when rolled out nationally, it would cost $12,000 to hedge the $400,000 house in the earlier example. At this price, it's less costly and risky than the stock hedges mentioned here, and a lot longer lasting than the LEAPS hedge. So look into it. If this or something like it is offered in your area, give it serious consideration.

Another possibility is an online futures market for trading real estate risk that's being developed by Ralph Liu, former head of the Asian derivatives operations of UBS and Chase Manhattan in the early 1990s, and architect of several Asian equity derivatives exchanges. This promises to be more of an insider's game but, if it succeeds, will probably spawn some mass-market derivatives that home owners might find useful.

Refinance

By early 2003, mortgage rates had fallen below 6 percent, leaving, oh, 50 million or so home owners wondering whether they should refinance. Slice a single point from a $200,000 mortgage and you save about $1,500 a year, or $45,000 over 30 years. But how do you know when rates have fallen far enough to make refinancing worthwhile? Does the difference have to be 2 percent, as financial planners used to claim? Or is it 1/2 percent, like some sharp-pencil serial refinancers seem to think? The answer, as this is written, seems to be somewhere in between. Computerization and competition have squeezed refinancing fees down to historically low levels, making it possible to refinance for less than 2 percent and still generate some savings. But the process will always involve a lot of variables and will never be cheap.

So start by finding out what's possible. If you're 10 years into a 30-year mortgage, for example, refinancing the remaining balance for another 30 years will cut your monthly costs but dramatically increase the amount of interest you'll pay over the term of the new loan. Meanwhile, going to a 15-year mortgage might not lower your payments sufficiently. And does your current mortgage have a prepayment penalty clause? If so, the added cost might make even a 2 percent difference inadequate.

If none of the above applies to your mortgage, call your current lender and ask if they'll consider lowering your rate for a small fee, in order to keep your business. They'll do this only if they've kept your mortgage—rather than shipped it to Fannie or Freddie for packaging—which gives you a roughly one-in-four chance of having this option. If you get lucky, it's possible that you can get a lower rate without the usual rigmarole of a new home appraisal, credit report, and so on. If your lender has sold your loan, refinancing means taking out a whole new mortgage to replace the current one. For this, either engage a good mortgage broker to help sort through the forest of options, or get familiar with a mortgage Web site, some of which are listed at the end of this book. Kiplinger's Mortgage Finder, for example, allows visitors to check the national average for various types of mortgages, and then drill down to find the most competitive rates in a given area.

As for finding the best rate, what does "best" mean, exactly? That's another complicated, somewhat subjective question because mortgage lenders muddy the waters by mixing rates (which you pay on the money you borrow) with points (which you pay up front to compensate the lender for the many things involved in making the loan). Each loan comes with a different combination of fees, including the following:

- **Discount points.** These are prepaid finance charges designed to raise the lender's return beyond the loan's stated interest rate. "Point" refers to percent, so one point on our $200,000 loan would come to $2,000. Generally speaking, the lower the interest rate, the higher the points.

- **Application fee.** This charge covers the initial costs of processing your loan request and checking your credit report.

- **Title search and title insurance.** Title search covers the cost of examining the public record to confirm ownership of the real estate. Title Insurance is a policy issued by a title insurance company that protects against losses caused by future problems with the title to the property. Be sure to ask the company carrying your present policy if it can reissue your policy at a reduced rate. This could save up to 70 percent of the cost of a new policy.

- **Attorney's review.** The fee charged by the lawyer who conducts the settlement.

- **Appraisal fee.** The cost of sending an appraiser to verify the value of your house.

Now, say that the fees and points come to $3,000 on your $200,000 refinancing and that your savings from the lower rate come to $1,500 a year. It will take two years to make back the fees, after which the savings begin to accumulate, which means the deal works if you plan on sticking around for a while. Some of the Web sites in the "Mortgage Rates and Home Prices" section of Further Reading on page 248 offer special-purpose calculators that let you plug in various deals to see what kinds of payments they translate into and how long it takes a lower rate to compensate for a given package of fees.

Pay It Off

If mortgage debt is the problem, then it logically follows that paying off your mortgage is the solution, right? Maybe, from a societal standpoint. But for an individual, the answer is a little more complicated. The reason mortgage debt has become the latest booster engine of the U.S. credit rocket is that it's such a great deal for the borrower. Consider that most forms of adjustable-rate debt, like business loans or credit card balances, move both up and down in sync with some benchmark interest rate. A business, for instance, might pay prime plus 1 percent, with the prime rate being tied to short-term Treasuries. If Treasury rates rise, banks raise their prime rate, and the business has to pay more. A 7 percent 30-year fixed-rate mortgage, on the other hand, doesn't rise, even if the prime rate goes to 15 percent. But if rates fall, you can refinance at, say, 5 percent, and lock that in no matter how high other interest rates subsequently go. And, icing on the cake, mortgage interest is tax deductible, knocking another point or so from the effective rate. This is the sweetest deal currently available in the credit markets, vastly better than the terms of either credit cards or auto loans. So if you have to owe money to someone, better your mortgage bank than a credit card issuer.

Still, with money market funds paying less than 2 percent, wiping out a mortgage with an effective (that is, after tax) rate of 5 percent is the same as earning a risk-free 3 percent a year. So if you the have cash sitting around, using it to pay off a mortgage might be worth several hundred thousand dollars over 30 years. To get a feel for the numbers involved, picture two neighbors living in identical homes, each with a $200,000, 6 percent, 30-year mortgage. One—let's call her Sheila— takes $200,000 out of savings and pays off the mortgage. She then takes the $1,200 a month she would have paid on the mortgage and deposits into a money market fund yielding 2 percent. Her neighbor Bob keeps paying $1,200 a month on his mortgage and lets his $200,000 ride in the same money market fund at 2 percent. He also deposits into the account the tax break he receives on his mortgage interest—about $300 a month initially, declining to zero at the end of 30 years. After

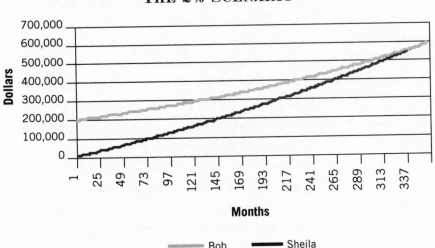

THE 2% SCENARIO

30 years they both own their homes free and clear. But their cash balances have done very different things. Bob's has grown steadily to nearly $600,000. Sheila's, fed by her monthly $1,200 check, has started slowly but finished strong, catching up to Bob at the end. This seems a little counterintuitive, given Bob's big head start, but such is the power of steady savings and compound interest.

As always with this kind of numbers game, the devil is in the assumptions. Scenario 1, for instance, assumes that both Bob and Sheila earn only 2 percent after taxes on their investments for 30 years. But what if instead of a money fund they buy long-term bonds yielding 5 percent? Bob, because he's earning more on a bigger early balance, holds his lead a little longer this time, and each finishes with over $1 million. But Sheila still catches up in the end.

THE 5% SCENARIO

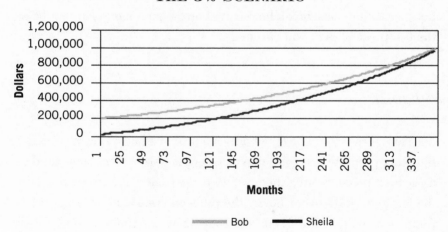

Now, one might make the argument that even 5 percent is way too low since many of the strategies in chapter 10 could yield considerably more, making paying off a mortgage a lot less interesting. But that would be mixing apples and oranges. Yes, some of the more aggressive ways of betting against the housing market will probably return more than 5 percent over the next few years. But they might lose money as well. Because paying off a mortgage is in effect investing risk-free (in the sense that you're guaranteed the savings that result from eliminating your monthly mortgage payment), you should compare those savings only with other risk-free alternatives, like money funds and high-grade bonds.

Then there's the assumption that both Sheila and Bob are debt-free other than their mortgages. That's a nice place to be, but not very realistic in today's world. If Sheila, for instance, pays off her mortgage but continues to carry a 12 percent credit card balance and an 8 percent car loan, while Bob uses his free cash to eliminate his high-rate debt, then the outcome shifts to his favor.

To sum up, paying off a mortgage makes a certain amount of sense when (1) That's the last piece of debt on your family's balance sheet, and (2) Your risk-free alternatives yield less than your mortgage. But because it's the most favorable way to borrow, your mortgage should be the last piece of debt you eliminate.

Swap It

Now, let's say you have not only a house in a hot real estate market but other properties as well, maybe a couple of rentals or some land or a vacation place. Selling them would make financial sense, except for the fact that unlike your home, the proceeds would be taxable. If the rental you bought for $200,000 back in saner times is now worth $400,000, your gain results in a $40,000 tax bill (or more, when you add in state and local capital gains taxes). Perhaps it still makes sense to sell, but with the government taking a guaranteed 20 percent right off the top, the case becomes a little less compelling.

Luckily, there are ways to defer—and maybe eliminate—capital gains on appreciated property. One of the niftiest is the Rule 1031 exchange. Under this IRS rule, you can sell one piece of investment real estate and swap the proceeds into another without having to pay capital gains taxes. As it says in the Internal Revenue Code:

> *No gain or loss shall be recognized on the exchange of property held for productive use in a trade or business or for investment, if such property is exchanged solely for property of like-kind which is to be held either for productive use in a trade or business or for investment.*

To understand how this works, let's take the above rental house and assume that you would consider selling if there were a way to avoid writing a $40,000 check to Uncle Sam. Let's also assume that you're open to retiring, eventually, to another part of the country. So you look around for great but less extravagant places, and decide on a gorgeous little town on the Oregon coast, where weakness in the local fishing and logging industries has made homes a steal. Then you put your rental on the market, and when it sells that afternoon for 5 percent above the asking price, you use the proceeds, via a 1031 exchange, to buy your Oregon retirement home. Not only have you captured the entire appreciation in your old rental; you've also gotten a great deal on a house you would have eventually bought anyhow. You rent it out until you're ready to relocate, satisfying the requirement that it be an investment property. And when you do eventually move in, the Oregon house becomes your residence and can, after two years, be sold free of capital gains taxes. You've thus captured the whole gain on your hot-market rental.

The main focus here is using Rule 1031 to get you out of appreciated investment property tax-free, but that just scratches the surface of its uses. If you've accumulated several pieces of investment property over the years, and managing them has become a headache, you can sell them all and use the proceeds, via 1031, to buy a single, easier-to-manage property, like a multiunit apartment complex with a resident manager. Same thing if you have several pieces of land, each with its own zoning and environmental headaches. Just exchange them for one big tract with a single set of regulatory issues.

Or say you or one of your parents has a single large property and no idea how to divide it up for those who will eventually inherit it. To avoid a nasty battle after the funeral, you can sell the property and swap the proceeds into a number of smaller ones, each earmarked for a different heir. The properties have to be "like-kind," which, to the IRS, means not your main residence. But they don't have to be identical. One can be a strip mall and the other a piece of raw land. As long as they're investment properties, the IRS is satisfied. You're also allowed to sell one property and use the proceeds for the down payment on a much bigger property (not the kind of thing you want to be doing at the top of the market, but nice to know about after it bottoms).

Rule 1031 exchanges aren't simple, however. Once the sale of the first property is completed, you have 45 days to identify the real estate you're swapping into, and 180 days to close the deal. Come in a day late, and the sale becomes a taxable event. And the price of the new property or properties must at least equal the proceeds from the property that's sold or the difference is taxable. Here are some other things to consider.

Identifying properties. Though you have to identify the new property within 45 days of selling the old, you don't have to make a final decision that soon. Instead, you can identify up to three target properties without regard to their total value. Or you can identify an unlimited number of replacement properties, as long as their total value is not more than twice the value of the property sold.

Closing the deal. You have to actually buy the replacement property within either 180 calendar days after closing on the sale of the relinquished property or the due date for filing the tax return for the year in which the relinquished property was sold. Miss the tax filing date (or fail to get an extension), and the IRS will show no mercy. Obviously, this isn't a do-it-yourself kind of thing. You'll need an IRS-approved middleman, called a "qualified intermediary," who handles the paper-work for a modest fee. Because the intermediary will be holding your money during the exchange, this isn't a relationship to be entered into lightly. So check prospects out, and make sure, among other things, that they have a fidelity bond or some other way to guarantee that your funds won't disappear.

Give It Away

The top of a market is a great time to donate real estate to charity because the resulting tax break is based on the appreciated value. In philanthropic circles, giving real estate (or stocks or jewelry) is known as a "gift in kind" because it's an asset rather than cold, hard cash. There are many variations on this theme, some of which offer a big up-front tax break, some of which allow you to live in your home after do-nating it, and still others that allow you to pass the affected property on to your heirs. Here are a few of the more interesting ones.

Conservation easements. Think of a piece of land as a bundle of rights, including the rights to occupy, use, lease, sell, and develop it. Each right has a market value, and each can be sold or donated via something called an easement. This is an agreement to transfer one or more rights from the landowner to someone who does not own the land but who cares about how it's used. The result is a kind of dual owner-ship, with one person holding title to the land but another having the right to control some aspect of it. Utilities do this all the time, acquiring easements that allow them to run power lines across farm pastures and subdivisions.

A conservation easement (or conservation restriction) is a legal agreement between a landowner and a land trust or a government agency that permanently limits uses of the land in order to protect some aspect of it. You might, for instance, contract with a charitable organization like the Nature Conservancy to donate the rights to certain kinds of development on your land. Say you prohibit logging, ranching, or home building. It's still your land, and you aren't required to open it to the public. But with the easement in place, it's less valuable as loggers, ranchers, and developers would have no reason to buy it. The difference between what it would be worth unencumbered and its new value is what you're donating and what you can claim as a tax break. The easement is granted to a trustee, who assumes a legal obligation to ensure that landowners comply with the restrictions in the easement. You continue to own and use your land, and can sell it or pass it on to heirs.

As development begins to encroach on the more interesting and pristine parts of the country, conservation easements are becoming a popular way for one generation to limit the things their heirs can do with family land. Ranchers are using easements to prevent their ranches from being turned into golf courses, and retirees are using them to keep their little piece of heaven on earth from becoming a subdivision after they die. Because it's a private deal, this kind of contract can be structured in lots of different ways. An easement can cover only a portion of the property, or it can restrict one thing here and another there. If you own 80 acres, of which 35 acres are wetlands, you can restrict development on only those 35 acres, and leave the other 45 free. In short, it's up to you to prohibit or permit whatever you want, and then to an appraiser to decide what this does to the market value.

But look before you leap. To earn a tax break, easements must be permanent, so be very sure that the rules you devise today don't crimp your style unduly in the future. Stories abound about trust administrators vetoing new buildings and roads on lands covered by easements. And make sure you understand the tax implications. Some easements reduce the market value of a given piece of land by 50 percent, which is pretty good. Others don't have nearly the same impact, especially if there was little prospect of immediate development. Sometimes prohibiting development actually enhances the value of a piece of land, in which case you get no tax benefit. And because before-and-after appraisals are tough when the issues involve things like what a lumber company might someday think a stand of timber is worth, the appraisal process may not go as smoothly as it did with the last house you sold.

Other Ways to Donate

If you're not interested in passing a given piece of land on to your heirs, but you prefer not to see it developed, you can donate it outright. With highly appreciated land, this is especially appealing because you might get a tax break that approaches or exceeds your purchase price. Commercial and residential properties can also be donated to a land trust, with the understanding that the organization will sell them to support its conservation work.

Remainder interest. Or you can donate a property now, with the provision that the recipient doesn't get it until you're through with it. In this arrangement, you donate the property during your lifetime but continue to live on and/or use it. When you die (or sooner, if you choose), the land trust gets the property. Doing it this way might be worth an immediate tax break, based on the fair market value of the property.

Charitable gift annuity. Here you donate a property to a charity, and the charity agrees to pay you regular amounts for life. You get a charitable income tax deduction at the time of the gift, based on the value of the land less the expected value of the annuity payments.

Bargain sale. If you own the right kind of property, you can sell it to a land trust for less than its fair market value. This generates some cash for you, avoids part of the capital gains taxes a full-price sale would generate, and entitles you to a charitable income tax deduction based on the difference between the land's fair market value and its sale price.

As you can see, the financial engineers have been busy in the charitable giving field too. So before you sign anything, you'll want expert help, including a good land trust, an accountant, and maybe a lawyer.

CHAPTER 13

MINIMIZE YOUR PROPERTY TAXES

From a cash flow standpoint, the fact that your house is over-valued is irrelevant. It went up, and now it will go down, and—other than the fact that down is less fun—until you sell, it's all just theoretical. The exception is your property tax bill; that's a real cash outlay that tracks your home's value. And lately tax bills have been soaring as two trends—both very bad from a home owner's point of view—intersect.

First, because many cities reassess the value of local real estate every few years, the recent surge in prices is only now inflating tax bills. Second, in the booming 1990s, relatively few municipalities felt the need to raise tax rates. But that changed after 2000, when falling revenues from taxes on retail sales and commercial property (where assessments are dropping), along with the added costs of post-9/11 homeland defense, have forced many cities to choose between higher property tax rates and fewer police officers, teachers, and firefighters. Most are choosing the former. New York City, as you know from chapter 5, raised property taxes by 18.5 percent in 2002. Atlanta raised rates by 50 percent, while out west, nearly every good-size Montana town either has raised rates or intends to.

"There are probably 60 to 70 cities of 100,000 population that are contemplating it today," David Brunori, editor of *State Tax Notes,* a nonprofit publication that tracks tax trends, told *USA Today* in December 2002. As a result, property tax bills in some places are starting to rival mortgage payments. In New Jersey, which admittedly is at the outrageous end of the spectrum, the annual tax on a $350,000 home in certain towns can run between $7,000 and $9,000.

This combination of higher rates and the lag in new assessments means that as the market value of your house falls to a more reasonable level, your tax bill might remain uncomfortably high. But it doesn't have to be that way. The bill the county treasurer sends you isn't necessarily the right number. In fact it's probably *not* the right number, and there are ways to get it lowered, often by a little and occasionally by a lot.

This is so because local governments don't spend a lot of time pondering the value of any one house; there are too many for that, and tax assessors are generally elected officials with a shortage of both time and staff. As a result, they rely on fast, back-of-the-envelope calculations that are easily distorted by a few high-priced sales in a given area and that often fail to account for differences that make one house less valuable than another. The National Taxpayers Union (NTU), a taxpayer advocacy group, estimates that as many as 40 percent of all properties in America are over-assessed. Because fewer than 5 percent of home owners challenge their assessments, governments have no incentive to be more meticulous. It's cheaper and easier to simply accommodate the squeaky wheels. The NTU estimates that half of those who appeal their tax assessment win reductions, which means the payoff for becoming one of those squeaky wheels rises along with your tax bill.

The key to a successful challenge is to figure out what your home is really worth, and the simplest way to do this is to hire a professional appraiser who will look at recent sales of comparable homes and make all the necessary adjustments to account for the differences between those houses and yours. This will cost a few hundred dollars, depending on the area and the appraiser, plus another few hundred for the appraiser to defend his or her number to the tax authorities. But with a little legwork, you can do this yourself. Try, for instance, asking a local real estate agent to show you the list of recent sales in the general area. The answer will probably be yes, with the agent hoping to build a relationship. Once you find some comparables, go over their descriptions for details like recent renovations, landscaping, oversized garage, and decking that may make them more valuable than your house. And be sure to note the problems with your house, like an unfinished or leaking basement or old fixtures, that wouldn't have been apparent to the county's drive-by assessors.

Once you have a sense of your home's true worth, compare it with the tax assessment. Don't be thrown if the assessor's number is only a fraction of your home's market value. Many towns use an "assessment ratio," which involves multiplying the value of a house by 25 percent or whatever to get the tax assessment. So you'll want to apply this ratio to your calculation of fair market value and then compare the result with the assessor's number. If there's a big difference (in your favor, of course), you have a case for an appeal, so contact the municipal authorities or the local tax assessor for printed material on how to challenge your taxes, fill out the forms, and get the ball rolling. From here, there are several ways it can go. The assessor can come out for a more detailed appraisal. Or you'll go there for a hearing. And don't be discouraged if the first answer is no. There are several levels of appeal, from local assessor to municipal tax court to state supreme court, and according to a 2001 study, your chances of success—and the size of the award—rise with each step up the ladder. Some excellent guides to this process available from the NTU and others are listed in Further Reading, page 243.

FURTHER READING

This book scratches many surfaces without delving too deeply. So if you're left wanting more, here, arranged by subject, are some sources that might help.

Bubbles, Manias, and Financial Panics

At the Crest of the Tidal Wave: A Forecast for the Great Bear Market, Robert R. Prechter Jr. (hardcover, $14.99). The Elliott Wave perspective on the development of financial crises. Ahead of its time when published in the mid-1990s, but spot-on today.

Extraordinary Popular Delusions and the Madness of Crowds, Charles MacKay and Bernard M. Baruch (hardcover, $9.98). The classic survey of the great bubbles of the past, including the Dutch tulip mania and the South Sea Bubble.

Manias, Panics, and Crashes: A History of Financial Crises, Charles P. Kindleberger (hardcover, $19.95). A more modern and theoretical look at why markets act the way they do.

Bear Market Investing

Bear Market Investing Strategies, Harry D. Schultz (hardcover, $49.95).

Conquer the Crash: You Can Survive and Prosper in a Deflationary Depression, Robert R. Prechter Jr. (hardcover, $27.95).

Infectious Greed: How Deceit and Risk Corrupted the Financial Markets, Frank Portnoy (hardcover, $27.50). The evolution of derivatives, as explained by a former derivatives salesman. His conclusion: In their current form, derivatives are less about efficiency than circumventing basic accounting rules, like the one requiring firms to show their liabilities on their balance sheets.

The Ultimate Safe Money Guide: How Everyone 50 and Over Can Protect, Save, and Grow Their Money, Martin D. Weiss (hardcover, $24.95).

When Genius Failed: The Rise and Fall of Long-Term Capital Management, Roger Lowenstein (hardcover, $26.95). The story of the biggest derivatives debacle—so far.

Bear Market Web Sites

Bear Market Central
www.bearmarketcentral.com

Beartopia
www.beartopia.net/earlybear.html

Prudent Bear
www.prudentbear.com

SafeHaven
www.safehaven.com

Cash

Savings Bonds Direct
www.publicdebt.treas.gov/ols/olshome.htm
www.publicdebt.treas.gov/of/ofbasics.htm

The SafeMoney Report
www.safemoneyreport.com

Everbank (Swiss franc accounts)
www.everbank.com

The Consumer Credit Bubble

CardWeb
www.cardweb.com/cardtrak

Loan Performance
www.loanperformance.com/library.asp

American Bankruptcy Institute
www.abiworld.org

Derivatives (Their Risks)

Bank for International Settlements
Tracks global derivatives exposure.
www.bis.org

Derivatives Study Center
A clearing house for derivatives statistics—including the exposure of individual banks—and regulatory updates.
www.financialpolicy.org

U.S. Treasury Derivatives Page
www.occ.treas.gov/ftp/deriv/dq402.pdf

Derivatives (Their Uses)

Lycos Finance Overview of LEAPS
finance.lycos.com/home/options/education.asp?options=aol

NASDAQ's LEAPS page
quotes.nasdaq.com/asp/option_index_leaps.asp

Nothing but Options
Funny illustrations and simple explanations to put a beginner at ease.
www.nothingbutoptions.com/education/default.asp

Options Institute
The Chicago Board Options Exchange educational site. Lots of basic information and free tutorials.
www.cboe.com/LearnCenter/OptionsInstitute1.asp
(888) OPTIONS

Option Tutor
More theoretical, for those who really want to know how these markets work.
www.ftsweb.com/options/optut.htm

Economic Statistics

Bureau of Economic Analysis
www.bea.gov

Census Bureau
www.census.gov

Bureau of Labor Statistics
www.bls.gov

Economic Statistics Briefing Room
www.whitehouse.gov/fsbr/international.html

Federal Reserve Board Statistical Releases
Source of the Z.1 Report, the most complete flow of funds analysis available.
www.federalreserve.gov/releases

Financial Services Fact Book
www.financialservicesfacts.org/financial/

Grandfather Economic Report
Great site. A concerned grandpa presents our financial situation in a series
of charts that are among the scariest things on the Web.
mwhodges.home.att.net

National Association of State Budget Officers
www.nasbo.org

The Housing Bubble

Housing Bubble
www.housing-bubble.com

Fannie Mae Watch
www.fmwatch.org

National Association of Realtors
www.realtor.org

Mortgage Daily
www.mortgagedaily.com

Realty Times
www.realtytimes.com

Mortgage Rates and Home Prices

Interest.com
www.interest.com/calculators

Domania.com
www.domania.com/index.jsp

Electronic Appraiser
www.electronicappraiser.com

Local Market Monitor
www.localmarketmonitor.com

Mortgage Bankers Association
www.mbaa.org

Office of Federal Housing Enterprise Oversight (OFHEO)
www.ofheo.gov/house

Property Taxes

National Taxpayers Union
www.ntu.org

Property Tax Online
www.propertytaxax.com

State Tax Notes
www.tax.org/tcom/state/stn.htm

Real Estate Exchanges and Donations

American Association of Retired Persons
www.aarp.org/foundation-plangift

Nature Conservancy
nature.org

Property Rights Foundation
prfamerica.org/ConsEaseIndex.html

Realty Exchangers
www.realtyexchangers.com

Stocks, Bonds, and Mutual Funds

ConvertBond.com
www.convertbond.com

NASDAQ's Exchange Traded Funds page
quotes.nasdaq.com/asp/etfsSector.asp

National Association of Real Estate Investment Trusts
www.investinreits.com

RealtyStocks
www.inrealty.com

EPILOGUE

Making predictions in print is a little like having kids; once you've sent them out into the world, you have no choice but to live with the result. This is especially scary when the predictions appear in a book because of the time lag between writing and publishing. Here, for instance, the last *i* was dotted in June 2003, while the first hardcover copy won't hit the shelves until October. The intervening months are likely to be very eventful, to put it mildly, which raises the possibility that at least some of what appears here will be irrelevant by the time the book is available, either because it has already happened or because things have veered off in an unexpected direction. A near miss of the first kind occurred in March, when a Federal Reserve Board governor rhetorically smacked around Fannie Mae and Freddie Mac, the dominant players in the housing bubble and the subjects of chapter 6. Their shares plunged, and I spent a weekend worrying that all this research and writing was for naught because the housing bubble was bursting half a year too soon. Advising people to short these stocks in October would look silly if they had already collapsed in April. So I sent an anxious e-mail to Doug Noland, author of the Prudent Bear Web site's Credit Bubble Bulletin. "Damn," I wrote, "just saw what happened to Fannie and Freddie. Looks like I may be a few months late with this book. . . ."

Doug, luckily in the office and able to respond right away, noted that it takes more than one Fed governor to pop a bubble of this size.

"In the grand scheme of things, we are very, very early in the process. . . . The mortgage finance bubble is in its 'blow-off,' so your timing will be perfect." I relaxed a little, and soon he was proved right. Interest rates stayed low, demand for new mortgages kept setting records, and within a month Fannie and Freddie were up big from the day of the Fed's harsh words.

Now the pendulum is swinging the other way, as the war in Iraq seems, thankfully, to be over. Our soldiers are coming home, oil prices are falling (the economic equivalent of a huge tax cut), home prices are still rising, and the stock market is experiencing a bit of a relief rally. An end to the carnage and uncertainty is welcome news no matter what your ideology or investment portfolio. And—assuming we take a breather before the next international crisis—it sets the stage for a stretch of relatively good times as people get back to the business of cashing out their home equity to fill their SUVs with newly cheap gas. So it's entirely possible that the second half of 2003 will see reasonably strong growth and that some of that glow may carry over into 2004, making the prediction of a recession in 2004 look premature at best.

But another good year will come with a price, which by now you can probably recite from memory: an extra trillion in mortgage debt, $10 trillion of derivatives, and $400 billion in the hands of foreign investors via the trade deficit. All told, we're looking at another $2 trillion in total debt grafted onto an already unstable national balance sheet. So unlike past recoveries, which have been unalloyed good news, you have to view this one with mixed feelings because the longer it lasts, the more serious the eventual consequences will be. It does offer one clear benefit, though: If you're shifting your finances into a defensive stance, another year of stability will give you the time make the transition gradually, at favorable prices rather than after the fact in increasingly inhospitable markets. Especially if you're thinking of selling your house, the tenor of the market makes all the difference.

So by all means cheer for peace in the Middle East and cheaper gas and higher home prices. But don't let these things—or ephemera like consumer confidence figures, stock prices, and the president's approval ratings—blind you to what really matters, which is the changing structure of our national balance sheet. Rising mortgage debt and falling home equity are real. Derivatives exposure, though hard to understand, is real. Recall from the last few entries in Scenes from the Current Bubble in chapter 6 that in the first quarter of 2002, we added $500 billion of new debt, with mortgages leading the way, which indicates that even after a decade of truly frenetic borrowing (and despite 9/11 and the Iraq war), we're not slowing down. Sooner or later this fact will migrate from the shadows to the front page. And when it does, you'll be ready.

INDEX

Underscored page references indicate charts and graphs.

A

ABS, 90–92, 92
ADM, 159–60, 159
Aetna Health, 157
Affordability of homes, decreasing,
    45–47, 46
Ambac, 174
American Century Global Gold, 143
American Century Utilities (fund), 165
American Dream Down Payment
    Initiative, 15, 96
American Real Estate Partners, 186
Apartment REITs, 192–93, 193
Apartment vacancy rates, 102
Appliance makers, short selling, 187–89,
    189
Application fee, 228
Appraisal fee, 229
Appraising home, 240–41
Archer Daniels Midland (ADM), 159–60,
    159
"Are 'Gifts' from Builders Inflating a
    Price Bubble?" (*Wall Street
    Journal* article), 100
Aristotle, 76
Arkansas state finances, 67
Arktos Fund, 208
"Asian Contagion," 123
Assessing home, 240–41
Asset Backed Securities World, 94
Asset-backed security (ABS), 90–92,
    92

AT&T, 156, 165
At the Crest of the Tidal Wave (Prechter),
    116
Attorney's review, 229
Auto makers, short selling U.S., 183–84,
    184

B

Bank of America, 179
Banking
    current system, 84–86
    old-style, 83–85
    securitization in age of, 125–26
Bank money market deposit accounts,
    135–36, 135
Bank One loans, 98
Bank Rate Monitor Web site, 136
Bankruptcies, rise in personal, 109,
    110
Bargain sale, 237
Barrick (mining company), 141
Barry, Dave, 71
Bassett (furniture company), 187
Bear market mutual funds, 206–9,
    208–9
Bear Stearns, 176
Beazer Homes, 181
Big Tobacco, 70, 93
Biogen, 184
Bloomberg report (2002), 65
Bloomberg report (2003), 103
Boeing, 213–14

Bonds
convertible, 167–69, _168–69_
debt and, 86–87
economic stimulation and, ideas for,
102
mortgage-back bond guarantees, 86
ratings of, 91
savings, 134–35, _136_
Series E/EE, 135
Series HH, 135
Boston home prices, _27_, 217. _See also_
Massachusetts housing market
Brendsel, Leland, 97
Bre-X Minerals disaster, 142
Browne, Harry, 148
Brunori, David, 239–40
Buffett, Warren, 75–77, 82
"Building in the Aftermath of the Boom
Gone Bust" (_Boston Globe_
article), 27–28
Bullion, gold. _See_ Gold
Bureau of Economic Statistics, 17
Bureau of Labor Statistics, 98, 106
Burns, John, 215–16
Bush, George W., 15, 96
Business cycle, 2–4
Business Week poll (2002), 100

C

California
home owner's net worth in, 44
housing bubble in, 28–31
housing market in southern, 28–31
office market in San Francisco, 20–21
Proposition 13 voter initiative in, 70
state finances in, 68–70
tobacco settlement and, 70
California Association of Realtors, 99
California Statewide Financing Authority,
93
Call options, 198
Capital gains, deferring, 232–35
Capital One Financial, 59–60, 96
Car manufacturers, short selling U.S.,
183–84, _184_

Case, Karl, 105
"Cash Out Now" (_Time_ magazine article),
98
Cash-out refinancing, 48–49, _49_, _107_
Cash preservation strategies
bank money market deposit accounts,
135–36, _135_
gold versus, 136–38, _138_
savings bonds, 134–35, _135_
treasury-only money market funds,
132–35, _132–33_
treasury securities purchased directly,
134, _135_
Cash-rich companies, investing in,
151–55, _154_
Catellus Development, 186
Cato Institute, 70
CBS MarketWatch Web site, 100
Center on Budget and Policy Priorities,
67
Center for Housing Policy, 98
Centex (home builder), 181
Charitable gift annuity, 237
Charles Schwab, 133, 143, 176, 203
Chicago Bridge (construction company),
185
Chile and U.S. dollar, 64
Cisco, 152–53, 155, 197
CitiFinancial, 59
Citigroup, 59, 82, 111
Clorox (consumer product company), 161
Closing real estate deal, 234–35
Colgate (consumer product company),
161
Collars in shorting derivatives, 198–200
Commercial REITs, 195–96, _196_
Commodity prices, 116
Community Reinvestment Act (1977), 14
Con Edison, 165
Connecticut state finances, 67–68
Conquer the Crash (Prechter), 116–120,
191
Conservation easements, 235–37
Construction companies, short selling,
184–85, _185_

Consumer finance companies, short selling, 176–78, <u>178</u>
Consumer products companies, investing in, 161, <u>161</u>
Consumers
  debt burden of, 57–61, <u>57</u>, <u>59</u>
  housing bust and, 57–60, <u>57</u>, <u>59</u>
  spending of, 30–31
"Consumers Sell Stock to Put Money in Real Estate" (*USA Today* article), 99
Convertible bonds, 167–69, <u>168–69</u>
Cormier, Claude, 141–42
Corporate investment. *See also specific names of companies*
  cash-rich companies, 151–55, <u>154</u>
  pricing-power companies, 155–59, <u>158</u>, <u>159</u>
  recession-resistant companies, 159–64, <u>159</u>, <u>160</u>, <u>161</u>, <u>162</u>, <u>163</u>, <u>164</u>
Countrywide Financial, 101
Covered calls, 199
Credit Bubble Bulletin, 122
Credit card
  defaults, 109
  loans, 89
Credit default swaps, 79
Credit enhancement, 90–91
Credit insurers, short selling, 173–75, <u>174</u>
Credit Suisse First Boston (CSFB), 90–91, 93, 179
Currency swaps, 79
Cushman & Wakefield report (2002), 20

D

Daimler Chrysler, 183–84
David W. Tice & Associates, 122, 207
Davis, Gray, 69–70
Debt
  bonds and, 86–87
  consumer, 57–61, <u>57</u>, <u>59</u>
  government, 61–62, <u>62</u>
  new, in 2003, 103

Defense spending and housing market, 25, 29–30
Deficit, federal, 61–62, <u>62</u>
Deflation, 43
DeKaser, Richard, 25
Dell, 153–56
Department of Housing and Urban Development (HUD), 12, 13, 14, 51, 102, 109
Derivatives
  Buffett's view of, 75–77, 83
  credit default swaps, 79
  criticism of, 81–83
  currency swaps, 79
  defining, 76–77
  exposure, 75–78, 82
  Fannie Mae's liabilities, 87–88, <u>87</u>
  gearing, 80–81
  historical perspective, 76
  interest rate swaps, 78–79, 83
  portfolio insurance, 79–80
  puts and, 198
  short selling
    collars, 199–200
    covered calls, 199
    ETFs, 204–6, <u>204</u>
    LEAPS, 200–204
    married puts, 199
    naked puts, 198–99
    overview, 197–98
    volatility spreads, 200
  stock options and, 76–77, 198
  total return swaps, 79
  value of U.S., 81–82, <u>81</u>
Digital gold, 144–46
Discount points, 228
Ditech.com, 50
Dollar, vulnerability of U.S., 63–66, <u>65</u>, <u>66</u>. *See also* Cash preservation strategies
Donating home, 235–37
Dot-com bubble, 105–6
Dot-com bust, 42
Down payment assistance (DPA), 51–52
Down payments, low or nonexistent, 49–52

DPA, 51–52
Drug companies, investing in, 162, _162_
Dukakis, Michael, 22
Dynamic hedging, 79–80

E

E*TRADE, 203
EasySaver, 135
Economy
  business cycle and, 2–4
  deflation and, 43
  expansion of, 1–2, 4
  fine-tuning, 2
  gross domestic product and, 28, 38,
    62–63, _62_, 82, 106
  housing bubble and, 2
  psychological factor in, 3, 117
  real estate and, 17, _17_, 105–7
  recession of, 1–2, 4, 21, 112–14, 176
  stagflation and, 148
Economy.com, 216
E-gold-based payment system, 145–46
Electric utilities, investing in, 162–63,
    _163_
Elite Rewards Platinum Plus MasterCard
    (MBNA), 59
Elliott, Ralph Nelson, 116
Elliott Wave Theorist newsletter, 116
Emcor (construction company), 185
Employment
  in construction industry, 106
  housing bubble and, 106
  housing bust and, 55–57, _56_, 106
Engineering companies, short selling,
    184–85, _185_
England, private property in early, 10
Equity Office, 19–20
ETFs, 166, _167_, 204–5, _204_
Ethan Allen (furniture company), 106, 187
Europe. _See specific countries_
EverBank.com, 151
Exchange-traded funds (ETFs), 166, _167_,
    204–5, _204_
Expansion, economic, 1–2, 4. _See also_
    Housing bubble

F

Fannie Mae and Freddie Mac
  current banking system and, 84–86
  debt sold outside U.S., 65
  debt-to-equity ratio, 86–88, _87_
  derivative liabilities, 87–88, _87_
  down payments and, low, 50
  first-quarter earnings in 2003, 103
  housing bubble and, 83–88
  LEAPS, 200–204, _201_
  loans, 98
  role of original, 86
  short selling, 171–73
FBR Asset Investment, 195
Federal Deposit Insurance Corporation,
    26, 136
Federal Financial Institutions
    Examination Council (FFIEC),
    111
Federal Home Loan Mortgage
    Corporation (Freddie Mac), 14,
    84. _See also_ Fannie Mae and
    Freddie Mac
Federal Housing Administration (FHA),
    11–12, 50, 102, 108
Federal National Mortgage Association
    (FNMA), 12, 14, 84. _See also_
    Fannie Mae and Freddie Mac
Federal Reserve Board, 5, 44, 48, 66, 85,
    102, 113
"Fed Weighs Alternative Stimulus Plan"
    (_Wall Street Journal_ article), 102
Feudal system, private property in, 10
FHA, 11–12, 50, 102, 108
Fidelity National Financial, 52
Fleckenstein, Bill, 147
Florida housing market, 216
Flour (construction company), 184
FNMA, 12, 14, 84. _See also_ Fannie Mae
    and Freddie Mac
Food-processing companies, investing in,
    160–61, _160_
Ford Motor Company, 183–84
Foreign currencies, investing in, 147–51,
    _148_

Foreign investment in United States, 64–65, 65
Forest City (property developer), 186
France, economic problems in, 149–50
Franklin Resources, 177
Freedom Loan, 50
Free Market Gold newsletter, 145
Friedman, Milton, 2
FFIEC, 111
Funds. *See also specific fund names*
    exchange-traded, 166, 167, 204–5, 204
    HOLDR, 166, 167, 205
    mutual
        bear market, 206–9, 208–9
        gold, 142–44, 144–45
        sector, 165–66, 167
Furniture makers, short selling, 187, 188

G

GDP, 28, 38, 62–63, 62, 82, 106
Gearing, 80–81
GE Capital, 179
General Dynamics' Electric Boat Division, 23
General Electric, 179
General Motors, 183–84
Genesis Program (DPA purveyor), 52
Germany
    economic problems in, 149–50
    trade deficit and, 65
Giving away home, 235–37
GM, 183–84
Gold
    bullion, 139, 139
    buying, 138–42, 139, 140
    cash versus, 136–38, 138
    cost of, 142
    digital, 144–46
    hedging policy, 141–42
    leverage and, 142
    mining stocks, 140–41, 140, 141
    mutual funds, 142–43, 144–45
    newsletters covering, 142–43
    Web sites covering, 140, 141

Goldman Sachs, 176
Goodman, Ellen, 24–25
Gorelick, Jamie, 97
Government Money Fund, 133
Government-sponsored enterprises (GSEs), 12, 14, 84, 86, 125
Great Depression, 11–12, 117
"Great Race from Office Space, The" (*Business Week* article), 19
Greece
    derivatives in early, 76
    private property in early, 9–10
Greenspan, Alan, 5, 82
Grizzly Short Fund, 208–9
Grocery chains, 163–64, 164
Gross domestic product (GDP), 28, 38, 62–63, 62, 82, 106
Grubman, Jack, 72
GSEs, 12, 14, 84, 86, 125

H

Harris, Don, 50–51
Health care REITs, 191–92, 192
Hedge funds, 93
Hedging
    dynamic, 79–80
    gold and, policy for, 141–42
    with puts, 198–200
    real estate, 222–27, 223, 224
Herman Miller (furniture company), 187
HFN, 52
HMOs, investing in, 156–57, 158
HOLDRs, 166, 167, 205
Homebuilders Financial Network (HFN), 52
Home builders, short selling, 180–82, 182
Home building, 21, 26
Home equity
    credit lines, 48
    loans, 1
    low, 47–52, 47
    refinancing and, 1
Home ownership, high, 52–53, 53

Home prices
in Boston, 27, 215
declining, 26–27, 27
income and, 46–47, 46
in Japan, 37
in Los Angeles, 31
resold home, 100
rising, 43–45, 44
in San Diego, 100, 223
Home sales
falling, 110–11
high, 41–42, 42
new, 100
Hong Kong and U.S. dollar, 64
"House-Poor Children" (*Boston Globe*
article), 24–25
Housing bubble
in California, southern, 28–31
characteristics of, 22
conditions for continuation of, 112–14
defining, 5
economy and, 2
employment and, 106
Fannie Mae and Freddie Mac and,
83–88
formation of, 3–4
identifying
caution about, 213–14
overheated local market and,
214–17, 214, 216
in Japan, 32–38
in New England, 22–28
Noland and, 125–27
scenes from current, 95–103
signs of
affordability of homes, decreasing,
45–47, 46
home equity, low, 47–52, 47
home ownership, high, 52–53, 53
home prices, rising, 43–45, 44
home sales, high, 41–42, 42
interest rates, low, 42–43, 43
Housing bust. *See also* Investing during
real estate bust
homeowner's options in
giving away home, 235–37

hedging real estate, 222–27, 223,
224
paying off home, 229–32, 230, 231
refinancing home, 227–29
selling home, 219–22
swapping home, 232–35
impact on
consumers, 57–60, 57, 59
debt, 61–63, 62
dollar, 63–66, 65, 66
employment, 55–57, 56, 106
local finances, 67–73
state finances, 67–73
scenarios of
Noland, 121–27
Prechter, 115–21, 119
signs of
bankruptcies, rise in personal, 109,
110
credit card defaults, rising, 109
home sales, falling, 110–11
mortgage-backed security market
troubles, 111–12
mortgage delinquencies, rising,
108–9, 108
regulations to avoid abuse in
housing finance, 111
slow-down in high-end housing
market, 110
Housing cycle barometer, 215
Housing market. *See also* Housing
bubble; Housing bust; Private
property; Real estate; *specific
U.S. housing markets*
California, southern, 28–31
cold, 215
cycle of, 3–4
defense spending and, 25, 29–30
Florida, 216
hot, 44, 214
Illinois, 213
Japan, 32–38
Massachusetts, 22–28, 213, 215
New York, 72
office, 18–22, 102
Oklahoma, 213

overheated, 214–17, <u>214</u>
overvalued, 214–17, <u>216</u>
Pennsylvania, 217
Rhode Island, 23
Seattle, 213–14
slowdown in high-end of, 110
undervalued, <u>216</u>
variances in, 213–14
Housing statistics, U.S., <u>21</u>
Housing, total value in U.S., 44
How You Can Profit from the Coming Devaluation (Browne), 146
HUD, 12, 13, 14, 51, 102, 109
Humana (HMO), 157
"Hurray for the Trade Deficit" (*Wall Street Journal* editorial), 101

I

Illinois housing market, 213
Income, real estate wealth versus disposable, 46–47, <u>46</u>
Infineon Technologies, 150
Inktomi, 19
Intel, 153
Interest rates
    declining, 1, 66
    deductible, 11
    low, 42–43, <u>43</u>, 102
    relative, 64
    swaps, 78–79, 83
Internal Revenue Code, 15, 232–35
Investing during a real estate bust. *See also* Short selling
    cash preservation strategies
        bank money market deposit accounts, 135–36, <u>136</u>
        gold versus, 136–38, <u>138</u>
        savings bonds, 134–35, <u>136</u>
        treasury-only money market funds, 132–34, <u>132–33</u>
        treasury securities purchased directly, 134, <u>136</u>
    convertible bonds, 167–69, <u>168–69</u>
    corporations
        cash-rich companies, 151–55, <u>154</u>

pricing-power companies, 155–58, <u>158</u>, <u>159</u>
        recession-resistant companies, 159–64, <u>159</u>, <u>160</u>, <u>161</u>, <u>162</u>, <u>163</u>, <u>164</u>, <u>164–65</u>
    foreign currencies, 147–51, <u>148</u>
    gold
        bullion, 139, <u>139</u>
        buying, 138–42, <u>139</u>, <u>140</u>
        cash versus, 136–38, <u>138</u>
        cost of, 142
        digital, 144–46
        hedging policy, 141–42
        leverage and, 142
        mining stocks, 140–41, <u>140</u>, <u>141</u>
        mutual funds, 142–43, <u>144–45</u>
        newsletters covering, <u>142–43</u>
        Web sites covering, <u>140</u>, <u>141</u>
    platinum, <u>147</u>
    sector funds, 165–66, <u>167</u>
    silver, 146–47, <u>147</u>
Investment companies, short selling, 175–76, <u>175</u>, <u>177</u>
IPOs, 95
Irrational Exuberance (Shiller), 105–6
Israel, private property in, 9

J

Jackson, Douglas, 144–45
Jacobs Engineering, 184–85
Japan
    economic problems in, 149
    home prices in, <u>37</u>
    housing bubble in, 32–38
    housing market in, 32–38
    keiretsu in, 33–34
    Ministry of International Trade and Industry in, 34
    Nikkei Index and, 35, 38
    private property in early, 32
    southern California's housing bubble and, 29
    trade deficit and, 65
    trade surplus, 149
    zaibatsu in, 32–33
Japan in the Passing Lane (book), 34

Job creation. *See* Employment
Joint Center for Housing Studies
    (Harvard University), 101
JPMorgan Chase, 178–79, <u>179</u>

K

Keiretsu (industrial alliances), 33–34
Keynes, John Maynard, 2
Kiplinger's Mortgage Finder, 228
Kiplinger's Personal Finance magazine,
    110
Kmart, 155–56
Kohn, Donald, 65
Kondratieff, Nikolai, 116
Kondratieff Wave, 116
Korean War and *zaibatsu*, 33
Kraft (food-processing company), 160

L

Law, John, 125
La-Z-Boy (furniture company), 187
LBOs, 94–95
LEAPS, 200–204, 225, <u>226</u>
Lennar (home builder), 181
Leuthold (fund operator), 208–9
Leveraged buyouts (LBOs), 94–95
Liu, Ralph, 226–27
Local finances, 67–73
Long-Term Capital Management (LTCM),
    87–88
Los Angeles home prices, <u>31</u>. *See also*
    California
Lowenstein, Roger, 87
LTCM, 87–88

M

McMahon, Fred, 26
MacArthur, Douglas, 33
Madison Avenue wealth, 71–72
Managed care providers, investing in,
    156–57, <u>158</u>
Married puts, 199
Massachusetts housing market, 22–28,
    213, 215
Maytag, 188

MBA, 49, 102, 108–9
MBIA, 174
MBNA, 59
Medical device makers, investing in,
    157–58, <u>159</u>
Medicare reimbursements, 191–92
Meiji Restoration, private property in, 32
Merrill Lynch, 72, 175–76, <u>175</u>, 203
Mesopotamia, private property in, 9
MGIC, 174
Microsoft, 152
MIGA, 93
"Millionaire tax," 67–68
Mining stocks, 140–42, <u>140</u>, <u>141</u>
Ministry of International Trade and
    Industry (MITI), 34
Minnesota's finances, 68
Minsky, Hyman, 122
Mississippi Bubble scheme, 125
MITI, 34
Money center banks, short selling,
    178–80, <u>179</u>, <u>180</u>
Money Game (Smith), 115, 189
Money market funds
    bank deposit accounts, 135–36, <u>136</u>
    treasury-only, 132–34, <u>132–33</u>
Money Report newsletter, 145
Moody Investor Service, 180
Moody's report (2002), 192
"More Buy Multiple Homes for Portfolio"
    (*Detroit News* article), 100
Morgan Stanley, 176
Morningstar, 143
Morris, Ian, 46
Mortgage-backed bond guarantees, 86
Mortgage-backed security market,
    trouble in, 111–12
Mortgage Bankers Association of
    America (MBA), 49, 102, 108–9
Mortgage borrowing, 57–60, <u>57</u>, <u>59</u>, 102
Mortgage delinquencies, rising, 108–9,
    <u>108</u>
Mortgage insurance programs
    FHA, 12
    HUD, 13

Mortgage packagers, short selling, 173–75, <u>174</u>
Mortgage rates. *See* Interest rates
Mortgage REITs, 194–95
M/PF Research, 193
MSF Holding, 93
Multilateral Investment Guarantee Agency (MIGA), 93
Multiplier effect, 85, 106
Mutual funds
 bear market, 206–9, <u>208–9</u>
 gold, 142–43, <u>144–45</u>
MyCommunityMortgage 97, 50

N

Naked puts, 198–99
National Association of Home Builders, 106
National Association of Realtors, 49, 106
National Down Payment Assistance Program, 52
National Governors Association, 67
National Taxpayers Union (NTU), 240–41
"Negotiability factor," 71
Nehemiah (church-sponsored charity), 50–51
Neighborhood Gold (DPA nonprofit), 51–52
New England housing bubble, 22–28
Newmont (mining company), 140
Newsletters, precious metals, <u>142–43</u>
New York
 finances, 70–73
 housing market, 72
 property taxes, 239
Nikkei Index, 35, 38
Nokia, 154
Noland, Doug, 85–86, 121–27, 172, 207–8
NTU, 240–41

O

Office of Federal Housing Enterprise Oversight (OFHEO), 14, 44, 214
Office market, 18–22, 102

Office REITs, 195–96, <u>196</u>
OFHEO, 14, 44, 214
Ohio state finances, 68
Oklahoma housing market, 213
Options Industry Council, 203
Oregon state finances, 67
Overcollateralization, 90

P

Parker, Dorothy, 39, 41
Pataki, George, 73
Paul, Ron, 136
Paying off home, 229–32, <u>230</u>, <u>231</u>
Pennsylvania housing market, 217
Pfizer, 162
Philip Morris, 93
Platinum, <u>147</u>
Portfolio insurance, 79–80
Prechter, Robert, 115–21, <u>119</u>, 191
"Prices Just Keep Plunging" (*Business Week* article), 97
Pricing-power companies, investing in, 155–58, <u>158</u>, <u>159</u>
Private property. *See also* Housing market; Real estate
 historical perspective
  England, 10
  feudal system, 10
  Great Depression, 11–12
  Greece, 9–10
  Israel, 9
  Japan, 32
  Mesopotamia, 9
  post-World War II, 12
  Reformation, 11
  Renaissance, 11
  Roaring Twenties, 11
  Rome, 9–10
  tenure laws and, 10
 tax code and, 15
  in United States, early 20th-century, 11
 U.S. government and, 12, 14–15
 value of all U.S., 17, <u>17</u>, <u>20</u>
Procter & Gamble, 161

ProFunds (fund operator), 208
Properties, identifying, 234
Property developers, short selling,
185–86, 187
Property laws, 9–10, 14
Property. *See* Private property; Real estate
Property taxes, minimizing, 239–41
"Property Taxes Squeezing Harder" (*USA
Today* article), 99
Proposition 13 voter initiative
(California), 70
Prudent Bear Fund, 122, 207–8
Puts, 198–99

Q

Qualified intermediary, 234–35
Quattrone, Frank, 72
Quigley, John, 105
Qwest, 154

R

Raytheon, 23
Reagan, Ronald, 23, 29
Real estate. *See also* Housing bubble;
Housing bust; Housing market;
Investing during a real estate
bust; Private property
disposable income versus wealth of,
46–47, 46
economy and, 17, 17, 105–7
hedging, 222–27, 223, 224
slowdown, 2
ubiquity of, 17
value of U.S., 17, 17, 20, 97
Real estate investment trusts. *See* REIT
combinations
"Real Estate Riches" (*Business Week*
article), 98
Real Liquidity, 226
"Realtors Pressured to Cut Commissions"
(*Wall Street Journal* article), 97
Recession, economic, 1–2, 4, 21, 112–14,
176. *See also* Housing bust
Recession-resistant companies, investing
in, 159–64, 159, 160, 161, 162,
163, 164–65

Redeker, Hans Guenther, 66
Refinancing
cash-out, 48–49, 49, 107
home equity and, 1
as home owner's option in housing
bust, 227–29
"Refinancing Boom Spells Big Money
for Mortgage Brokers, The"
(*Wall Street Journal* article),
101
Reformation, private property in, 11
Regional banks, short selling, 180, 181,
205
Regulations to curb housing finance
abuse, 111
REIT combinations, short selling
long/short
apartment, 192–93, 193
bad, 194–97, 195, 196, 197
commercial, 195–96, 196
good, 191–93, 192, 193
health care, 191–92, 192
mortgage, 194–95
office, 195–96, 196
overview, 190–91
retail, 196–97, 197
Relocating home, 221–22
Remainder interest, 237
Renaissance, private property in, 11
Renting home, 220–21
Retail REITs, 196–97, 197
Rhode Island housing market, 23
"Rising Home Prices Cast Appraisers in
a Harsh Light" (*Wall Street
Journal* article), 99
Risk of swaps, 78–79
Roaring Twenties, private property in, 11
Rome, private property in early, 9–10
Rowland, John, 67–68
Rule 1031, 232–34
Rydex (fund operator), 208

S

Safe Harbor Fund, 207
Salomon Smith Barney, 72
San Diego Association of Realtors, 100

San Diego home prices, 100, 223. *See also* California
San Diego Regional Planning Agency, 100
San Francisco office market, 20–21
Savings bonds, 134–35, 136
Seattle housing market, 213–14
Sector funds, 165–66, 167
Securitization
    asset-backed security and, 92, 92
    banking in age of, 125–26
    credit enhancement and, 90
    defining, 84
    loans and, nonstandard, 89–90
    next-generation deals, 93–95
    overcollateralization and, 90–91
Selling home, 219–22
Series E/EE bonds, 135
Series HH bonds, 135
"Shelter from the Storm" (*U.S. News & World Report* article), 96
Shiller, Robert, 105–6
Short selling
    appliance makers, 187–88, 189
    auto makers, U.S., 183–84, 184
    bear market mutual funds, 206–9, 208–9
    construction companies, 184–85, 185
    consumer finance companies, 176–78, 178
    credit insurers, 173–75, 174
    defining, 171–73
    derivatives
        collars, 199–200
        covered calls, 199
        ETFs, 204–5, 204
        LEAPS, 200–204
        married puts, 199
        naked puts, 198–99
        overview, 197–98
        volatility spreads, 200
    engineering companies, 184–85, 185
    ethics of, 189–90
    Fannie Mae and Freddie Mac, 172–75
    furniture makers, 186–87, 188
    home builders, 180–82, 182

investment companies, 175–76, 175, 177
    money center banks, 178–80, 179, 180
    mortgage packagers, 173–75, 174
    property developers, 185–86, 187
    regional banks, 180, 181, 205
    REIT combinations, long/short
        bad, 194–97, 195, 196, 197
        good, 191–93, 192, 193
        overview, 190–91
    title insurers, 182–83, 183
    tool makers, 187–88, 189
Silicon Valley, 19–20, 25, 29
Silver, 146–47, 147
Silver Institute, 146
Sklarz, Michael, 216
Smith, Adam, 115, 189
Southern Company, 165
"Space Race, The" (*Boston Globe* article), 18
Special-purpose vehicle (SPV), 90
Spieker Properties, 196
Sprint, 165
SPV, 90
Stagflation, 148
State finances, 67–73
Stock market, 1, 66–67
Stock options, 76–77, 198
"Subprime" market, 14
Sun Microsystems, 19
Swapping home, 232–35
"Sweat equity" programs, 15
Swiss franc, 148, 148, 151
Switzerland's economic situation, 151
Sysco, 160–61

T

Tax assessment, 241
Tax code, 15, 232–35
Tax deferrals, 232–34
Tech bubble, 105–6
Tech companies, 19–20, 23, 25, 67. *See also specific names*
Tech stock crash, 42
Tenure laws, 10
Thales, 76

TheStreet.com, 181
Thornburg Mortgage, 195
Tice, David W., 122, 207
Title insurers, short selling, 182–83, 183
Title search and insurance, 228
Tobacco settlements, 70, 93
Tool makers, short selling, 187–88, 189
Total return swaps, 79
Trade balance, 64
Trade deficits, 65, 101
Trading down home, 219–20, 219
TreasuryDirect, 134
Treasury-only money market funds,
    132–34, 132–33
Treasury securities purchased directly,
    134, 136
Turk, James, 145, 151

U

UltraBear Fund, 208
UnionBanCal, 101
Union Bank of California, 224
United Health Care, 157
United States. *See also specific housing
    markets*
    dollar and, vulnerability of, 63–66, 65,
      66
    foreign investment in, 64–65, 65
    private property in early 20th-century,
      11
    stock market, 1, 66–67
    trade deficit, 65, 101

Ursa Fund, 208
USA Today survey (2003), 100
U.S. Treasury Money Fund, 133

V

Vacancy rates, 20, 25, 102
Vanguard, 208
Volatility spreads, 200

W

Wall Street wealth, 71–72
Wal-Mart, 155, 163–64
"Wal-Mart effect," 155
Wealth effect, 106
Wells Fargo, 51, 224
When Genius Failed (Lowenstein), 88
Whirlpool (appliance maker), 106,
    188
William the Conqueror, 10
World Bank, 93
WorldCom, 156
World Trade Center attacks, 42, 72
World War II, private property
    after, 12
Wyeth Medica, 184

Y

Yahoo Finance, 188

Z

Zaibatsu (banking/industrial entities),
    32–33